Praise for *Patchwork*

"A generous, brave, and powerful sharing of the shadowed part of one woman's life."

—PATTIE C. S. BURKE, author of *Women and Pedagogy: Education Through Autobiographical Narrative*

"Just as the Sleeping Beauty pricked her finger on a fateful spindle and fell into a cursed hundred years' sleep, Mary Jo's suppressed memories of childhood abuse lay dormant for years until awakened. How Mary Jo chronicles her painful process from denial to full consciousness is both raw and delicate, using the woman's touch with a needle, stitching through pain, to create a searing patchwork and a final understanding of love."

—KATE FARRELL, Author and Storyteller

Patchwork

A MEMOIR OF LOVE AND LOSS

Mary Jo Doig

SHE WRITES PRESS

Published 2018
Printed in the United States of America
ISBN: 978-1-63152-449-3
ISBN: 978-1-63152-450-9
Library of Congress Control Number: 2018946478

For information, address:
She Writes Press
1569 Solano Ave #546
Berkeley, CA 94707

She Writes Press is a division of SparkPoint Studio, LLC.
All company and/or product names may be trade names, logos, trademarks,
and/or registered trademarks and are the property of their respective owners.

Names and identifying characteristics have been changed to protect the privacy
of certain individuals.

For my parents, Joe and Audrey; my sisters, Jackie and Bonnie; and my children, Jocelyn, Chip, Keith, Polly, and Susan, with profound love and deepest gratitude for each of our days.

Part of the task of composing a life is the artist's need to find a way to take what is simply ugly and, instead of trying to deny it, to use it in the broader design.

—Mary Catherine Bateson, *Composing a Life*

Prologue

Bovina Center, New York, October 4, 1991

I snuggle into my favorite chair on this autumn evening, a moonless sky outside my window, and open the latest issue of *Newsweek*. Relaxed and contented, slowly leafing through pages, I pause to read an article, when sudden tension surges into my body and flows into my right hand. I stare as my fingers transform into a claw, as rigid as the cultivator I use to wrench deep weeds from my garden.

My breathing becomes ragged. My exhalations transform into whimpers. I gasp as the now-frantic energy coursing through my body forces me to jump up and begin pacing back and forth, seemingly endlessly, until, much later, calm gradually returns to me.

As I drop into my chair and stare at my softening fingers through still-flowing tears, I silently wail, *What . . . just . . . happened?*

The universe remains quiet.

I am forty-nine years old and about to uncover a long, tightly tangled thread that will tug me, one knot after another, back to my childhood.

Part I

Chapter 1: ONE WEDDING RING

Manhattan and Center Moriches,

New York, 1940

The diamond was stunning, nearly a carat. Surely my mother's brown eyes sparkled as beautifully as the precious marquise-cut in the sterling setting my father held out to her. "Audrey, will you marry me?"

It was early evening, after work, and they sipped a cocktail in a quiet Manhattan bar. Although some misgiving might have niggled at her belly, my mother, twenty-six, believed this was likely her last chance to marry. She gave him her lovely smile, showing the even white teeth I always admired, and said, "Yes, Joe." She believed this would work out fine; her lifelong dream, after all, was to become a wife and mother.

I wonder what my father's dreams were. Did he look beyond having finally captured this slim, brunette beauty? How did he feel about being a husband? Did he think about having children? What career did he have in mind? Did he even consider these important, practical questions? I'll never know those answers, yet I do know one fact for certain: they planned to live happily ever after.

My parents worked at 20th Century Fox Studios in early 1940 in New York City, where they met four years earlier. My father, twenty-eight, was a stock person and my mother was a secretary. He asked her for a date when he first met her, but she was still waiting for her best friend's brother, Shep—the love of her young life—to finish law school. When Shep became engaged to someone else shortly before his graduation, my mother's heart nearly broke.

Perhaps the Fox grapevine took the news to my father, for he asked her out again. This time she accepted, and they soon dated regularly. Sometimes they went for walks, or for dinner, or to the theater to see Fox films, for it was the golden age of the industry and they were part of it. By all my mother's fond accounts, those years with Fox were exciting and romantic. I was proud that my parents had been there.

Yet five decades later, as I write their story in my tiny cabin in the Blue Ridge, I sense silent shadows present during that romantic evening. In truth, while the gorgeous ring sparkled as if brand new, it had previously adorned the hand of my father's first fiancée, Corinne, who had recently broken their engagement. *What was her reason?* I muse.

I wonder if my mother's unrequited love for Shep stole slivers of joy from the special moment for her. Did either think of someone else as he slid the ring onto her finger?

I easily see his charismatic response to her gentle "Yes, Joe," and her sweet smile. He was slim, handsome, and charming, a few inches taller than her five-foot-four, seemingly attentive and affectionate, his dark hair already thinning and receding, his eyes bright and warm, his smile snaggle-toothed.

"You remind me of Aunt Madeline," he told her affectionately as they sipped their drinks, his hand holding hers, perhaps looking at the diamond shine between his fingers. My mother liked the comparison, for she was fond of Madeline, his paternal aunt, a petite, wispy-haired dynamo of kindness and caring.

My father grew up in the Bronx, at 1121 Findlay Avenue, and rarely talked about his family: Joe, Sr., short, portly, ostensibly amiable, but often absent from home as he chauffeured for a wealthy Connecticut family; his mother, Josephine Daly, who died when he was thirteen; or his soft-spoken, seemingly pleasant brother, Matt. My mother told me in later years she always felt uneasy with Joe, Sr. I venture to guess now that beneath his seeming charm, she sensed how much he devalued women.

He talked often, though, about his stepmother, Mary, the large-boned, pure-Irish dumpling of a woman with twinkling, Delft-blue eyes whom his father married a few years after Josephine died. Two decades younger than her new husband, Mary, fresh off the boat at Ellis Island, as the family used to say, became a warm and loving presence in the lives of then-sixteen-year-old Joe and fourteen-year-old Matt.

Ready for a break, I save my computer document, grab my jacket, hurry out the door, and start walking briskly on the path toward the top of my mountain. A third of the way up, I freeze when I see a yellow-and-black garter snake curled on the path. He looks innocent, and I know he won't hurt me, but I've learned that innocent appearances sometimes conceal inner demons.

Circling well around him, I continue until, panting, I reach the mountaintop. Standing still as my breathing quiets, I turn in a slow circle to look out at the entire mountain range. I inhale the pure air and think of the next chapter I will write, about the weekend my mother took my father home to meet her parents. I see my grandparents relaxing in their cozy living room filled with furniture now passed on to their grandchildren. Grandma Davis sits on the sofa, her hand-crocheted afghan a colorful backdrop behind her, and Grandpa relaxes in his chair by the bay window, pipe smoke rising lazily as he puffs quietly. The serenity and timelessness of that scene, along with the knowledge of having been well cared-for in that place, slowly envelops me until I'm fully anchored in the tableau. One day I will create a quilt with heart-shaped leaves that represent each person who was important in my life. The hearts for my Davis grandparents will be close to each other and prominent.

I exhale and sigh at the sweet memory, then walk slowly down to the cabin. I notice that the snake is gone.

A few weeks later, my parents took the train from Penn Station after work on a Friday afternoon and arrived in the early evening in Center Moriches, on Long Island's south shore, bordering Great South Bay, seventy-five miles from Manhattan.

My shy, soft-spoken grandparents, Clarence and Edna Cartright Davis, met them at the railroad station, standing by their car when the squealing train arrived. They hugged my mother when she stepped off the train and smiled at my father. "Hi, Joe," my grandfather said. "We're glad to meet you. We've heard nice things about you from Audrey."

My father, also shy, felt uneasy in this first meeting, yet he wanted to make a good first impression. He smiled broadly, extended his hand confidently to each of my grandparents, and said, "It's nice to meet you both."

Grandpa nodded and said, in his gentle, deep voice, "Yes. Well, let's put your bags in the car and get on home."

My father carried their weekend bags to the black Ford Coupe and stowed them. Four miles later, Grandpa turned into the driveway of a large, stately white home on Lake Avenue, steered the car halfway around the driveway circle, and parked near the huge bed of orange daylilies.

"Come on in," my grandmother said, smoothing her flowered housedress after the ride. My grandparents, followed by my parents, entered the back mudroom, walked through the low-ceilinged kitchen, passed by the round, claw-foot oak table and chairs in the dining room, and went on into the homey living room, immaculately cared for by my grandmother.

I slide back to that time before my birth to imagine that welcoming room and hear their nuanced voices. I know the softness of my grandmother Davis's handmade afghan—its beautiful, lacy squares in primary colors crocheted together with black yarn—smoothed on the back of the overstuffed couch, the centerpiece of her living room.

In front of the couch stood a one-of-a-kind coffee table Grandpa had crafted from a thick slab of white, gray-veined marble, supported by an ornate, cross-shaped, walnut-stained wood base. Grandpa's overstuffed easy chair was nestled into the bright bay window, with a large padded footrest in front. A tall wooden Zenith floor radio stood to the left, near several built-in wall shelves that held a few books, some knickknacks, and a lamp.

My father lit my mother's Viceroy filter, then my grandmother's Old Gold, then his own Lucky Strike while Grandpa filled his pipe, tamped down his tobacco, and ignited it. While the unforgettable sweet scent of Prince Albert permeated the room, they each had a brief respite to think about what to say next.

My mother took the lead as they sought common topics. She chatted about some of Fox's new releases in 1941: *Blood and Sand*, with Tyrone Power, Rita Hayworth, and Anthony Quinn; *How Green Was My Valley*, with Roddy McDowall, Walter Pidgeon, and Maureen O'Hara. Then Grandpa asked my father, "So, Joe, what kind of work do you do at Fox?"

My father cleared his throat. "Well, I . . . work in the stockrooms. I unload the trucks and replenish the supply shelves."

Grandpa puffed thoughtfully on his pipe for several seconds. Joe broke the silence by adding, "I also attended a semester of college after high school but withdrew because it wasn't interesting. I wanted to start earning money."

Grandpa puffed some more. Was he wondering about what I think of now: Since Joe possessed no specialized work skills, how would that affect his and my mother's future?

My mother and grandmother each lit another cigarette, and my grandfather changed the subject. "Well, Joe, Audrey probably told you I served in the navy after I graduated from high school. Now that Hitler's escalating this terrible war, will you be enlisting?"

My father again cleared his throat, "Uh, Mr. Davis, since Audrey and I are getting married, I've decided not to. I want to be with her."

Grandpa silently puffed what might have looked like smoke signals and stared far away. Silence reigned until my grandmother invited everyone to the dining room.

With relief, each person rose and followed her to the table, where she served coffee and cake and the conversation easily shifted to how delicious her cinnamon-nutmeg confection was.

The next day, my mother drove my father to Westhampton Beach to show him the stunning homes of movie stars and other wealthy Fire Island residents. Later they walked around the quaint hamlet of Center Moriches and saw the boats docked in the nearby canal, the many roads that led to Great South Bay, and several of the homes my grandfather, a lifelong carpenter, built.

Grandpa's father, Spicer Davis, also a lifelong carpenter, built a residence for each of his three sons—Archie, Fred, and his youngest, my grandfather, Clarence—as they started their adult lives. The lovely white two-story house that Spicer built for my grandparents, the home my mother and her future husband visited, was where they lived out their entire lives.

On Sunday afternoon, following my grandmother's delicious every-Sunday pot roast dinner, my mother and father prepared for the train ride home to their respective apartments. As my grandparents said goodbye at the train station, if they had reservations about their daughter's betrothed, they kept them to themselves.

My parents married on August 10, 1940, in a simple ceremony before a justice of the peace and a few close friends and family members. As my mother's maid of honor, Alice, and my father's best man, his more rounded brother, Matt, stood near, my razor-thin father slipped a narrow sterling band on my mother's left hand.

Amid warm, festive well wishes, they left for a honeymoon camping trip in the Adirondack Mountains, a favorite place where my mother had often vacationed with her friends. The happiest time in their marriage had opened.

Chapter 2: THE LONE STAR

Pasadena, Texas, 1941–42

My parents continued working at Fox, where my mother earned $17 weekly and my father $15. They furnished their apartment on Joralemon Street in Brooklyn with a small, sturdy maple dining table and four chairs, an overstuffed brown sofa, and other modest miscellaneous furniture. In their spare time, they enjoyed cooking, movies, and camping.

Fox strictly mandated that married couples could not both work there. Since my father's wage was lower, he sought civilian employment at the Brooklyn Navy Yard. Shortly afterward, though, in mid-1941, my mother experienced pervasive morning sickness early in her pregnancy with me and resigned, thus severing their pleasurable connection with that dazzling time in the film industry. Quickly, the horrific attack on Pearl Harbor thrust our country into war, as Joseph Stalin became *Time*'s Man of the Year, Henry Kaiser preached "full production for full employment," and Wendell Willkie sought to build relations with Russia. Two months before my birth, the military draft board sought all able-bodied young men.

My father's wish to avoid the draft had been well-secured by his new job at the Navy Yard. Shortly after Pearl Harbor, though, my father met a man planning to move to work in a Texas defense plant. My father decided he also wanted to. My mother was agreeable, in part because her brother, Gene, was stationed in Texas with the army. As my parents planned their move, my grandparents decided to relocate, too, just until the war was over. So my grandparents and parents drove 1,700 miles from New York to Pasadena, Texas, in four days, arriving three weeks before my birth.

In Pasadena, my grandparents rented a small house for themselves and my parents. My father found factory work making plastic parts used to manufacture war materials. They settled into a new lifestyle in this wartime climate, hugely different from New York State.

I entered into my parents' story at 10:21 a.m. on February 5, 1942, in Pasadena, Texas, where the weather was recorded as sunny and in the seventies. My mother was so heavily medicated that she did not regain consciousness until the next day. When I was finally placed in her arms, she likely gazed unbelievingly at her new, rosy, eight-pound daughter, a big baby for my one-hundred-pound mother. I imagine her pretty smile when she gently smoothed my sprinkle of dark hair, took hold of every finger and toe, and cooed at how soft and perfect they were. When I grasped and held her finger, she would have alternated laughter with tears of happiness.

Ten days later, my father took us home.

On a warm Texas afternoon, I slept outside in my small black canvas carriage. When my mother came to check on me, she noticed a snake circled around one carriage wheel and called Grandpa. "Pop, come see the pretty snake." He took one look, ran to get his hoe, and quickly killed it.

Sorrowfully, my mother said, "It was so beautiful."

He replied gruffly, "Audrey, that was a coral snake. They're deadly." My mother grabbed me from the carriage.

I have studied my mother's old Kodak photographs of our small family during those Texas months. It's easy to see that Mom took good care of me. My eyes were large and brown, and she tied a tiny ribbon around a clump of dark hair on top of my head, making a little waterspout. My clothes were clean; my smile was happy.

I look closely at my parents' smiles and especially into their eyes, those windows into the soul. They look happy. Their smiles do not reflect a deep, glowing happiness, but neither do they appear to be two people pretending to be happy. I see a bond. One or the other holds me, and they stand fairly close to each other.

Yet, along with these sunny photos, other forces frightened my mother and grandmother: the endless numbers of tarantulas both outside and inside the house, the coral snakes and rattlers, and the constant smell and appearance of mold on the furniture, a consequence of 1942's long, hot summer without air conditioning. Then my mom contracted a mild case of malaria.

"That's it, Joe," she told my father. "I don't want to live in Texas anymore."

He didn't argue. In October 1942, eight months after my birth and just as the Manhattan Project was starting to develop the atomic bomb, my family packed up the 1939 Dodge and we moved north. I see now that the reasons my parents left Texas paled in comparison to the troubles that waited ahead.

They never returned to Texas, but all my life I ached to revisit the birth state I could not remember.

Chapter 3: COCOON

Sandy Hook, Connecticut, 1942–45

We moved 1,700 miles from Texas to Sandy Hook, Connecticut, to live with my father's aunt Madeline and uncle Henry. Aunt Madeline's mother, Grandma B., in her eighties, also lived with them in what I remember as a somber, silent house with dark furniture. While Aunt Madeline's disposition was sunny, my great-grandmother—who sat in an overstuffed chair in the living room most of the day, wearing long, dark dresses, her white hair pinned on top of her head—had ebony-colored, tempestuous eyes. Once, I was crying as I walked past her, and she barked, "You stop crying *right now* or I'll give you something to cry about. *Be quiet!*" I obeyed instantly.

Family are the people who usually comprise the first important circle we enter in life. If we are fortunate, we're contained in a warm, nurturing vessel where we grow in healthy ways. A few weeks after my great-grandmother slammed me with her fury, I tumbled down her basement steps into total darkness, an event I later saw as a physical manifestation of my accidental stumble that day into my grandmother's rage, part of a thread of dark undercurrents I'd later find woven throughout my father's family. Already, though I was physically present in that house, I had silently moved deeper within myself in order to feel safe.

Somehow, that sourness bypassed my sweet aunt Madeline. If she was caring for me while my mother was out and I inadvertently got snared in a situation with Grandma B., she swiftly swooped me up and transformed the next moments into something light and pleasant, like giving me some ice cream or kind words: "There, there, don't cry now. Everything's okay."

I loved my days with Aunt Madeline, who played and giggled with me, while gently reminding me to be quiet and not upset Grandma B. We lived with them briefly while Uncle Henry helped my father find work. Soon after my father started his new factory job, my parents rented an apartment in Sandy Hook. I have no memory of missing that dark house, just Aunt Madeline. Decades later, I would create a quilt for my writing room, one that remarkably resembles the one on this book's cover. I fashioned a heart-shaped leaf for Aunt Madeline and affectionately attached it to the graceful plant that symbolizes my tree of life.

Our new home, in Fred and Ella Reiner's duplex, brought my mother a staunch new friend: Ella. We joined the Catholic Church that year, an event that evolved from Ella's deep Catholic faith and persuasive skills. When my parents married, my father was—and remained throughout his life—a lapsed Catholic, while my mother had been a lifelong practicing Methodist. Whatever caused them to choose a civil, rather than religious, marriage ceremony in 1940 was remediated in Connecticut three years later, when they wanted to have me baptized. I easily hear the devout Ella saying, "Audrey, you've got to join the Church so you don't raise that child in sin. You've *got* to get her baptized."

Ella would have called Father William Collins, pastor of her church home, St. Rose of Lima RC Church in Newtown, and invited him to meet my mother and me. I was too young to understand anything about religion, of course, and couldn't know my future would hold a difficult, guilt-ridden relationship with the Catholic Church following some poor life choices I'd make. Sometimes I have wondered, if Mom hadn't met Ella, would she would have raised her children in her Methodist faith? Would those Methodist roots have led me on to better pathways? I'll never know that answer, but I like to think so.

I learned as a young child that the Catholic Church was the one, real, and true church and grew up feeling sorry for people of other faiths. Did they not know they were doomed to hell? Wouldn't they convert to Catholicism if they knew?

I memorized my catechism lessons:

Who made the world? God made the world.

Who is God? God is the Creator of Heaven and Earth and all things.

Did God have a beginning? God had no beginning. He has always been and He always will be . . .

Yet memorized knowledge didn't lead to an awakening of my spirit. That would happen many decades later, in a much different way. As a child, I believed God was a stranger who resided far away and was busy with others who needed Him much more than I. Yet I never doubted that I could trust my parents or the church.

My mother attended church each Sunday, while my father attended with us on occasional Easter Sundays. Through the years, I felt little sense of his being either devout or spiritual, although we never spoke of such substantive matters.

In late 1943, when I was almost two, my parents renewed their marriage vows. I open the Bible that Father Collins inscribed for them and read his words:

> *To Audrey and Joe, with the sincere hope that God will send them many of His choicest blessings.*
> *—(Rev.) William J. Collins, Feast of the Immaculate Conception, December 8, 1943*

Within are tangibles that my mother tucked between the razor-thin pages: a *New York Times* clipping announced that Father Collins later became vicar-general of the Catholic archdiocese of Hartford, Connecticut, then another notice, of Father Collins's picture and obituary, on October 16, 1959. I have no recollection of Father Collins, but I know I saw him once, for my baptism certificate holds his signature eleven days after he officiated my parents' renewed marriage vows. Unsurprisingly, Ella Reiner is listed as my sponsor.

Then I find a paper-thin, pressed clover with three leaves attached; the fourth has broken away to the bottom of the page. A memory stirs, from when I was an early teen and my sister, Jackie, was about nine.

Mom loved hunting for four-leaf clovers. "Jackie, Mary Jo, come over here!" she called out enthusiastically. "They bring good luck," she reminded us, in case we'd forgotten. But I didn't remember Mom's placing them in her Bible until I discover several this day. My heart warms as I sense her belief that they were gifts of grace, worthy of space in her holy book.

And then a Connecticut memory returns and makes me smile.

I sat on Ella Reiner's back porch steps, as my mother and Ella talked and sipped coffee in the kitchen. Idly, I picked out a clothespin from the nearby basket and dropped it through a space between the step boards, where it softy thumped to the ground. *Well, that was fun*, I thought, and dropped several more into the invisible darkness.

In a while, Ella and my mother stepped out onto the porch.

"You've been a good girl today," Ella said, smiling widely and handing me a crispy cinnamon-brown Mary Jane cookie.

Ella's raspy voice intimidated me, but I liked her fading red hair and freckles and Mary Jane cookies.

My mother said, "Tell Ella thank you." I did.

The next day, clothes hung on the line between the back porch and a big tree in the yard as we approached. Ella smiled at us. "Hello! Did either of you see anybody drop some of my clothespins down through the step?"

Uh-oh. I've been bad. I froze, as my mother looked at me sternly. "Did you do that?"

I nodded fearfully and watched Ella closely to see if I was in danger. She stepped outside the door and sat down beside me.

"That's okay, Mary Jo," she said gently, in her croaky voice. "Just remember that if you put all my clothespins under the steps, I can't hang up my laundry. Please don't do that again. Okay?"

"Okay." I broke out into a relieved smile.

My mother prompted, "Tell Ella you're sorry, Mary Jo."

"I'm sorry, Ella."

Ella said, "Thank you. You're a good girl, Mary Jo," and handed me a cookie. After she and my mother went inside, I picked up a clothespin and pondered, *She wouldn't miss just one more, would she?* I looked around to be certain no one watched as I slyly dropped the clothespin into the space. I never did it again.

Ella couldn't have known how her kindness soothed my soul that day, or that she had shown me a new aspect of a world I rarely experienced in the growing clouds of tension, anger, and fear that floated in the oxygen of our home. I already knew I was a bad girl, yet Ella laced a small golden thread into my dark beliefs that day. Others through the years would pick up her thread and expand it further, until one day I would assimilate that giving kindness whenever possible lightens darkness. Just as Ella didn't know she gave me a memory I'd never forget, we often never know the impact of our kindness on others. What we are able to know is that we can never err by giving kindness and compassion wherever and whenever we can. Later in life, I would tenderly stitch a heart-leaf for Ella onto my quilt.

Some weeks later, Ella cared for me for several days, then one morning took me home. Soon my father opened the front door for my mother, who walked inside, carrying a pink bundle the size of a loaf of bread. My mother removed her coat, with Ella's help, then sat on the couch with me and arranged the baby in her lap.

"Mary Jo, this is your new sister, Jackie." I was shocked; maybe somebody had told me there would be a new baby, but, if so, I hadn't understood.

I stared at a face smaller than my doll's. Later, I'd learn Jackie had been a preemie, only four tiny pounds at birth. "You can hold her hand if you want to, but be gentle."

I reached over to touch. "That's good, nice and gentle," my mom said. I touched Jackie's hand and squeezed a little; she cried out.

"No. Be gentle, Mary Jo," Mom said firmly, pulling my hand away. As she and Daddy started talking to Ella, I took my sister's hand and held it again, thinking I was gentler, but Jackie started crying.

Suddenly, my father jumped up and grabbed me by the arm. His dark eyes were mean and scary. I began crying, too. He pulled me to my room and took off his belt. I screamed while he hit me. When he stopped and slid his belt back on, he glared down at me and said angrily, "Don't ever hurt your sister again, you stupid kid. Do you hear me?"

I froze.

"Now stay here until I tell you to come out!"

I believe on that day, alone in my bedroom, I first spun my cocoon, wrapping it around to hold me in a quiet, gray place where I didn't feel afraid. I was alone and numb, yes, but I felt safe being there. I don't remember leaving my room that day, but I know my mom must have come to get me for supper.

Days later, my mother and I were home, as usual, in the living room, where there was now an infant crib. My new sister lay on her back, squalling.

"What's the matter with her, Mommy?" I asked quietly, staring at my sister's wispy, dark hair and red, scrunched-up face.

My mother placed her hand on Jackie's tiny legs, strapped to rigid braces held fast by a bar that kept her feet separated. Spread-eagled on her back, she couldn't move. "She doesn't like her brace," my mother said, as Jackie wailed more loudly, as if in affirmation.

"Why does she have it?" I asked, puzzled.

My mother smoothed Jackie's hair, saying, "Everything's okay, Jackie," but her tense, too-loud words didn't comfort my sister. I watched her small chin quiver in a rhythm that matched her trembling sobs. I wished she'd shut up for a while. Our house used to be nice and quiet before my parents brought my sister home. Now everybody was upset all the time, and this unhappy baby was apparently the reason.

"Jackie has club feet," my mother said. "Her feet turn in, and she won't be able to walk unless we get them straightened with the brace."

I looked from Jackie back to my mother, who was so thin and had dark circles beneath her eyes. Because we stayed home all the time and didn't see many people, Jackie was the only baby I remembered ever seeing. I didn't know anything about babies or club feet. Her legs looked like chicken bones. How would she ever walk on them anyway? And her huge brown eyes looked so gloomy, almost like she already knew her journey through life might be wretched.

"Do they hurt?" I asked.

"No, she just doesn't like not being able to move her feet," my mother said sadly. "At least she doesn't have to wear them at night."

Things soon got worse. A few weeks later, I was in the kitchen with my mother, crying about something. She was holding Jackie, who was wailing, too.

"Mary Jo, it seems like you cry all the time now," my mother said, her words seeming to explode. "I'm going to send you to nursery school so you can have more attention. I just can't give you enough now."

What did that mean? Her distressed voice frightened me, and when, a few days later, a dark-haired lady came to visit, she really scared me. My mother introduced us. "Mary Jo, this is Dorothy. She's going to take you to nursery school tomorrow."

Dorothy bent onto her knees in front of me, smiled, and said, "Hi, Mary Jo. You'll have a nice time playing with other kids in nursery school." Dorothy seemed nice, but I stared down at the floor and didn't say anything. She talked more with my mother, then said, "Bye, Mary Jo. I'll see you tomorrow."

"Did you like her?" my mother asked after Dorothy left.

"No," I blurted, pouting. "I don't want to go *anywhere* with her."

Yet the next morning, after a loud battle of wills, my mother placed me firmly on Dorothy's backseat. Dorothy talked nicely to me as she drove, but I was so mad and scared, I didn't answer. I just wanted to go back home with my mother. When the car stopped and Dorothy opened my door, she reached in and took my hand and we walked toward a white building. Suddenly, I stood paralyzed in a big room with a lot of kids, having no idea this place was an important circle of growth and nurturance for children: school. The kids were noisy, scattered all over, some playing with toys, some laughing, one crying. Nearby, a boy stared at me. I pulled back toward the door, but Dorothy tugged me over to him and said, "Mary Jo, say hello to Charlie."

I didn't want to talk to Charlie. When he said hello, I knitted my brows and glowered at him, my lips pursed tight.

Another lady called to Dorothy, who turned and said, "I'll be right back." Charlie started talking to another boy, so I looked around and spotted a quiet corner, walked over, sat on the floor, and stared down. I felt better as I quickly wrapped myself in the secret cocoon I'd created when my sister had come home from the hospital. Inside my cocoon, I went to a faraway place where I felt safe, where I wasn't scared anymore. I had just rejected the environment that might have had a chance to help me grow socially.

I used my cocoon for all the days I was there. I didn't know how many days that was, probably a lot. When I told my mom every morning that I didn't want to go, she said, "I'm exhausted, Mary Jo. Jackie has colic; that's why she cries all the time. You have to go."

I soon stopped saying I wanted to stay home. It never happened. Sometimes, though, I wished my mother would just smile like she used to. She had such a pretty smile, but the truth was, my nice mom was never the same after Jackie's birth.

As Jackie grew, my mother worried when Jackie didn't walk or talk when I had. In the year following her birth, my mother learned Jackie was mentally delayed. Later, as a young adult, she was further diagnosed with mental illness: schizophrenia.

Years later, when I was a young mother, Mom confided in me that when she happily told my father she was expecting Jackie, his face darkened.

"Get rid of it," he said coldly to her. I never forgot those atrocious four words.

Mom shrieked, "Get an abortion? I would *never* do that!"

Ironically, Mother Nature gave her the opportunity to follow his wishes when she started to miscarry at eight weeks. Instead, she became a tigress for her unborn child, getting medical help that enabled her to carry her pregnancy to near term. This all happened, she told me, about the same time she found out my father was seeing another woman. I was so horrified by her disclosure, I never asked for more details. It does seem to me, though, that following Jackie's birth, our home became a house without laughter.

Deeper truths of my family's functioning as we journeyed forward in Sandy Hook surfaced as daffodil bulbs do each spring, but they did not bloom into sunny yellow flowers. The dark side of my father's family revealed itself in seeds I would guess at but would never know for certain until years ahead. The promise of joining the potentially rich, nurturing Catholic church community would not come to be. And while my parents were blessed with two daughters, my mother—who essentially raised us by herself—had strength for Jackie only and often not even enough for her. Yet, despite the darkness, Aunt Madeline and Ella radiated a kindness and caring that would, in time, bloom and flower.

Chapter 4: AIRPLANE

Troy, New York, 1945-46

When I was three and a half, my father announced he had been hired as a salesman by a man who manufactured aluminum storm doors and windows. Mom began to perceive that my father didn't hesitate to change jobs if he heard of one that paid better. Thus, we moved once again—217 miles, from Sandy Hook, Connecticut, to Troy, New York.

As with Connecticut, I have few clear memories of our time in Troy. One vivid recollection, however, shows how our family life was evolving into further violence. On a day my father came home for lunch, we sat in three chairs around the maple table, my father in one chair, I in another, and my mother, with Jackie on her lap, in the third, facing my father at the head of the table.

I had eaten half my peanut butter and banana sandwich, then said, "Mommy, I can't eat anymore."

My father glared at me. "Don't be stupid. You eat the rest, or you'll be sorry."

I looked away from his mean eyes. "I'm full, Daddy," I said, in a small, pleading voice.

"Eat it, you stupid brat!" he said more loudly, as he leaned down to take off his brown shoe.

Uh-oh.

Mommy, holding Jackie, shouted, "Stop, Joe!"

I picked up my sandwich and took a small bite, chewed for a long time, then swallowed. The rubbery ball went down reluctantly, but then I gagged and spit it onto my plate. "I can't," I said, starting to cry.

He jumped up, grabbed me, and started hitting my bottom with his shoe. Mommy yelled at him to stop. "Shut up!" he yelled back. I wailed until he let me go; then I ran to hide in my room, covering my ears so I couldn't hear them hollering at each other.

My mother told me when I was older that, as a bride, she believed a wife should never challenge her husband's decisions, especially in front of their children. But her feelings changed as he became increasingly harsher with Jackie and me. I shiver and protectively wrap my arms around my waist as I remember, still feeling the fear always inside my belly when he was home. And I think of how his heartless parenting skills so deeply affected my little sister.

My second memory contrasts richly with the first and makes me chuckle. Within the important life circle that holds friends and other social interactions, my mother became friendly with our next-door neighbors Ray, Evva Mae, and their three young daughters. One day, I was playing with the two oldest girls, Rae Ann and Annie Mae, at their house, when Evva Mae said, "I'm going to run over to Audrey's house for just a minute. Now, you girls be good while I'm gone." When the back door closed behind her, we looked at each other. We were alone, free from supervision, and could do whatever we wanted—a first for me.

Annie Mae looked at us and said, "What do you want to do?"

Rae Ann didn't hesitate. "Let's have some cookies. Mommy hides them up there." She pointed to a cabinet that went to the ceiling and said, "On the top shelf, in that cabinet."

"But somebody's got to climb up on the counter and get them," Annie Mae said, looking at me.

I stared up at the cabinet. Those cookies might as well be on the moon, for as high as that cabinet was. "Me?"

They both nodded. "You're the smallest. We'll help you get up there."

I hesitated; then, because I wanted them to like me, I said doubtfully, "Well, okay." Rae Ann and Annie Mae boosted me clumsily onto the counter, as I grabbed the cabinet edge to keep from falling. Then I stood up shakily, held on with a death grip, and opened the cabinet door.

"There they are!" Rae Ann and Annie Mae both shouted. Soon I handed them a package of Oreos. The girls helped me safely off the counter (getting down was easier than up, I learned), and Rae Ann showed me how to twist open my Oreo and lick the delicious icing off each cookie. "They should put more icing inside," we agreed. I, in fact, would have been happy just to eat icing and forget the wafers altogether.

Rae Ann was just reaching for her third cookie when the back door burst open. Evva Mae looked at us with wide eyes, then said, "You got those cookies down by yourselves from way up there?"

Rae Ann and Annie Mae nodded yes. I owned up to nothing; instead, I braced myself for punishment. As I wondered how bad it would be, Evva Mae extended her hand to Rae Ann, saying firmly, "Well, you're just lucky no one got hurt climbing up there. Now, give me those cookies; you've had enough."

Rae Ann handed the package back. I began to breathe again and looked at Rae Ann, who grinned back at me, her teeth covered with mushy chocolate cookie. Evva Mae, with her nurturing disposition, showed me, as had Aunt Madeline and Ella Reiner in Connecticut, that within that small circle of kind people, I was safe from severe punishment when I'd done something bad, as opposed to when I was home. I didn't understand yet that other homes were much different than mine, but I never forgot those rare, unexpected moments of compassion when they happened.

Most days after breakfast, my mother sent me outdoors to play while she took care of Jackie and the house. Our front yard was close to the busy road, so I had to stay in the backyard. There, I created a hideout under the porch, where a lattice ran from the porch floor to the ground. I was a little chubby but managed to wriggle through a small side opening, plunk down cross-legged on the dirt, and play. I liked that I could see out but no one could see me. I was cool in the summer heat and also invisible in what I now see was an alternative cocoon, one of many I would wrap around myself for decades as I became increasingly invisible.

The final Troy memory is precious and also bittersweet, a time when my father took me flying with him. He'd become friends with a man named Al Reed, who owned a small Piper Cub. Al invited our family to go for a plane ride, but when the big day arrived, my mother stayed home with Jackie. Just my father and I met Al at the grassy regional airport.

I remember small fragments of an exhilarating, sometimes dizzying time in the air. I sat alone in the rear of the plane, staring out my tiny window, while my father and Al schmoozed up front.

I smile with affection at my young, innocent self that day, as I recall feeling like Tinker Bell flying above the Earth. Although the flight gave me an amazing new perspective on my world, I wouldn't fly again until I was in my fifties. By then, I would have completely forgotten about that day many decades earlier.

After we landed, someone—probably Al—took a picture of my father and me. My father stood behind me, his hands on my shoulders. We both smiled broadly, and our eyes shone. This became a standout moment in my childhood; my father and I had a great adventure together, and he seemed to like being with me that day. He was charming, as he always was around his buddies, and he did not call me stupid even once.

In her book *In the Body of the World,* Eve Ensler tells us, "Stupid is a word that gets into you, into your blood and your being. It gets into your cells. It is a violent word, a catastrophic word, a stigma, a scarlet letter *S,* and sadly it was my father's favorite word for me."

Ensler's words speak with brilliant clarity to all who have been devastated by this particularly insidious label. When "stupid" seeps into our psyche, it poisons our self-respect and causes us to feel not only dumber than a floorboard, but also worthless. Did my father know that his word choice would affect my life for decades? Maybe, but probably not. I share this with you, dear reader, with the hope that you were never a target of the word or that a child you know has never been called stupid. If so, you can know that such language was not your fault, or the child's, and that neither of you was stupid.

Decades passed before I slowly emerged from the "stupid" snakeskin that smothered me and I could accept I was intelligent. I've wondered sometimes how my life would have unfolded if I'd known that fact decades earlier; even today, the word can grip me at unexpected times and make me nauseous with anxiety until I figure out what has happened and self-talk through the situation.

The plane ride, sadly, is the single good childhood memory of my father that I retain.

Chapter 5: BOOKSHELVES

Center Moriches, New York, 1946–47

Near my fourth birthday, the storm-door-and-window business folded and my father lost his job in Troy. By then, my mother was weary of packing up her family of four to move every year or two.

"Joe, I want to move back to Center Moriches, near Mom and Pop," she told him. "I need help with the kids, and you're hardly ever here."

Grandpa offered to apprentice my father in his carpenter trade and told my parents he would rent them the sizable apartment upstairs in his home. While my mother was elated to move back to Center Moriches to be near her parents, my father—though happy to return to New York, where he'd lived his entire life before moving to Texas—was uneasy with the thought of living and working with his in-laws. From that first day in 1940 when my grandfather had met my father, the awkward moments that resulted from his questions about my father's work and non-enlistment in the service had, in fact, gelled into a lifelong uncomfortable relationship that would deteriorate progressively over the years.

How did I feel about leaving Troy? I looked through my mother's photos for that answer and found three small shots outside a house I have no memory of. Mom wrote, "The family preparing to move to Center Moriches" on the back of each. My mother, unsmiling, looks very tired as she holds Jackie. Both Jackie and I stare into the camera, expressionless. My father's countenance is a mixture of seeming happiness diluted by something I cannot interpret. Pretend happiness, maybe.

The Dodge transported us—for our final move, my mother hoped—220 miles from Troy back to Center Moriches, where we settled into Grandmother and Grandpa's apartment. Here, we opened a new, long chapter; in fact, my mother would live out the rest of her life on Long Island.

My grandmother's mother, Adelaide Cartwright, a widow in her seventies, also lived with my grandparents; my grandmother Davis cared for her. Grandma Cartwright's dear heart petal is also fastened on my quilt. I remember my mother and grandmother Davis giving me a bath one day in the large porcelain kitchen sink. Grandma Cartwright didn't help but stood off to the side, talking quietly with my mother and grandmother. I recall feeling embarrassed about being naked, yet it was pleasant to be with these women.

This was the summer of 1946, I was four years old, and they were wondering if I was old enough to enter kindergarten. My mother called the school to inquire.

The office secretary said, "We won't have a kindergarten class until next year. Your daughter will be five then, just the right age to start. Give her another year; she's too young for first grade this year."

My mother was disappointed. She still felt as she had when she'd sent me to nursery school: that she needed others to help care for me. My little sister was, in fact, growing ever more demanding of my mother's attention.

Unwilling to accept a no, Mom called the school again and asked to talk with the principal. "My daughter is bright, and I know it will work out fine," I heard her say.

"He'll think about it and let me know," she said to my grandmother when she hung up.

Three days later, my mother was ecstatic when the principal told her, reluctantly, that he would try me out in first grade at age four and a half. If he believed it wasn't working for me, he would send me home to restart the following year. I, of course, had no idea what any of this meant, but I saw that my mother was happy, and because I liked to see her that way, I decided this must be good.

By the tender age of four, I had learned that whenever I couldn't avoid my father when he was home, he might not hurt me if I used a soft, saccharine voice to please him. I didn't fear my mother, but I worked hard to please her, too, because she sometimes rewarded my efforts with a smile. I derived some self-worth from the knowledge that I could help her feel happy. And so, at this point in my young life, I slipped into a care-taking role for both my parents, with the occasional reward of feeling as if I had some value, or that I was alive, or real. Yet I had made a high-priced decision, albeit unconscious, to be a caretaker. None of us understood that within me resided a spirit that was uniquely mine, like a tiny diamond that, if nurtured and polished with caring, could sparkle with multiple passions and talents and rich, varied feelings. Instead, that gem would lie dormant within me for five more decades.

"Mary Jo, look what just came in the mail," my mother called out happily one day. She opened a package to reveal white fabric with delicate red lines.

"I'm going to make you a dress for the first day of school with this material," she said, as she unfolded pieces in strange shapes. "It's precut," she went on, "so all I have to do is sew these pieces together. When I'm done, you'll have a new dress."

"It's pretty, Mommy," I said, wondering how this flat material could ever become a dress.

"Ah, here's the collar," she said, holding up two white half-ovals. "And this is bias tape to decorate the collar and the red bodice."

During the days that followed, I stood quietly nearby watching the dress come to life under the guidance of my mother's fingers and her feet, as they pumped the treadle on her Singer sewing machine. Soon, my dress was done.

"Now, cross your fingers and try it on, Mary Jo," she said, frowning slightly, her own fingers crossed. She slid the dress over my head, then said, "Stand back and let me see how it looks."

In a few seconds, she smiled broadly. "It fits beautifully," she breathed. Again, she was happy, so I was, too.

Although we didn't exchange conversation or teaching of skills, as my mother constructed my dress, I nevertheless learned that a person could transform fabric into a dress, something I thought was as amazing as a newborn kitten. This was, I now believe, the seed that bloomed into my lifelong pleasure in and love of creating clothing and, later, quilts from all kinds of textiles.

As the first day of school approached, we counted down. Mom was eager, and I was looking forward to wearing my new dress. Finally, the big day arrived: I'd been bathed, shampooed, and dressed in my pretty dress, my reddish-brown, shoulder-length hair was braided, and I held my new red lunch box. My mother posed me outside my grandmother's back door for a picture of a smiling me. Holding her Brownie box camera, she winked one eye closed and said, "Say cheese, Mary Jo."

I've often studied that old photo. There are few photographs of me that I like; this is one. Yet the expression on my face compels me to study it closely. Half-smiling, lips together, my head tilted slightly downward with skinny pigtails framing my face, I'm most fascinated by my eyes. Looking directly into the camera, with a hint of happiness, they are also distant and reserved. While writing this story, I spent an afternoon looking through a box of family pictures, searching for one of me with a big, broad, spilling-over-with-happiness smile. I didn't find one, not even in the years before Jackie's birth. That same reservation was always there, prevalent through the decades. Even today, I see it in some photographs. I no longer feel shame when I see that old expression, though, for now I know its roots.

I entered a new phase of life: public school. First grade was located at the other end of town, in the huge white Presbyterian church basement. I vividly remember sitting at a desk near the front of the room, my fold-up seat attached to the desk behind me, feeling as strange as I had in nursery school. Why was I here with all these kids whom I didn't know? However, I quickly learned that our teacher, Mrs. Havens, told us everything we needed to do and when to do it. I wondered if I was in school just for one day or if I'd come back another time. I still wanted to be home with my mother and grandmothers.

I learned those answers in time and got used to school, yet I never lost the feeling of being very different from the kids whom I saw laughing and playing together. As I had in nursery school, I stayed quiet and invisible and hoped nobody would notice me.

Yet there was one part of first grade that absolutely thrilled me. I was learning to read, and I *loved* reading books. I believe today that the stories my mother read to Jackie and me helped lead me to that moment in school that birthed my lifelong passion for books.

Each morning, Mrs. Havens asked, "Who wants to read to the class today?"

I loved that question! It was the singular moment of each school day when I became alive and assertive. I raised my left hand, held it at the elbow with my right hand, and then shook it vigorously back and forth so Mrs. Havens had to see it. Sometimes I called out, "I do, Mrs. Havens! I do!" I so wanted to read to the class that I burst from my cocoon and let myself be both seen and heard. Mrs. Havens couldn't have overlooked the fact that reading was deeply meaningful and important to her otherwise-silent student, who in all other ways passively blended in with the walls. She often called on me; in the glorious moment when I heard my name called, I was exhilarated. When she didn't, I struggled with profound disappointment.

Look, Jane, look. See Spot run. Even now, in my eighth decade, I smile whenever I think of those wonderful first words. They are deeply etched in my memory, sharing space with the blossoming joy I felt in first grade when I finally learned to read.

One day Mrs. Havens handed us each something she called a report card. "Put it in your lunchbox, and give it to your parents tonight," she told us.

I handed it to my mother, who sat right down and opened the envelope. Glancing down at the paper, she looked up at me and smiled. "You've done well, Mary Jo. I'm very proud of you."

I'm very proud . . . Those words felt as delicious as Thanksgiving pumpkin pie. There was a negative notation that we didn't talk about because it probably didn't seem important then. In this first, and in every subsequent, report card in my elementary school years were noted the words *emotionally immature.* I didn't know what that meant but intuited it wasn't good, and felt ashamed. Not until junior high school would I understand the meaning of the term, when it reaffirmed my core belief that I was stupid.

Meanwhile, at home, my father's apprenticeship with Grandpa Davis and Uncle Gene wasn't going well. He was miserable, and, worse, Grandpa didn't like him, nor did Uncle Gene.

One night he yanked open the apartment door and snapped, "Audrey, I can't take this anymore. I hate working with your father, and I hate carpentry, too. Tomorrow, I'm looking for another job. I'm done!"

In my room, I slid into my cocoon as I heard further words. "And I can't stand the way he's so damn cheap with the electricity and the heat," my father continued. "We're getting out of here as soon as I get another job!"

My mother said, "But, Joe, I don't want to move—"

"There are no buts about it, Audrey." They argued a while longer, and then I heard him stomp down the stairs, slam the front door, and squeal out of the dirt driveway.

When my mother came to my room to hear my prayer, her eyes were red. I knelt by my bed:

Now I lay me down to sleep. I pray the Lord my soul to keep. If I should die before I wake, I pray the Lord my soul to take. Amen.

She tucked me in, kissed my cheek, said good night, and clicked off the light. After she closed the door behind her, I tossed a long time in the darkness, wondering what would happen to us now.

Chapter 6: SHADOW PLAY

Mastic, New York, 1948–50

M y father stirred up his charming side by giving the mirror a toothy smile. He had dressed in a white shirt, a tie, brown slacks, and polished dark brown leather shoes. I watched from the hallway, carefully out of sight, knowing he could change from that nice man to the mean one faster than a lightning flash.

Sweetly, he said to my mother, "Wish me luck, Bup." I hated that nickname, understanding when I was older that it bore covert, abhorrent disrespect. He kissed her noisily, the sound of a chirping bird, and drove off to the Center Moriches Appliance Store. The owner hired him that day to sell a brand-new product: television sets. My parents started house hunting and soon purchased a two-bedroom bungalow five miles away, in Mastic.

Today, I think of recent drives through that small town. Despite improvement efforts by present-day home- and business owners, my stark perspective remains: the homely bones of an area carelessly tossed together, a hodgepodge of buildings and garish lighting up and down the main highway. My perception may also echo, in part, the fundamental desolation of our lives there.

We lived on Park Avenue, seventy-five miles from Manhattan's vibrant Park Avenue. The contrast was dramatic. Mastic's Park Avenue was remote, with bare, weedy fields on both roadsides. Beyond the bleak, one-mile drive to our house was a tiny regional airport, where cracked concrete hosted abundant weeds in and around it. Yet during our first summer, Jackie, Mom, and I discovered a wild blueberry patch in that middle of nowhere that astonished us with abundant, sweet fruit.

I felt proud that we owned this house and loved the honey-colored, polished maple furnishings in the bedrooms and living room that came with it. My parents needed to bring just the small maple kitchen table and chairs they bought as newlyweds, and our clothes, dishes, linens, and toys.

Since we'd moved from the Center Moriches school district, I transferred to second grade in West Moriches, into a white, annexed building that was part of the large William Floyd school system. The following year, my mother enrolled Jackie in kindergarten and I entered Mrs. Badalado's third grade.

I recall little about that school year, except a haunting, recurring dream: I sat quietly at my desk in Mrs. Badalado's classroom, always aware I was a very bad girl. Without warning, each day she hurried to my desk, pulled me out of my seat, and dragged me down the aisle to her desk chair, where she tossed me over her lap and spanked me in front of the entire class. I cried and wailed.

After the spanking, I always woke up and, strangely, felt relief from the pain of knowing I was such a bad person. I didn't mention this dream to anyone until many years later.

Sometime during those months, my mother brought a delightful and lovable surprise into our home, a registered Welsh terrier named Sir Corcoran of Wales; we called him

Corky. Before Corky came to live with us, there was just the swing set, some toys in the sandbox, and a cat, which had recently had kittens and homesteaded near the basement door. But now there was Corky, a happy, vibrant being who filled our house and backyard with his energy and joy.

Corky had thick, wiry tan-and-black hair and fat, round, stumpy front legs. His face was unusual, with a jaw so square it looked like a fur-and-mustache-covered rectangular shaped box. His *woof* was short, deep, and loud but not scary.

We'd always had pet cats, but Corky was our first dog and I adored him. We played together in ways the cats wouldn't: he loved to run and chase sticks, he sat when I told him to, and he always stayed close to me. Each day after school, when I pulled open the chain-link gate, he ran to me with sloppy kisses. Corky was like the best friend I'd never had, and he made me laugh out loud, a rare sound in our house.

One day after the bus dropped me off and I walked the mile home, Corky wasn't waiting for me. I ran inside, where Mom told me someone had left the gate open and he'd gotten away. Two days later, he was found at the side of the highway, killed by a car. I cried so hard, Mom decided we wouldn't get any more dogs because it was too hard to lose them. When I stitched my dear doggie's heart patch onto my quilt years later, I smiled remembering the joy he brought to my life.

Then something exciting happened. My father, who'd been selling televisions for more than a year, brought a Motorola home for us. Until then, I had visited the neighbor's house every day so I could watch *Howdy Doody* and *Pinky Lee* with the three neighbor kids. Now, with our own TV, I could watch at home and also discovered *Hopalong Cassidy*, *The Milton Berle Show*'s Uncle Miltie, who made me giggle, the wonderful puppets on *Kukla, Fran and Ollie*, and Ed Sullivan's *Toast of the Town*—and who could ever forget the announcer saying, in his baritone voice, "And now, it's the Loooooone Ranger . . . and Tonto"?

One Saturday, though, my father came home from work at Heller's Appliance Store during the day, slammed the back door shut, yanked open the refrigerator door, grabbed a Ballantine beer, and said, "I've been fired."

Mom crumpled into a kitchen chair. "Why, Joe?"

My father raised his right hand and batted air toward her face. "Oh, he got mad because he found out I've been selling TVs on the side. He said he hired me to sell for him, not be his competition."

Tears welled in my mother's eyes. "So now what?" She reached for her Viceroys.

Sensing trouble, I scurried to my room, but not before I heard his next words. "Aw, don't worry, Bup," he said, softening. "I've got a line on a better job. I met this guy Dressel, who sells real estate, and he's paying the kind of money I want. I'm gonna see him tomorrow."

Dressel hired him the next day. Our life soon changed in ways I liked. My father stayed out most nights with sales prospects. He also brought home new friends, and, shyly, I liked them. Hans and Gretel had a little girl named Monika; tall, thin Fred had a quiet, pretty wife named Norma; and short, burly Henry's wife was Helen, who told my mother lots of gossip. They came to our house on weekends when my father was home, where everybody drank beer and laughed a lot.

We'd never had company like this. Yes, there'd always been my grandmother and, occasionally, Aunt Mac, who was Jackie's godmother and Mom's friend from when she worked in Manhattan. A few times a year, Aunt Mac rode the Long Island Railroad out to visit us. She had pretty blue eyes, curly red hair, big, bright white buckteeth, and smelled like the purple lilacs that grew alongside our bungalow. She laughed a lot, too; I loved her company.

During one visit, I heard Aunt Mac tell my mother, "The subway fare just increased to ten cents; a lot of folks aren't happy." That wasn't a problem for Aunt Mac, who worked as an executive secretary for an economist named Alan Greenspan and lived comfortably in her Manhattan apartment. When she saw me in the doorway, she said, "Mary Jo. I've been wondering if you'd like to learn to knit."

I had always loved watching Aunt Mac's fingers flicking yarn around her clicking needles whenever she visited. I didn't know if I wanted to knit, but did know I wanted the time with her. "Yes!" I said.

She pulled a hank of bright red yarn from her knitting bag. As we sat together on the couch, I pulled yarn from the hank; she rolled it into a ball, then cast stitches onto a needle.

That completed, she put a needle in each of my hands, her arm around my shoulders, and placed her hands over mine. Ever so slowly, we knitted together. Despite my clumsiness, Aunt Mac was patient, though she often chuckled as we progressed. By the end of that afternoon, I could knit and purl by myself; my big, loose stitches already looked better than they had when I'd started.

"Keep practicing," Aunt Mac encouraged, her eyes twinkling as she smiled at me. "You're doing fine."

I warmed to her words and within days transformed that itchy red yarn into a scarf with slightly irregular edges caused by some dropped stitches. Too, I warm to that sweet afternoon so long ago, snuggled up close to Aunt Mac on the maple couch, when she taught me a skill I would enjoy throughout my life. I loved seaming Aunt Mac's heart leaf onto my quilt in later years. When I look at it, I smile because I can still hear her knitting needles clicking.

I liked hanging around when Helen and Harry visited on weekends. Harry and my father sat in the living room, drinking beer and watching baseball games on television. My father, a lifelong Yankees fan, would yell things like, "Those Brooklyn Dodgers are bums!" or, "How about Joe DiMaggio, setting a record with three consecutive home runs?"

On the next commercial, he ranted about Harry Truman's reelection upset. "Tom Dewey's my man."

Harry agreed.

Yet I liked listening to Helen's gossip more, so I sat quietly at the kitchen table as Helen and my mother prepared an onion dip. When they finished, I scooped a big glob onto my finger. As I licked at the scrumptious, smooth, salty cream, I heard my mother say softly, "I don't have a good feeling about Joe and Fred spending so much time together. Do you know what they're up to?"

"Oh, Audrey," Helen said tenderly, "you don't want to know what those two are doing. You would be terribly upset."

What are *they doing?* I wondered, alarmed. I looked at my mom, but she'd turned away and said nothing more. Helen changed the subject.

Looking back on Helen's warning words all those years ago, I could guess what the two might have been doing, but never knew for sure. Once, during a loud argument, I heard my mother accuse my father of taking advantage of poor people. He and Fred may have had a scheme to elicit money from the many disenfranchised people in our area. What I do know now, though, is that my father had been wandering down a shadowy path for quite a while by then. I believe his connections with his new employer and his friend Fred were likely catalysts that caused him to step through the door into life's dark side.

In early 1950, Mom became pregnant. "I'm doing everything I can so this baby will be born healthy," she told my grandmother.

"The baby will be here for Thanksgiving," she told Jackie and me. As that holiday approached, my parents talked about names: a girl would be Bonnie Jean; a boy, which my father really, really wanted, would be Joseph John III. As the end of November arrived, I remember my mother, who had grown huge and uncomfortable, often saying, "I can't wait for this baby to get here."

I, on the other hand, couldn't imagine having another sibling. I already had a sister and wasn't close to her, so what would be different about another one?

My sister, Bonnie Jean, was born on November 26, 1950, during a heavy snowstorm. I stared at my father later that evening as he ecstatically told Jackie and me that Bonnie was small, with light brown hair, and "absolutely beautiful." I was fascinated by his animation, something I had never seen him exude the way he did about my new sister.

While my mother recuperated in the hospital, Jackie and I both contracted chicken pox. When my father brought my mother and Bonnie home, Mom whisked her right into their bedroom, where my sister remained behind the closed door. Two weeks later, healthy again, Jackie and I met our new sibling for the first time.

Then Jackie got whooping cough and Mom had to quarantine Bonnie again. Sitting on my bed one morning and watching Jackie whoop and bounce involuntarily up and down on her bed to the rhythm of her coughs, I burst out laughing.

When she caught her breath, she glared and hollered, "Stop laughing at me! I hate it when you bug me!"

"Well, don't have a cow!" I retorted, taken aback, although I stopped laughing.

With Bonnie's arrival, we had outgrown our small bungalow. My father painted the entire house, making it look nicer than it ever had, and it soon sold.

Chapter 7: TURTLE TRACKS

Center Moriches, New York, 1950–55

"We're buying a house on Senix Avenue, just one street over from Mom and Pop's house," Mom told me one afternoon, her cheeks flushed with happiness.

"Can I have my own room?" I asked hopefully.

She shook her head. "There are three bedrooms: one for your father and me, a tiny one for Bonnie, and a medium one for you and Jackie."

"Can't I have the smallest one? Pretty please," I begged.

"It's better if you and Jackie share a room."

I did not want to share a bedroom with my five-year-old sister, yet my mother's words silenced me. I probably sulked until she yelled at me to stop.

The house was a weathered, two-story, cedar-shingled structure with an enclosed front porch on a quiet residential street. Downstairs contained a large kitchen, dining room, and living room with a broad staircase up to the three bedrooms and bath. Jackie's and my room was L-shaped, enabling my mother to arrange our beds so we couldn't see each other when we climbed into them.

After our move I explored our new neighborhood, where I discovered a nearby wooded area behind a small subdivision of ranch houses. A narrow, trickling stream flowing through the hushed space enthralled me, as did the solitude. I grew to appreciate, after a rainfall, the pungent scent of wet leaves, as well as the dappled sunshine on sunny days. One day I almost stepped on a box turtle before I saw it. In silent awe, I watched the fascinating creature disappear into his shell; then, as I waited and watched, his little head emerged and he slowly walked forward. From then on, I searched every day for turtles in what became magical treasure hunts for me.

I'd carry a few home, where, beneath our horse-chestnut tree, I built a turtle pen from chicken wire. Mom said I could keep each turtle two days. She gave me lettuce and raw hamburger meat, which my terrapin friends devoured. I also cut a small opening in a cardboard box and flipped it upside down in the pen so my turtles would have a place for solitude, failing to comprehend they already carried that place on their backs.

I loved watching my turtles, their honey-colored lines defining squares on their molasses-colored shells, slowly lumber along the grass on their claw-like toes and webbed feet. The males had red eyes, while the females had brown eyes, like mine. I became fascinated by my turtles' ability to close themselves into their shell with their hinged front opening. Once, when Myrtle the turtle would not open her shell, I cautiously tried to open it with my fingernail.

"C'mon, Myrtle. Open your door so I can see inside," I pleaded, but Myrtle would not budge. Although an early teenager now, I could not yet have verbalized that Myrtle and I shared something in common: similar ways to protect ourselves when frightened.

If people could have peered into our house the way I tried to see my turtles' inner world, they would have seen five miserable people. Jackie's body was small and thin and felt hard as stone. Although it had been years since I'd watched her wailing in her crib and the leg brace was long gone, Jackie was nearly always unhappy.

My father was rarely home, and my mother was always busy, distant, or nervous as she struggled alone in a role that so needed two people. Daily life centered on Jackie's mood, rarely positive. If Bonnie or I caused Jackie to cry or yell, Mom told us to leave her alone. If Jackie and I argued, Mom told me to stop because I was the oldest. When Bonnie and Jackie fought, Mom took Jackie's side because she was disabled. If Bonnie and I bickered, my mother took Bonnie's side because she was the youngest. Always there was a winner and a loser. I was, of course, the consistent loser because I was oldest and "should know better." I couldn't possibly comprehend then the deep divisions this dynamic created between my siblings and me, nor can I believe now that my parents understood this outcome.

Mom told me in later decades how guilty and responsible for Jackie's retardation she'd always felt, and said she'd believed that if she gave Jackie her way, that would somehow compensate for Jackie's handicaps. Later, she understood how badly that theory backfired. Yet even if they'd had a strong, happy marriage, neither of my parents possessed the skills to meet Jackie's complex needs. It seemed our family was always bickering, mildly or intensely, and that we'd all slid into a deep well of negativity. My father escaped by not coming home, my mother had no escape, and we kids had no idea of any other way to be.

Mom would later learn that when she started miscarrying Jackie, she was given the drug diethylstilbestrol (DES), a synthetic form of the hormone estrogen prescribed to pregnant women between 1940 and 1971 to prevent miscarriage and related complications from pregnancy. Later research revealed that when daughters in utero were given DES, they had a high risk of developing adenocarcinoma of the vagina and cervix, and breast cancer.

Today, the National Cancer Institute says of DES Daughters: "DES is now known to be an endocrine-disrupting chemical, one of several substances that interfere with the endocrine system to cause cancer, birth defects, and other developmental abnormalities. The effects of endocrine-disrupting chemicals are most severe when exposure occurs during fetal development." That statement raised, for me, a world of potential explanations for my sister's disabilities, yet, as I write this book, Jackie in her eighth decade has remained healthy and cancer-free.

Pretty, dark-eyed, blond, and lithe, Bonnie was my father's favorite child. Yet when he came home in a foul mood and Bonnie greeted him with the same saccharine voice I used to try to please him, he'd yell, "Shut up and get out of here!" Sometimes he'd smack her, devastating and confusing her with the strange love-hate relationship between them.

I understood in later years that, because I acted out in some ways that resembled my father's ways, my mother often directed her frustration and anger toward my father at me. In the therapeutic world, it's called displacement of anger.

"You're just like your father," she'd holler. I didn't experience my father as a very nice man, because he targeted me with so much anger and degradation. If I was like him, that meant I was not a nice person either, right? My deep self-hatred was reinforced. Even though my mother's intention was to motivate me to act better, the opposite occurred because the words were so hurtful.

If, as a quilter, I could stitch a priceless new gene into every newborn's genetic code, it would give each child the wisdom to know that sometimes parents, peers, and others of influence are wrong in what they say or do. They're not perfect and that's okay, in most instances. The gene would also provide the wisdom to know when these people are wrong.

The most harmful part of our family dynamic, as I see it in today's sunshine, was that we were each effectively cut off from any lines of affection or other positive interactions. We were silent, sullen, angry, mean, or sarcastic with each other.

Now, like Myrtle, I close this small glimpse into our home.

Our move returned me to the Center Moriches school system in the fifth grade, where I rejoined kids I remembered from first grade. I smiled shyly and said hello, as if glad to see them again, noticing they looked much the same. In the interceding years, though, my weight had slowly climbed and I was then twenty pounds overweight.

"We should talk to Dr. G. about a diet for you," Mom said one morning when she noticed my dress was too tight. A few days later, I sat quietly in his office, feeling shamed, jittery, and invisible as they talked about my weight problem.

"Here's a diet that should help," Dr. G. said, handing my mother two sheets of paper. "Come back in a month, and let's see how you do."

Vaguely, I recall some changes in the food my mother served us, but no conversations about portion sizes or the idea that if I didn't sit in the rocker, reading a book every day, and instead got up and moved around, that might be helpful. I recall still eating cupcakes the bakery truck delivered weekly. But mostly I remember that I lost no weight and continued to hate my body. The pain of that self-loathing was alleviated only when I separated from thinking about my overweight self, which was most of the time. Body awareness was a concept I would not know about for decades, in part because I unknowingly lived outside mine. I did know I'd never look as good as the slim, pretty girls I went to school with.

Later that year, Mom bought me a bicycle as an early birthday gift. I wonder now: Did she believe this would be a way for me to lose weight? I never asked, and she didn't say. Either way, I loved riding my blue bike on the long, flat roads all over our neighborhood. I may have lost a little weight; if so, I don't recall that, but weight loss *was* ahead in my future.

I believed all families were like my family, until I formed some friendships in our new neighborhood. Jeannie, a year younger than I, lived across the street in a big tan stucco house, and we became friends. We both loved reading and shared our Nancy Drew and Cherry Ames books. Her father, Ed, was what my mother called "salt of the earth," like her own dad. Ed was always home when not at work, devoted to his wife and daughter, puttering with small projects around the house. I visited Jeannie's house more than I invited her to mine because I liked her kind, soft-spoken parents.

Another man my mother considered "salt of the earth" was Uncle Matt. For several summers, he and Aunt Diane, along with their daughter, Bethany, rented a cabin in the nearby Hamptons where Grandpa B. and his wife, Mary, stayed. One summer Sunday, all ten of us rode in two cars to the ocean on Fire Island in Westhampton Beach. We unloaded our stuff onto the sandy asphalt parking lot—blankets, towels, umbrellas, toys, coolers of food, thermoses of drinks, and fold-up chairs—and trudged them up the boardwalk and down the stairs to the hot, dry sand. The sun bore down on us relentlessly as we staked out our place, spreading blankets, chairs, and umbrellas out on the beach like an incoming wave slowly crawling across the shoreline. Then I ran to the water. Some days it was calm and I could run right in, unafraid, while on other days waves thundered down. One of those waves could, I knew, easily knock me down, spin me around crazily, and pull me away from shore in the dangerous undertow.

Once in a while, on a day when the ocean was calm and clear, I pulled a green rubber diving mask over my eyes and paddled around in shallow water to see what lay on the sandy bottom. A variety of shells, stones, and beverage containers left behind by visitors lay randomly scattered and partly covered by sand. A few times I saw ahead of me a shadow that filled me with sudden terror that a shark might lurk nearby. I'd frantically leap up and race toward shore, then look back to see that the shadow was simply another human who'd been standing nearby. I exhaled in relief, not yet knowing that some humans were already dangerous shadows in my life.

One morning Uncle Matt said, "Bethany and Mary Jo, want to go fishing today?" I knew nothing about fishing but said yes. Soon the three of us sat in a small outboard motorboat, *putt-putt*-ing across the quiet waters of nearby Great South Bay, as wind blew our hair across our faces.

In a while, Uncle Matt slowed the boat and said, "Here's a good place to stop." I wondered why he had chosen this spot, which looked no different than any other in the huge body of water, but said nothing. He anchored, gave me a pole, put his arm around my shoulder and patiently showed me how to cast out the line. I was awkward, yet during the next few hours, as we rolled gently in the waves, we caught several small fish— snappers, I think—which we took home and ate for dinner.

While I saw no shadows in the water that day, I did see, for the first time in my life, how food found its way to the table. As usual, I ate too much that night, unaware of the link between the quantity I ate and my weight. Sadly, my shame, at how over-weight my body was and how large my clothing sizes were, was disconnected from food.

Late that summer, as Uncle Matt and Aunt Diane prepared to return to Syosset from the Hamptons, they invited me to come with them to visit so I could play with their daughter. I was thrilled when my parents agreed. My aunt and uncle were attentive to me, and I remember vague slivers of play with Beth-any. Though I remember few other details of the visit, I fondly recalled it as a highlight of my childhood.

I joined the Center Moriches Library, located in an older, white two-story house on Main Street. A ten-minute walk from our home brought me to this place I loved, where I discovered new worlds. Soon I signed out two books every other day, came home, curled up in the platform rocker, and read until dinnertime.

When my father failed to come home for dinner, which was nearly all the time, my siblings and I cheerfully ignored his strict rule that children should be seen and not heard. That rule was, for me, equally as silencing as when he called me stupid. Later in life, as I grew to understand the roots of my paralyzing silence and lack of expressive skills, I understood how vital it was to nurture a child by listening carefully and talking with respect in return.

Mom believed my father was usually taking potential cli-ents to dinner or having a drink to celebrate a deal. A few times she remarked, "I hope he's not taking advantage of some poor black family." My father sometimes chuckled about manipulat-ing a family who couldn't afford to buy a home into a purchase that would end in profit for him and probable foreclosure for the purchaser. It's hard to admit that I would smile at his story as I sought his approval. It is also profoundly sad to see now the cruel values I blindly accepted as okay.

Along with business, my father may well have been seeing other women—or men, as I would later learn from an unlikely source in my twenties. Although our mother wished for a happy family sitting around our dinner table, she knew by then it wasn't possible. Those silent meals when he was home were so strange, as I think of them now, with little conversation even between my parents. Mostly, though, he wasn't there and his plate steamed all evening above a large pot of simmering water. If he wasn't home when Mom went to bed, she sighed, turned off the gas burner, and put his plate in the refrigerator.

In 1953, I entered seventh grade—the year my school offered Home Economics to girls and Wood Shop to boys—and my lifelong love affair with textiles and spools began. As I walked into the Home Ec room that first day, my eyes fastened on the six sewing machines that lined a wall of huge windows. Like a parade of miniature train cars, they would transport me into a thrilling new world of fabric and thread, where I would learn cherished, lifelong skills.

Our attractive, blond-haired teacher, Mrs. Forster, informed us, "We'll sew the first half of the semester and cook the latter half. The second semester, you'll take Shop and the boys will take Home Ec." I rolled my eyes when I thought of the boys cooking and sewing, for I looked through a narrow lens of adult male and female roles then: essentially, men worked, mowed the lawn, and washed the car while women stayed home, raised children, cooked, and cleaned.

I daydreamed as Mrs. Forster talked, picturing her in her own home, calm and gracious as she prepared delicious meals and sewed for her family. She was the adult I wanted to become: a talented homemaker.

"For our sewing project, I'll teach you to make an apron. You'll need to purchase a pattern, fabric, and thread," she said.

My heart plummeted. *An apron? Yuck!* I'd tried Mom's apron on once, and my mirror had shown me that I looked fat and frumpy. But eventually I resigned myself to the fact that an apron would be my starting point.

Mrs. Forster showed us how to operate a sewing machine, how to pin fabric pieces together, and how to stitch straight, five-eighth-inch seams. Mom took me to Woolworth, where we chose a simple apron pattern with a gathered skirt and waist tie. As Mom leafed through the patterns in a deep drawer beneath the counter, I stared wide-eyed at the beckoning world within.

We carried a bolt of pink cotton to a saleslady, who unrolled it with a *thump-thump*, then measured, cut, folded, and handed me a yard. I carried the fabric and matching thread to the fair-haired cashier and watched her punch her white cash register keys.

"That will be $1.48," she informed us. Mom paid, the checker smiled as she handed me my small bag of treasures, and I said, in my artificially sweet voice, "Thank you."

At home, I tenderly placed my purchases on the dining table, the brown bag beneath the fabric like a serving dish, the spool resting neatly in its center. All weekend long, each time I walked by, I paused to touch the soft fabric and enclose my hand gently around the small spool. On Monday morning, I could barely wait for class, where we showed each other our fabrics and patterns amid the happy hum of *oohs* and *aahs* filling the air.

After Mrs. Forster showed us how to carefully unfold the tissue-paper-thin pattern, smooth the pieces with our hands, place them on our fabric, and insert straight pins at right angles to the pattern's cut lines, she told us to pin our patterns on our fabric. She walked around the room, checking our work, helping where she needed to. When she got to me, she said, "This looks good, Mary Jo." My heart swelled with pride.

Next, she handed out sewing scissors, demonstrating how to hold the closed blades and extend the handles to the recipient.

"Use these only to cut fabric; any other use will dull them," she concluded.

When I placed my scissors on a cut line, fear suddenly froze me. *If I make a mistake, I'll ruin my apron before I start.* Fortunately, aside from a few wobbles on my cutting lines, which I quickly learned I could camouflage by sewing a nice straight seam, I cut my pieces adequately, with much relief.

We progressed from basting through stitching to the day my apron was finished. The moment felt magical: I'd made an apron, and I was delighted with how, well, *real* it looked. Yes, I'd had to tear out some seams to make them straighter, but I'd learned I could correct a mistake. In later years, I'd realize that carefully following a pattern and attentively stitching the anticipated garment became a metaphor for how I lived my life. I'd also discover, to my sorrow, that I could not correct all my mistakes by ripping out stitches.

Sadly, the sewing portion of my class ended and we switched to cooking. While I liked learning to make French toast, my hands ached to create clothing I would actually like—and wear. I walked to Woolworth one afternoon after school, looked through the catalog, chose a gathered-skirt pattern and baby-blue cotton fabric with matching thread, paid, and hurried home.

I smoothed the fabric on the dining room table, followed the cutting-out process as I'd been taught, and carried the pieces upstairs to the now-retired Singer sewing machine. When, a few days later, I stared critically at my completed skirt, I felt as exhilarated as I had after I'd made the apron.

Disappointed that a gathered skirt didn't allow my chubby body to look as svelte as my growing interest in boys wished for, I went on to make another skirt, simply for the love of creating. Then I made a blouse, which involved setting the sleeve into the shoulder curve; after ripping out stitches several times, I got it right. While I was not happy with how I looked in my handmade clothes, I was proud to wear them.

Seventh grade was also the year Mom announced, "I always wanted to take piano lessons, but we couldn't afford them, so I want you to learn." I'd been playing the clarinet in school for a few years and liked music, so I agreed easily. Mom hired Mr. Ninow to come to our home each week to tutor me.

Tall and nice-looking, he was also kind and patient. "Now," he said quietly, in his pronounced German accent, as my first lesson ended, "you must practice at least thirty minutes every day. I will know if you haven't."

That would be embarrassing, I decided. So I practiced faithfully and enjoyed the rewards.

I'd taken lessons nearly two years when Mr. Osborne, my junior high school music teacher, stopped me after band practice one afternoon.

"Mary Jo," he said, his blue eyes the size of quarters behind his thick glasses, "would you like to play a duet with Carolyn for your graduation ceremony? You'd play the piano, and she'd play her violin."

"Uh, what song would we play?" I stammered, stalling for time. Carolyn, who was in the most popular clique in our class, whose father was the school custodian, who had gorgeous clothes that her rich aunts bought her? Carolyn and *nobody me*? I was terrified.

"'Unchained Melody,'" he replied. "It's one of the most popular songs this year."

While I shook at the thought of being onstage with Carolyn, I thought of all the people who would be in the audience. My terror approached crisis level. Mr. Osborne saw something was wrong.

"I know you can do it," he said, the father of four cute, redheaded kids. His words warmed me. "You'll do a great job," he added, smiling.

I melted. "Okay," I said, though I still wondered how I could do this monumental thing.

I practiced the song endlessly, terrified I would blunder during the performance. When the day arrived, I felt surreal, unable to believe junior high was really over and that high school awaited in September. I walked into the auditorium with my family—pleased that my mother had purchased the pretty pink organza dress I wore, yet ashamed of my plump body—never suspecting the afternoon would bring me two extraordinary surprises. Soon, Carolyn and I were introduced to the audience. I trembled as I slid onto the piano bench while she assuredly lifted her violin to her shoulder. I nodded at her, and we played our opening notes. My fingers soon relaxed into the slow keyboard waltz they'd memorized, and I forgot everything except the loveliness of this song. Too soon, it ended. Our audience applauded rousingly. I joined Carolyn and together we smiled and bowed to our audience. This was my first surprise: I had played well.

Then we took our seats with our classmates on the auditorium stage and the ceremony commenced. After the main speaker addressed us, Mrs. Cox, the Latin teacher, began presenting achievement awards. I was thinking about how relieved I was about the song as I half-listened to her present the awards for science, then mathematics. "And now, the Balfour award for excellence in English goes to"—she paused—"Mary Jo . . ."

I thought I'd heard my name. *No.* Not me.

The girl next to me elbowed my arm and hissed, "Go! Get your award." My core belief that I was stupid fought fiercely to control me and I must have appeared shell-shocked as I walked toward Mrs. Cox. I mutely emulated what I'd seen the earlier recipients do: receive the medal with one hand and shake Mrs. Cox's hand with the other. Unbelieving, I returned to my seat and opened the small, square blue box. Inside lay a narrow, one-inch-long sterling medal with the word *English* raised across the bottom. Above the word was a shelf of books, with an open book and a lamp above it. Engraved on the back was *CMHS—1955*. It was my second astonishment of the day.

Had I dug into the colliding feelings within as I sat through the rest of the ceremony, I would have heard the intense, cold words in the voice that had said repeatedly to me through my life so far, *But you are so stupid. How could you have won that award?* Yet beneath the painful words was surely another, nearly mute voice that would have said, if only I could have heard, *You are not stupid and never have been. Doesn't the medal help you see that you are a smart girl?*

Outgrowing the destructive label of stupidity is long and tedious. The prevention is so much easier: to erase this unnecessary word from everyone's vocabulary and always find genuine ways to compliment or otherwise mirror each small or large success to a growing child.

Although I saw my mother's proud smile after the ceremony, I recall no compliment from my father. Yet memory can be selective; it's hard to imagine he didn't respond. Likely, he bragged about my medal to his friends because he'd have seen it as a positive reflection on him. The heartbreaking fact for us both, though, was that my father never experienced the true, deeper joy of a parent who lovingly praises and supports each small achievement his child makes through the years—the ones that help her grow into a confident adult.

After writing the first draft of this chapter, I opened my jewelry box, where the medal rested in repose in its original blue box, never removed. I opened the cover and moved my thumb gently over the tangible piece of precious metal that tried to tell me in the eighth grade something I could not fathom: that I was smart at something, that I was worthy of recognition. But back then, the tiny object simply collided with my terrible self-image.

Today, if I could return to that day, I would take that medal from the box after the ceremony, put it on a sterling chain, and feel proud to wear it often. Instead, although I kept it, I rejected it and hid it in a dark corner all those decades.

I paused and suddenly wondered, *Is it too late to wear it?* My answer was instantaneous: *Of course not!* I slipped it onto my favorite chain and fastened it to embrace my neck for the very first time—fifty-eight years later.

Chapter 8: BRICK WALLS

Center Moriches, New York, 1955–59

I n September 1955, Argentina ousted Juan Perón as I drifted into high school. Mom wanted me to take academic courses for college; I'd become the first person in our family to earn a degree, something she'd ached for at my age. Because I loved reading and writing, I decided to become an English teacher—a notion that, in truth, I could not envision.

Too busy to play two instruments, I decided to drop my piano lessons but continue with the clarinet. One day after band practice, I heard two girls talking about another girl, Sheila, in our band. She was blond and blue-eyed, the daughter of a successful businessman, and chubbier than I was.

"Isn't it sad that someone so pretty is so fat?" I heard one girl say to the other. The concept that you could be fat and pretty at the same time seemed impossible to me, but it spurred me to wonder if there was any hope for me.

"Mom, am I pretty?" I asked her later that evening.

"You're pretty enough for normal purposes," she replied, smiling. *Does that mean yes or no?* I wondered but didn't ask. Later, when I studied my shoulder-length bob in my mirror, my remote brown eyes, and my half-smile, with one front tooth overlapping the other, I knew I was not pretty.

Soon, though, I set aside that concern, as one of my classmates, Pam, and I became friends. Pam lived in adjacent Manorville, a wilderness with mostly open land, few houses, and plenty of forest.

One Friday afternoon, as we bumped along on the school bus to her house, Pam stopped snapping her bubble gum and said, "Little Bit, have you ever smoked?" Pam had created the nickname because she was four inches taller than I.

"Nope," I said. "Have you?" I'd never thought about smoking.

"Oh, sure," she said quickly. "Let's have a cigarette when we get home."

"Okay," I said, feeling uncertain. Yet I thought Pam was groovy, so what could be wrong with smoking if she did it?

Behind the barn, she lit up a Marlboro and inhaled by hissing through her teeth, then exhaled perfect smoke rings as she handed me the cigarette. I took a cautious, small drag, breathed in, and promptly choked. Pam, with her nasal Long Island accent, laughed so hard she sounded like a quacking duck.

"I'll never . . . smoke . . . again," I gasped in a strangled voice.

Pam said, "It gets better, Little Bit. I choked my first time, too."

I hated the acrid smell, the bitter taste on my tongue, and the whole stupid process, yet I persevered until I was hooked. Somehow, my mother suspected and one day asked, "Are you smoking, Mary Jo?"

I wanted to avoid an angry confrontation. "No."

Sternly, she said, "Honest?"

Oh. The rule was, we'd never get in trouble if we told the truth. If we said yes when Mom asked, "Honest?" the answer was definitely true.

I mumbled, "Well, I've tried it a few times," and braced myself for trouble.

She said, "If you're going to smoke, I'd rather you do it in front of me than behind my back."

Wow, I thought, *isn't that something?*

"How many cigarettes are you smoking a day?" she asked.

I divided the real number by four. "Maybe two a day," I said, praying she wouldn't ask, "Honest?"

"Okay, I'll give you two cigarettes a day if you promise to smoke them only at home." She pulled two Viceroys from her pack and looked into my eyes. I nodded, speechless; her response was so far from what I'd expected. I accepted them and said, "Thanks, Mom."

Two cigarettes a day was not enough, of course, since I was already addicted. I smoked my mother's daily ration at home and also bought my own Viceroys for twenty-three cents a pack. Soon, though, the Virginia Slims advertising snagged me like a fat, wiggly worm baiting a naive fish: *You've come a long way, baby!* I smoked them for fifteen years.

The advertising was seductive, and I was strongly drawn to the idea of having come a long way, yet, in truth, every report card still noted, "Emotionally immature." And while my grades were good, learning held little meaning or value. School was like home: I was detached and incurious. My more accurate mantra would have been *You've got a long, long way to go, baby!*

I was, however, thrilled when those Virginia Slims trimmed me down to a size four without dieting. I felt more attractive then, anguishing only because I was flat-chested compared with my peers. One day I joyfully discovered padded bras in Murray's Department Store and bought one. The next day, I wore a tight sweater with my skirt, and when I walked into homeroom, the boy who sat behind me tapped my shoulder and said, "Wow, your boobs got big last night. How'd that happen?"

"Shut up, Mahlon!" I hissed viciously, my cheeks flaming. I

clutched my notebook tightly against my chest all morning, then hurried home for lunch and changed into my AA cotton bra. Mother Nature could take her sweet time, I decided, mortified.

Then a new friendship unexpectedly arrived in my life and I felt even better about myself, like I might be almost as okay as the popular girls in my class. Toward the end of my junior year, I dated Doug, who was unpopular, pale, and skinny, with pimples and hands that tremored, as he smoked and drank coffee incessantly. Then a new boy, Cliff, moved to town and joined our class. He was an athlete, cute, and friendly with everyone, and seemed to enjoy talking to me. Doug noticed this and asked me if I'd like him to step aside so Cliff and I could get to know each other. His offer astounded me, and at first I demurred so I wouldn't hurt his feelings. Within a few weeks, though, he told Cliff and me that he was withdrawing from his and my relationship.

After that, Cliff and I began to date steadily. I soon wore his senior ring on a chain around my neck and felt popular at last. I had a cute boyfriend. He was busy with practice after school on the soccer and baseball teams. Though he was not a starter for either, I gazed lovingly at him as he sat on the bench, and if he was called to play, I cheered loudest.

Between sports, each day after school, Cliff and I walked to town, arms around each other. He'd pull open the door to Pete's Candy Kitchen, where we hung out, mostly just the two of us, until we had to go home for supper.

Pete the Greek, as everyone called him, stood behind the counter, gripping a lit cigar between his teeth. The sizzling sound of grease and the beefy burger scent on the grill behind the counter always greeted us, but mostly we sipped vanilla Cokes or creamy root beer floats. Cliff and I snuggled close to each other in our booth, pulled out our cigarette packs— my Virginia Slims, his Marlboros—ordered our drinks, and got together change for the jukebox. Some of our favorite songs that year were Bobby Darin's "Mack the Knife," Dinah

Washington's "What a Diff'rence a Day Makes," Johnny Mathis's "Misty," and Ricky Nelson's "Never Be Anyone Else but You." And everyone engaged in heavy foot tapping when Johnny Horton's "The Battle of New Orleans" started playing.

Sometimes we did pranks, like putting salt in the pepper shaker. The next day Pete would yell at us, but we never got into serious trouble.

My father was rarely home during my high school years. He still sold real estate with Dressel, the longest job he'd ever held. Most evenings he was with prospective clients, with friends in bars, and probably with other women. If someone had told me that my parents' marriage was a shell, I would have been surprised. In reality, though, Mom had been a single parent for years. Decades would pass before I understood that my parents' union modeled for me what a marriage was like. Had I known how well-programmed I was to follow a similar path, to become an overfunctioning single parent, I would have been stunned.

During that time, my mother, encouraged by a friend, applied for a job at nearby Brookhaven National Laboratory, a huge federal research facility in Calverton, and was delighted when she was hired. "I'm going to work for two reasons," she told me. The first was to send me to college, which made me proud. The second was a shock initially, but I soon accepted it: she had hired a lawyer to arrange a divorce in Mexico.

Now that Mom was working, I had to go home every day after school to babysit for my sisters and start supper. I reluctantly agreed when my mother told me this, but I quietly decided I would take a speedy walk to Pete's after school with Cliff, have a quick vanilla Coke, a few songs, and some cigarettes, then hurry home, with no one the wiser. I soon learned I was the unwise one, for on the second day, when I got home,

Bonnie and Jackie had gotten into an angry physical fight. I yelled at them both, and they in turn ran to our mother the minute she got home.

"I thought I could count on you to do this," she said, furiously slamming her purse on the yellow Formica counter.

"I want to be with my friends for just a little while," I whined.

She didn't take a breath before she spit out, "This job is going to send you to college. Have you forgotten that?"

Well, I had. Some of my sullenness melted, and now that she was home to take over, I faded away to my bedroom, where I realized how trapped I felt by this babysitting business. Being with my friends was the only good part of my life, and now . . . Yet from then on I came home right after school each day.

When the annual carnival returned to town, I couldn't wait to go. Cliff and I planned to go on Saturday night with some other guys he knew. When I told my mother, she said firmly, "No. You absolutely cannot hang around with a big bunch of boys like that. Tell Cliff you can't go, unless he wants to go just with you."

I was enraged. I called Cliff and told him what Mom said. He made no offer to change his plans, and we coolly said goodbye. He'd disappointed me, yes, but it was my mother I was so furious with that I shook as I ran up to my room. How *dare* she tell me what I could and could not do!

I decided I'd rather die than be treated that way. Sobbing, I tiptoed to the bathroom, opened the medicine chest, took out the aspirin bottle, filled a glass of water, and gulped aspirins between sobs. I had no idea how many I'd taken when I finished the glass of water, but I thought it was enough to end my life.

I returned to my room and lay down; in the darkness, my anger slowly diminished. Then a small ache of worry gripped me and grew. Did I *really* want to die? Maybe not. Minutes later, I decided I definitely didn't want to die. Yet I changed into my pajamas, climbed into bed, and clicked off the light. When my sister came in later and said good night, I murmured the same to her and wondered if I'd wake up in the morning.

I never told anyone what I had done. The next day, I woke feeling groggy and sluggish, but, since it was Saturday, I stayed home. Later that night, I felt better. And pretty lucky.

As graduation approached, Fats Domino topped the charts with his hit "Whole Lotta Loving." Pam and I, the youngest members of our class, regularly heard through the grapevine that there was, indeed, a whole lot of loving going on; every few weeks, another girl's name moved through the rumor mill as having gone "all the way." With so many new names on the list, we began to think we should consider joining it. Pam went first, and I soon followed.

Why did I decide to have sex with Cliff? I ask myself now. I was curious, I knew that my best friend and many of my peers were having sex, I believed I loved my boyfriend, and I liked his family, too. They were a close family, Cliff told me, and since I didn't know what a close family was, I believed him. I found no significance in the frequent drinking in their home, for alcohol was a regular resident in mine, too.

Mom took me to Murray's Department Store to buy my senior prom dress, a long, strapless baby-blue gown. I didn't recognize the slim, attractive brunette who looked back at me from the dressing room mirror, but I loved the way she looked.

Cliff, incredibly handsome in his tuxedo, arrived on prom night in his brother's Pontiac. We drove the mile to school, where we spent an evening unlike one either of us had ever experienced. Our arms around each other's waists, we walked into our school gymnasium, transformed into a paradise of crepe paper, flowers, streamers, and balloon decorations. We stood still a while, enchanted by the scene of our classmates, dressed up as we'd never seen them in all our years together. The evening felt surreal, yet soon we entered into the magic and danced through the night.

In 1959, we had no parties after a prom that we knew of, so when 1:00 a.m. arrived and friends began to leave, we said good night and left, too. Cliff drove down Lake Avenue and parked by the bay, where we stayed close and intimate until the sun creased the misty morning sky over the water.

Yearbook staff were snapping candid photos all over school while photographers were taking class pictures, as well as honor society, sports, and other extracurricular group shots. It was always exciting when the yearbooks arrived; this year was more so because it was my last one.

Finally, I held mine in my hands: a slim red leather book engraved with *Center Moriches High School Yearbook 1959.* Quickly I leafed to the senior pictures and found mine easily in the early pages. I wanted to see how my picture looked and read the words beneath it, hoping they said something really nice about me.

I glanced at the picture and deemed it okay, then read the words below. Stunned, hurt, and then furious, I stared unbelievingly at eight words some unknown person had written to summarize my high school legacy: "How sweet and fair she seems to be."

Although I'd thought myself invisible, like my childhood turtles in their shells, someone saw me as a "seems to be" girl. I'd tried so hard to be a nice person but had obviously failed. Who had written that mortifying remark? I wanted to tell off that person, but no one could give me a name. Yet I also knew I could not, if the time came, speak anger to anyone outside my home, where, by contrast, I was angry most of the time. The destructive emotion of anger is a terrifying mountain for many of us to scale, yet it is also where hopefully we learn that anger can be a constructive emotion, too—one that is important to convey in positive ways, whenever possible, and release. Since I learned this, I have sought to convey anger in as kind a way as possible to others because it was so destructive in my own life. I also believe that repressed anger can make us very ill.

Today, as I gaze into the glittery, dark eyes and joyless smile of my sixteen-year-old self, my heart hurts for her. When my eyes move from her face to the words beneath the photo, I wonder again who created that assessment. I'd still like to talk with that person, probably a teacher, but now for a much different reason: I've realized the statement was astute and accurate. I was definitely a "seems to be" girl. I seemed to be a lot of things—all the things I wanted to be or thought I should be—but even I didn't know who I was. My fragile personality was merely a façade I created to try to get others to meet my most basic need: to be liked and accepted.

I tried to please everyone I met and adapt to whatever I thought people needed from me in order to make me feel liked. When I quietly observed the popular girls in our class—pretty, well-nurtured, full of confidence—I wondered what it would feel like to be one of them.

Four decades later, I would learn that answer.

Shortly before graduation, Cliff called to say, "I'm not coming over tonight. I'm hanging out with Steve."

I was feeling quite possessive of him since we'd become intimate and replied nastily, "Well, Cliff, who do you love—Steve or me?"

We broke up that evening, and soon I heard he was dating a Leila from Riverhead. My boyfriend had dumped me, and I was a nothing again. I smoked and brooded and was so cranky when my sisters battled that they became quiet whenever I was around. I slid into my shell and avoided the graduation parties I'd been planning to go to with Cliff. The summer suddenly stretched long and lonely ahead.

Chapter 9: BOXES

Oneonta, New York, 1959–62

I worked that summer as a checker in our local supermarket, Bohack's, walking the mile to and from home. I earned fifty cents an hour—for about a week, until the afternoon Harry, the store manager, told me, "Mary Jo, I made a mistake about your pay. We pay the boys fifty cents; girls earn thirty-five cents an hour."

"That's okay, Harry," I said, in my best people-pleasing manner, meant to convey, *See how nice I am? You're not a bad person, Harry.* I already knew that women in my world were not valued and had just learned we didn't receive equal pay, either.

I smile now, remembering what happened three decades later when I encountered a similar professional salary inequality. My response was again polite, but I no longer gave myself away. Instead, I respectfully requested what I needed and received everything I asked for, including a $10,000 raise.

But during that precollege summer, my life centered on work. At day's end, I was tired and discouraged because I had no date to look forward to. I wasn't interested in other boys and vaguely thought I had a problem with the Catholic teaching that you give yourself to your husband only. I'd thought Cliff was my future husband. What now?

During those gray, transitory days, I was thankful my father seldom got in touch, for his visits shredded me emotionally. He couldn't accept the divorce and, though he was seeing another woman—Lil, from Mastic—told me tearfully on one occasion, "There's just no love like your first love." When he left, I sobbed for an hour or more, grieving for the family we might have been. I would later understand that he'd long shaped me into being his confidant, a form of caretaking, and much more. Thus, I believed on some level that his failure was, in part, my failure.

What did he expect would happen? I wonder now. Any vestige of a happy marriage had disappeared long before. A recent event had likely brought my mother to her moment of truth: my father had gotten himself into a financial deal that ended with the other party threatening a lawsuit against him. To head off possible loss of his biggest asset, our house, he signed it over to my mother, assuming she'd sign it back to him later. When she told him a few months later she was filing for divorce and keeping the house, he was outraged, while my mother felt immense relief in knowing she would have a home for her family. In hindsight, she was wise, for the house was all she'd have. He never provided child support, except for a few dollars here and there.

My father moved in with Lil, and, honestly, I didn't miss him, nor did Jackie. Throughout our decades, even today, if I ask Jackie a question about our father, she looks grim and says quietly, "I don't want to talk about him." My father's relationship with Bonnie had appeared more positive than Jackie's or mine, and now she acted out in angry ways toward my mother. And my mother? She didn't miss the loneliness, the neglect, or the infidelity, although in later years she talked occasionally about some of the good, early times they'd shared before it all went acerbic.

Meanwhile, I prepared to leave for college. Mom and I had fun shopping for clothes, a footlocker, and other necessities that I placed visibly in my bedroom as tangible affirmations that I was really moving. My roommate, Ella, from the Hudson Valley, and I corresponded and looked forward to meeting.

Aunt Mac joined Mom and me for the 250-mile trip into the Catskill Mountains, to Oneonta, known as the City of the Hills. I'd chosen this state university over urban Albany State because I preferred rural living. When we arrived, I stared reverently at those hills, where I would major in secondary English education.

Ella, sultry, with long dark hair that fell over her face, had already arrived. From the start, I had trouble relating to her. She'd written that she was engaged and would go home each weekend to see her fiancé. In fact, she spent all her spare time either talking with or writing to him. I, still hurting from Cliff's breakup, found it easy to disengage from Ella's life.

I quickly became overwhelmed with what I told my mother was homesickness. Later I would understand that—having been abruptly thrust from the only life I'd known—I was not homesick, I was just plain terrified. The powerful, controlling structure of home life was gone; I alone was responsible for myself now, for the first time in my life. Fortunately, the basic structure of a college schedule helped reshape my routines, which got me started and allowed me to gradually shed my homesickness. Within a few weeks, I'd made some new friends on my dorm floor—Bobbie, Peg, Gail, Sue, and others—faces I still see in my mind today, although we've lost touch. As I got to know my fellow English majors in our classes, I suddenly knew more peers than ever before and felt exhilarated.

As I settled into campus life, I soon discovered I'd brought weak study habits with me, so I worked harder. Yet, as the end of my first semester approached, knots took residence in my stomach when I recalled test grades: some D's and C's, and some lonely A's and B's. Terrified by the prospect of probation, I prayed for a C average.

My deeper panic, I'd understand later, was that probation would affirm that I was stupid, just as my father had declared all the days of my young life. I was determined I would *not* fail at college, still not knowing that I was intelligent.

When my transcript arrived with a bare C average, I was profusely relieved but not happy. It wasn't good enough; I vowed to do better the following semester—and did. My average climbed closer to a B and continued upward for the next two semesters.

My social life expanded when friends invited me to go to City Hall, a college bar in town, where we met boys from nearby Hartwick College and some townies. I was overwhelmed the first time I entered City Hall's cave-like interior, filled with a mammoth cloud of smoke that shrouded the entire room, wall-to-wall bodies, loud music, and shouting voices. But I returned each weekend and soon met Bill, tall, dark-haired, and nice-looking. He introduced himself and asked if I attended Hartwick or Oneonta.

"I'm a freshman at Oneonta," I replied self-consciously in my saccharine voice. "An English major."

When Bill smiled, I noticed his teeth protruded slightly. "No kidding! I want to be a science teacher." His dark eyes smiled. He also lived on Long Island, not far from my town, in fact. At the end of the evening, he drove me back to campus. He was nice, and I decided I liked him.

Each day, we spent time together on campus. When Thanksgiving vacation neared, Bill drove me home, but first we stopped in Jamesport to meet his parents. Bill had one older sister, also a teacher, married, with two young children. Bill's mom welcomed me warmly; his father smiled and grasped my hand, saying, "Bill has told me nice things about you." The inner unease I always felt with new people melted away with them.

We left and drove to my house, where Bill met my mother. After he returned home, she said to me, smiling, "He's a nice boy, Mary Jo."

The few vacation days flew by, and soon Bill pulled in to my driveway again. Although we'd talked each day of vacation, we chatted easily the entire ride back to Oneonta.

My friendship with Bill felt right in so many ways. Back at school, though, I was coming to terms with the fact that whenever Bill reached affectionately for my hand, I took it but felt inner distance between our entwined fingers. After a date, I returned his tender kiss but not his obvious warmth. Yet I liked Bill and our wholesome friendship and kept hoping those negative feelings, whatever they were, would pass. When they didn't, I became passive. I didn't return his phone calls, and our relationship faded slowly from my gentle neglect. I was sad but not sorry when he stopped calling; I didn't have to worry about those nagging feelings anymore.

Then I met Carl, slim, blue-eyed, and blond, studying pre-med at Hartwick, and the same pattern unfolded. Carl took me on nice dates and was obviously fond of me. I liked him just as I'd liked Bill but felt the same distance. Once again, a promising romance faded away.

Who can help me figure out what's wrong with me? I wondered. A member of the Newman Club, our Catholic campus organization, I called a priest at St. Mary's parish and made a Saturday appointment. On that snowy morning, I slogged down the hill from campus with a heavy heart, carrying the terrible sin I would soon confess. As I sat waiting for Father O'Brien, my stomach clenched with dread.

After half an hour, a white-haired man in a black robe opened the door and said, "Mary Jo? Come in."

I nodded and walked awkwardly into his cramped white

office, wondering what all those piled-high papers on his desk could be. He gestured to a chair beside his desk, where I sat down, crossed my legs, and folded my arms across my chest as he sat behind his paper stacks.

"What can I do for you this morning?" Father O'Brien asked. His matter-of-fact tone intimidated me immediately. I inhaled and stammered through my story: how I'd dated my high school sweetheart for two years, how in our senior year we'd "gone all the way," then broken up before I'd come to college, and how I wished I'd kept my virginity. He pursed his lips and shook his head slightly but said nothing. I pushed on.

"I've dated two really nice guys here but couldn't feel close to either of them. I'm not sure what's wrong with me but think it might be because I've been taught you only give your body to one man, your husband. What can I do?"

As I write today, I feel an ache that the priest didn't connect with my need for compassion, didn't understand the self-loathing and shame I was filled with, didn't convey forgiveness to me for my mistake. What I heard instead were neutral words that are now cloudy, something like, "Well, let's pray together; then you can pray for forgiveness every day."

I trudged up the hill sobbing, dragging my problem back with me—a now-heavier problem because *he* knew what I'd done, too. By the time I yanked open the door to my room, I'd angrily decided to stop dating. And that's exactly what I did.

The remainder of my freshman and then sophomore years passed amazingly quickly. My grades steadily improved, I had a nice circle of girlfriends, and we enjoyed many fun activities together. We played bridge, exercised in the dorm hallway, and taught ourselves to do the twist to Chubby Checker's hit song. Someone's stereo blasted the words as we held towels across our behinds, pulling them back and forth to get the right twisting motion. After dozens of repeats, howling laughter, and critiques, we agreed we'd gotten all the right moves.

I joined the Mask and Hammer Club, the theatrical group, where I tried out for a part, but my too-soft voice disqualified me, so I worked behind the scenes with props and makeup. I joined the Young Democrats and enthusiastically campaigned for John F. Kennedy. My marks continued to improve and included an honorable number of A's.

I formed a close friendship with a dorm resident assistant, Emily. She was an English major, too, a warm and bubbly woman engaged to Bruce, about to graduate with an MB from Duke. She had a car and took me everywhere with her, including a trip to Gloversville to meet her parents, sister, and brothers.

They were a warm, close family, and I loved my time with them. As Em drove us back to Oneonta one Sunday, she encouraged me to apply to become a resident assistant in our junior year. "You would have a free room for the year, and I'll give up being an RA so we can be roommates." That's just how it worked out.

One afternoon, I peeked into my mailbox window and saw a letter. I spun the combination, then slid out the envelope. When I saw Cliff's handwriting, I gasped and shoved the paper into my pocket.

More than four decades later, I can still viscerally feel how the mattress felt beneath me as I sat on my dorm bed—legs extended and gut churning—staring out my window that day.

Throw it away. Just rip it up and dump it in the garbage, I thought. But I hesitated, questioning why my ex-boyfriend had written. Curiosity won, and I tore open the letter. Now in the navy, stationed at the Great Lakes, he was sorry we'd broken up and hoped we could be friends again. I crumpled the letter and held it like a baseball in my two hands. *How many times did I hope for this moment two summers ago? But do I want this now?*

Frozen, I knew the answer. *Throw it away.*

But I didn't listen.

Strangely, I have little recollection of our reunion. I remember his coming to campus on his next leave, looking more handsome than I'd remembered, yet exuding the aura of being a different person now. We lived in opposing environments—he on a naval ship, I on campus—unaware that we were growing into dissimilar people. As we embraced and kissed, I felt a mix of awkwardness, familiarity, and uncertainty. Yet by the time he returned to Newport, the strangeness had disappeared and we'd reverted to our previous familiarity.

The rest of my sophomore year sped by. Cliff and I kept in touch daily. In May I went home to work at Bohack's again and saw Cliff whenever he got leave.

In September of my junior year, I returned to Oneonta as a resident assistant, delighted that Em was my roommate. I resumed my studies, yet now was distracted by Cliff. As I spent precious time writing letters to him, talking on the phone, thinking about him, I wondered why I didn't feel about him as I had in high school. Yet I plodded on, thinking this reunion with him was probably the answer to all those prayers Father O'Brien had told me to say. *It will work out*, I thought, not knowing then that those were my mother's words about her engagement to my father.

Then I entered into a slow downhill slide. I saw I was going to fail an English course—unheard-of for me—and pushed harder, yet found no way to relate to medieval English. I shocked myself when I simply gave up and accepted that I'd fail. About the same time, I started feeling physically strange and suddenly realized with horror my period was late.

Two nights later, when all was quiet on our floor, I sat at the hall phone and dialed the number at Cliff's barracks.

"Hello," a male voice said. I asked for Cliff and gave my name.

In a moment, he said cheerfully, "Hi! This is a nice surprise."

"You might not think so when I tell you why I've called," I said heavily, having no idea what he'd say about my suspicion.

"Why? Are you okay?" he said, apprehension sneaking into his voice.

"I feel strange, different, and I'm two weeks late," I said. "I think I might be pregnant."

Several seconds of silence passed. Then, enthusiastically, he said, "Well, we'll just have to get married, won't we?" He sounded happy. *I'm glad you're happy*, I thought, *because if you dumped me I wouldn't know what to do.*

I withdrew from college in the middle of my junior year. I told Em just before we left for mid-semester break that I wouldn't be back. She was devastated. Otherwise, no one knew but Cliff.

I was on the last leg, seventy-five miles on the Long Island Railroad, of my final trip from college. My belongings waited in temporary storage until I returned to Oneonta to move them. Mom waited at the train station to take me home for what she believed was a weeklong break. I dreaded, more than anything I could remember since I'd talked with Father O'Brien, telling my mother why I'd withdrawn.

It was cold and dark by the time she pulled her orange Volkswagen Beetle onto the soft, silent driveway at my grandfather's house, where she and my sisters lived in the upstairs apartment. As we trudged, laden with my baggage, up the stairs, she said, "I'll bet you're hungry." In the kitchen, she offered me some chicken and rice she'd prepared earlier.

My stomach was queasy. "Just a cup of tea. Thanks, Mom."

Soon, two fragrant cups of Lipton steamed the air as we sat at the small kitchen table. "Tell me how the semester ended up," she asked, her eyes proud.

"I did fine in all my classes except Medieval Lit. I just couldn't get it," I said, pursing my lips, giving no further details as we lit cigarettes and exhaled smoke toward the ceiling.

"That's too bad, but I'm glad the other courses went well," she remarked.

"I think I'll get a D in Medieval, but the others should all be A's and B's," I replied.

She nodded. "Any special plans for your break?"

I took a long drag on my Virginia Slim, inhaled deeply, and slowly exhaled. "Cliff's coming home for a long weekend, so I'll spend some time with him," I said, subdued.

She puffed on her Viceroy. "Well, I hope *we* can have some time, too," she said, sounding mildly irritated. She had never said it, but I knew she didn't like Cliff. I never asked why, because, as far as I could see, he was a cute, nice, average guy. Now I believe she saw a dark side that I failed to see.

"We'll have time, I promise." *Oh, Mom, you have no idea how much time we'll have. . . .* My stomach was little comforted by the warm, sweet tea.

Inevitably, the next morning arrived and I heard Mom run water into the copper teakettle, then thump it onto the gas stove. I lay still, thinking, *I wish I could sleep through today and wake up tomorrow to life as it was weeks ago—not pregnant but studying hard, making my mom proud, achieving the degree she's worked hard for me to have.*

Abruptly I recalled a conversation nearly three years earlier when Mom had urged me to ask my father to help with my college expenses. I'd worked the past two summers, and Mom was saving, too. I'd pushed the fear-filled words from my mouth the next time I saw him, trying to sound as if I were asking for something small, like a pack of gum. "Can you help me with some college costs?"

He'd snorted, waved his hand at me as if brushing away a pesky mosquito, and replied with derisive words I still hear today: "Nah, you'll just quit so you can get married. That money would be wasted."

Now, nausea filled my belly when I suddenly realized I was living up to—or, more accurately, down to—his low expectations. I groaned, then thought, *I've got to face this day* and pushed myself heavily from my bed.

Mom had already eaten, so I made a cup of tea and a slice of toast as she worked around the kitchen. Her adorable new dog, Duffy, the first since Corky had died, was a small black mixed breed who trotted into the room and dropped onto the floor with all four little paws splayed into a double split. He looked at me through strands of fallen fur, in his cute pose; I couldn't resist smiling.

After my final bite of toast, I glanced at Duffy again and thought he looked worried. "Mom, I need to tell you something."

She looked over at me from the sink, where she pulled the last dish from the drainer and clattered it onto the stack in the cupboard. She kept silent eye contact. Did she know already what was in the air?

"I've withdrawn from college . . . ," I said, watching her carefully.

Her parentheses-shaped eyebrows rose as her big brown eyes widened. Upon receiving news she didn't want to hear, she typically got upset and tense and her voice grew louder, but now she said nothing.

"I'm pregnant," I said softly.

Her slim body froze briefly, and then she began to shake her head from side to side. Devastated by her silence, I grabbed my cigarettes with a tremoring hand, lit up with my Lady Zippo, and puffed. "I'm five weeks late, and I feel strange."

She stared at me, blinked, and looked away.

I pushed on: "I called Cliff last week and told him. He sounded happy and said we should get married . . ."

She picked up the Comet can on the sink, sprinkled several shakes, and started scrubbing while I watched. When the sink was clean, she walked to the stove and scoured it with vengeance. By the end of the day, she'd not spoken more than a dozen words to me but had thoroughly scrubbed every inch of the now-immaculate kitchen.

The next morning, Mom looked despondently at me when I sat down across from her at the table.

"Morning," I said timidly.

She said wearily, "Good morning. I guess we're going to plan a wedding." Her tone implied it was more like a funeral.

I pursed my lips, looked into her eyes, and nodded slowly.

Chapter 10:

PINK BABY BLOCKS—JOCELYN

Center Moriches, New York, 1962

We were stunned when Cliff's parents opposed our marriage. New York law for marriage certificates required that the man be twenty-one and the woman eighteen. I was almost twenty-one, and Cliff was five months younger.

"You're *not* old enough yet; I *won't* sign this," his mother asserted, as she dropped the consent form on her kitchen table. Her Irish eyes blazed.

"Me, neither," Cliff's dad added sternly, his usually warm eyes dark and murky. I was shocked; I'd never anticipated this and looked at Cliff, who was studying the green Formica table surface. I interpreted their no to mean they didn't like me, which time would prove correct.

As he drove me home, Cliff said confidently, "Don't worry. They'll come around."

He was right. A few days later, they signed their consent, although they repeated that we were too young.

I sip hot tea and think those red flags would have caused any emotionally healthy young woman to forget marriage and raise the child as a single parent, or release the baby for adoption. Single motherhood was shameful in the 1960s, though; if anyone had encouraged me to consider those options, I would have said, "I'm Catholic. I have no other choice."

Even though I'd been a lapsed Catholic since my talk with Father O'Brien in college, I had a naive belief that my name was placed on a master list somewhere in the universe as a Catholic and that I could never be anything else. Yet when Cliff suggested we marry in his Episcopal church, I agreed, believing a Catholic priest would never marry us. I didn't care what church we were married in; it was simply imperative that we wed without delay. We explained our situation to Cliff's priest, who scheduled the ceremony in two weeks.

Did we love each other? Today I know how terribly immature we both were and how Catholic guilt trapped me. Whatever love was between us had little breadth or depth, and events would make that clear fairly soon. Meanwhile, Cliff and I obliviously chose our matching wedding bands. My mother took me shopping for a wedding outfit; I chose a navy-blue suit as I briefly thought of gorgeous white bridal dresses, but who could wear one in my condition? Mom arranged for a small sit-down dinner at a local restaurant after the ceremony.

On February 2, 1962, three days before my twenty-first birthday, I rose to a dreary, rainy day. *Today is my wedding day*, I thought, as

I watched rivulets meander down Mom's kitchen window. The words felt dreamlike. I had always imagined my wedding day would be filled with happiness, yet I felt little joy; rather, this was a necessary event to give the baby, who I could barely believe was in my body, a legitimate birth. *We're doing the right thing*, I told myself.

Few knew about our quiet afternoon wedding. My mother and sisters, and Cliff's parents and brother, were the sole attendees. I didn't tell my father about the marriage because I didn't want to hear his smug "I told you so" as I moved ahead the best I knew how with my life.

After the ceremony and tasty though subdued dinner, we borrowed Cliff's parents' Buick and left for a weekend honeymoon in Newport, Rhode Island, where Cliff was stationed on a destroyer at the naval base. We went sightseeing in Newport, visiting the lovely old stone church where Jack and Jackie Kennedy had married, drove out to the Bouvier compound overlooking a dramatic, rugged coastline, walked in town, and then returned to Long Island, where we'd rented a tiny apartment above the Center Moriches Bakery.

We moved into the apartment and visited briefly with each of our families, and then Cliff's leave ended. He returned to Rhode Island, and my solitary life as a navy wife opened.

I thought our apartment was cute: three rooms lined up like train cars, one window in each. The kitchenette was like a dollhouse, papered with a green-ivy-on-a-trellis pattern on white. The window over the sink, with a minuscule counter on each side, faced a drab concrete building next door. A miniature refrigerator and stove stood next to the sink, while a petite dropdown tabletop hung from the opposite wall.

After I cleaned the apartment, I found little to do each day. Without a car, I was limited to walking to nearby destinations, where I soon bought some yarn at the five-and-dime store and cast on stitches to knit a baby afghan. I finished it quickly, then purchased yarn and a pattern for an infant sweater.

Yet after a few weeks of profuse knitting, I was restless. I missed going to classes but told myself that part of my life was over. I decided to apply for work. Without a degree, my only tangible work skill was my typing, so I took a Civil Service test and was soon interviewed. When I left, I saw the other woman who took the test with me called in for her interview. I knew she had scored higher than I, so I expected she would be hired. Thus, I was surprised and delighted when I was offered the clerk-typist job in the district attorney's office. I gratefully accepted, yet I lamented for the other woman, unable to suspect no other reason for my hire over her than our different skin color.

This was an early moment of my awakening to feelings of compassion for others who encountered discrimination because of race, socioeconomic status, or other situations beyond their control. I couldn't yet imagine that I would, in the near future, enter those troubled waters myself and, as a result, choose a career that reflected my desire to help others.

For the present, though, I mused how I'd always loved reading mysteries and told myself this work mattered because it mirrored my interest in investigation and prosecution. While I was not *Perry Mason*'s Della Street, whom I admired, I was content to type and file letters and reports about criminal proceedings. I also liked my two coworkers, Frieda and Mary, for their sense of humor, friendliness, and warmth.

One morning, embracing a stack of filing, I said, "Frieda, I'm going down to file these."

"Sure," she said, "go ahead."

One arm wrapped around the files and the other holding the cold metal handrail, I carefully traversed the creaky steps to the huge, dank basement. For nearly an hour, I shelved files in the twenty-foot-long rows of folders, then started to climb the stairs. I stopped when a thought struck: *I wonder if there's a file for anyone with my maiden name here.*

I was stunned to find one with my father's name on it. *There must be another man with the same name*, I rationalized. My hands trembled as I pulled the folder. *Put this back and forget about it*, I told myself. But I was too curious and slowly opened it, holding my breath, knowing full well the fact that a folder existed meant that my father had been charged with a crime.

The documents revealed his recent conviction for making sexual advances to a man in a public restroom. Sickened, horrified, I read he had been fined and given probation. A sudden heaviness rushed through me, and I dropped into a sturdy wooden chair, my thoughts swirling dizzyingly. *How could this be? My father, a criminal? No! How could he want sex with a man, a stranger?* The word *homosexual* surely shadowed my troubled thoughts. Society's attitude was so vicious toward gay people in the 1960s that I couldn't conceive of him as part of such a despised demographic. He was my *father*—not a great father, but not some monster, either.

My eyes dropped to my lap, where the file lay—silent, tangible proof that canceled any denial.

Minutes passed, and then a sound overhead triggered a terrifying thought: *Frieda could come downstairs at any moment to do her own filing.* I stood shakily and slid the folder back into its hiding place.

Upstairs, I finished the day at my desk, still dazed by what I'd learned downstairs. *Should I tell Mom about this?* I wondered. *No*, I decided, *she's already overwhelmed. I'll protect her from his criminal behavior.* It never occurred to me my mother might have known or that her knowing might be contributing to her nervousness, the word she always used. I simply assumed she didn't and, subsequently, never told anyone. In time, I "forgot." For several decades. Until I learned that my father's diagnosis was not in fact "homosexual."

My pregnancy advanced into my eighth month, and one Friday afternoon Frieda and Mary surprised me with a baby shower. I'd never had a shower and was deeply moved by their kindness. They didn't know I'd "had to get married" or of the shame that smothered the joy I wished I felt.

Their gift was a high chair with a pretty green-and-yellow design on the plastic seat and back. Releasing happy tears, I hugged them tightly; then, on that unforgettable, lovely summer afternoon, I departed, with no idea it was my final day of work.

The following morning, I woke alone, as always, feeling sick and feverish. I tossed and slept all day. When my mother visited that afternoon, she was alarmed by my high temperature and called my general practitioner. He was on vacation, it turned out, but his stand-in, Dr. Jones, told her to bring me in. I don't recall his diagnosis but cannot forget that he prescribed sulfa.

When I woke the following morning, my stomach was so swollen and hardened, it caused the onset of labor. Dr. Jones ordered me to the hospital while someone contacted Cliff in Newport. Several hours later, I gave birth to our sweet preemie, a four-pound daughter. In my drugged state, I smiled at Dr. Jones after her delivery and said, "Can I make you some coffee? You've worked so hard." Bemusedly, he thanked me and said he'd take a rain check, thank you. As my baby was whisked away from the delivery room, I felt no alarm that I had not seen her, held her, or heard her cry.

Then a friendly blond nurse wheeled me from the recovery room to my room, saying, "Your little girl is gorgeous!"

I beamed. "Thank you. I'm glad, because she's going to be my only child. Giving birth is *hard* work!"

The nurse laughed, a sweet, wind-chime sound. "Oh, you wait. You'll change your mind in time." I said nothing because I knew better.

Cliff arrived in early evening, on emergency leave. Tears

ran down my cheeks as I said softly, "Oh, God, I'm so glad you're here!"

"No more than I am," he murmured gently, as he wrapped his arms tightly around me and kissed me. "Are you okay?" he asked, his hazel eyes apprehensive as he looked into mine.

"I'm good," I said, sitting up painfully. "This was the hardest thing I've ever done, though, and I just want you to know we are not having any more children."

He chuckled. "One child is fine with me. When do we see her?"

I shook my head. "I don't know. Soon, I hope." And so, happy to be together, we waited innocently to see and hold our daughter . . . until our world shattered.

A doctor strode in, quickly introduced himself, shook hands with Cliff, and said, "Your daughter has a problem that we're trying to figure out. She's not passing food through her body, and we don't know why yet." He expanded briefly, then said, "I'll be back when I know more."

He disappeared as quickly as he'd arrived. I stared at Cliff, who stared wordlessly back at me, our joy transformed into alarm. As we asked each other questions we could not possibly answer, a nurse entered the room. I gazed at her through tears as she said gently, "The doctor thought you'd like to see your daughter."

She and Cliff helped me into a wheelchair. "She's in an incubator, and we're feeding her intravenously," she informed us, as she pushed me down a hallway, Cliff walking beside me, holding my hand.

When we reached a huge observation window, I stopped breathing as I stared at a naked, doll-size body taped to multiple tubes, whose face was turned away. As I write these words and remember, my body collapses into itself, just as it did at that moment in the hospital hall. I looked up at Cliff as he stared, too, clearly as terrified as I.

Today I imagine our infant beneath her trappings, an absolutely beautiful, miniature four-pound girl. Jocelyn's head, a tiny globe no larger than an orange, was covered with wispy strawberry-blond fuzz. Her eyes were the deep blue of calm tropical waters, her skin pink and translucent, and her minute fingers and toes were perfect.

"I'm very concerned about her," the specialist said matter-of-factly, following our visit.

No! I screamed silently within, denying any truth to his chilling words. I desperately needed to hear his compassion, his hope, and his reassurance that he could make Jocelyn better. Instead, I saw only his reserved eyes and heard his hard words.

Hours passed painfully. After watching my roommate embrace her son every few hours when a nurse brought him for breastfeeding, I finally cried because my empty arms ached with grief. A compassionate nurse asked if I'd like to be moved to another ward. "Please," I begged, and was just being moved to the surgical floor when the surgeon strode in again. "I suspect your daughter has an intestinal blockage, which is critical. I'm going to do emergency surgery within the hour, unless food passes through her body before then." It didn't.

I shuddered as I imagined a scalpel cutting Jocelyn's skin. *How can her tiny body endure the invasion of a knife? What kind of welcome into life is that?* My mind silently screamed over and over with fright and pain until, finally, the doctor returned and said, "Her large intestine was closed off in three places, like sausage links. We've opened them, and now we'll wait for a bowel movement. That will tell us there are no more blockages."

Life stopped then.

The hours, the day, and then another day passed in a fugue. Someone told us there were more blockages, that Jocelyn had a second operation. After, when she lay taped and tubed like a broken doll in her incubator, the doctor said, "I'm not optimistic." My entire life now centered on my daughter's large intestine. My desperate, silent plea—*Jocelyn, please have a bowel movement*—was to her and to God.

Once, during all the days Cliff and I sat by our daughter's incubator, as my hand touched the glass that separated us, a nurse came by and said kindly, "Would you like to touch her?"

Tears spurted from my eyes. "I would love to touch her," I choked. None of our family had had any physical contact with Jocelyn. I hadn't known we could, nor had I known enough to ask.

"You can touch your baby any time you want to," the nurse said gently, looking into my eyes with compassion. She showed me where to reach my forefinger through a small opening in the incubator and ever so lightly stroke my child's skin. The moment filled me with wonder. I had never caressed anything so beautiful and precious. So smooth, silky, soft. *Your priceless life cannot end, Jocelyn. It has just begun. We will get through this, my dearest daughter.* Now that I had this fragile, sacred connection with her, I believed I could pass my love, my strength, and my profound wish for healing to her through our bond of touch. Surely that would heal her body.

A month before Jocelyn's birthdate, newspaper headlines reported the plight of Sherri Finkbine, host of a Phoenix children's public television program. Finkbine had taken thalidomide—a drug recently revealed to cause severe birth defects—to treat nausea and morning sickness during her current pregnancy. In July, her search for a legal abortion in the United States opened a national debate between pro-life and pro-choice voters. Every avenue Finkbine pursued denied her request; she eventually flew to Stockholm, where the procedure was legal. On the day Sherri Finkbine's child was aborted, Jocelyn was born.

I followed the Finkbine story closely. In 1962, as today, I was pro-choice. I could not have terminated Jocelyn's life, despite her birth defect. In the heart-stopping day-to-day unfolding of Jocelyn's life, I often thought of Sherri Finkbine and, while I struggled to respect her decision, I was desperate for my imperfect child to live.

On day ten, when Cliff and I arrived at the hospital, the doctor came out to the waiting room and said, "The baby is very grave. Please wait out here."

Robot-like, Cliff and I paced in the busy waiting room. About midday, the doctor pushed through a door and said, "I'm sorry. She has died," words cold as an Antarctic air blast.

I wailed loud and long, the first cry that had escaped my body since Jocelyn's birth. Cliff wrapped his arms around me and laid his cheek on my head, wordless, but I could feel no comfort. The sounds that came from the depths of my soul seemed very far away, sounds that someone else was making—not I.

Today, I find profoundly sad the lack of staff to inform us about our opportunities for closeness with Jocelyn—we lost precious time to physically touch, comfort, and bond with our daughter, and she lost out by not receiving those loving connections. We were physically excluded from our daughter's last moments of life, in the absence of professionals who could have let us know she was near death. There was also our own inability to save our child, as well as the loss of the precious life we would never know or share, to accept.

We stood at Jocelyn's funeral, eyes fastened on the tiny, angelic white casket, overcome by searing, endless pain. Then we said "amen" and walked away, leaving our baby behind in the desolate ground beneath late-August sunshine.

Cliff and I pretended to start living again in the few days we had before he returned to Newport. As I look back at us then—two barely-twenty-one-year-olds, so innocent and shallowly rooted in life—I feel compassion for us both. We knew nothing about grieving or the importance of talking about our horrific loss, and so neither happened. Would it have made a difference? I cannot say yes or no, but I can say it would not have hurt.

Because I'd never held Jocelyn and now never would, I often embraced a pillow and cried quietly into it, pretending I was holding my baby. I had no picture of her, either, although the memory of her beautiful self was and is today forever imprinted on my brain. Did Cliff have those feelings? If so, what were they like for him? I'll never know.

I sometimes thought of Sherri Finkbine, too, and in time understood the core of my agony. She was able to make a choice about her medically compromised child. We were not. If we could have, we would have chosen life for Jocelyn, even if she were disabled.

In the years ahead, I would cut out a perfect miniature heart for Jocelyn, to appliqué onto my quilt.

Chapter 11: BLUE BABY BLOCKS—CHIP

Newport, Rhode Island, 1962–63

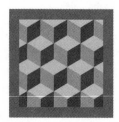

After Jocelyn's death, I moved to Rhode Island, where Cliff had rented a three-room apartment for us in Portsmouth, adjacent to Newport, in a lovely old house with a sprawling front lawn. I took another Civil Service exam and began work as a clerk-typist in the household shipping department at the naval base. I felt happier working, meeting other service families, and building new friendships. Though we had, in fact, been married nine months by the calendar, I felt for the first time as if, instead of existing from visit to visit, we were truly married. We got up together each morning, ate breakfast and my prepared dinner together, sometimes shopped or saw a movie, or played his favorite game, cribbage, and then went to bed together. This was the lifestyle I had envisioned for a good marriage—one of daily togetherness and the sharing of small activities. I didn't yet realize that a good marriage comprised varied lifestyles. I saw that many families chose to be part of our military for decades—the lifers, as they were called. Had I been curious enough to learn more about the broader navy way of life, I might have anticipated how short-lived our quotidian togetherness would be.

During my postpartum checkup, my obstetrician said, "I know your first child had a birth defect, but there's no reason why you can't have another perfectly healthy baby." His gentle words were a healing salve for the wound in my heart.

Eight months later, in April 1963, my body prepared for another child within its soundless depths. I watched the buds on the maple tree outside our third-story window grow infinitesimally as each day passed. I felt slightly fuller. Could I dare believe? At times I felt ecstatic; at other times, terror gripped me. Surely this child would be healthy and normal. I couldn't have another critically ill baby, could I? No! *Or could I?*

A second cycle silently passed, and I was certain. *Please, let this child be healthy*, I begged my Creator. Yet if I were fully honest, I would acknowledge that, in the silent nadir of my soul, my hope was for a son. Another daughter might feel like Jocelyn's replacement, and she could never be replaced. But I told anyone who asked that I'd be happy with either sex, just a healthy child. A few weeks later, Cliff and I, holding hands, were cautiously pleased when my pregnancy was confirmed.

Within days, the phone rang one evening after dinner and Cliff was ordered to report to the base within the hour. His ship, the USS *Roberts*, was getting under way that night.

"Where are we heading?" he asked.

"You'll find out after we leave port," he was told.

He tossed clothes in his duffel bag, and we drove hastily to the base. After a quick, apprehensive embrace, I watched his long legs dash up the gangplank with other sailors. Terror filled my belly; Cliff had never been called out like this in such haste. Part of that fear mingled with my newly acquired knowledge from Jocelyn that we can lose a loved one at any time. *Will I ever see him again?* I wondered after he'd disappeared into the ship. *Is there* anything *in my life that I can still control?* I brooded over those questions as I drove home with my hands in a death grip on the steering wheel to control my shaking. I also wondered where in the world was the apparent life-or-death situation Cliff was heading toward.

The next day, at work, we learned that the nuclear-powered attack submarine *Thresher*, the leading boat of her class, based in Groton, Connecticut, had disappeared. Faster, quieter, and able to dive deeper than any submarine ever built, she'd been designed to discover and destroy Soviet submarines. In 1962, the Soviet Union was our greatest enemy, and this submarine had tested so well that several more had been ordered to form a fleet. The day before, April 10, 1963, *Thresher* and her crew of 129 had been engaged in deep-diving tests near Boston, when all contact was lost. The USS *Roberts* and two other destroyers had been ordered into the Atlantic to search for any sign of the sub.

We listened to dismal radio reports all day. A few pieces of debris on the surface near where *Thresher*'s last contact had occurred were all that had been found. I thought of each man aboard, dedicated to his country, with family on the homeland, and felt the individual losses as much as if I had known each one personally. I knew if Cliff never returned home from a mission, my world would end.

Days later, I stood mutely on the pier and watched the *Roberts* burbling slowly—and sadly, it seemed to me—toward her slot. I keenly felt an aura that seemed to emanate from the gunmetal-gray ship: she had failed in her mission to find the *Thresher* and her crew. Much wiser that day about our military, its purpose, and this staggering loss, I knuckled away tears and returned to work. I'd see my husband later that night, unlike the families in Groton whose loved ones would never return.

The 1963 loss of the *Thresher* remains, as of this book's publication, the worst submarine disaster in US naval history.

A few weeks later, Cliff quietly pulled the front door closed behind him and removed his bright white sailor hat. The pasta sauce simmering on the stove infused the little kitchen with the fragrant scents of tomatoes and spices. "Hi, how was your day?" I asked cheerfully, musing how handsome he looked in his navy-blue uniform. Then I looked at his normally smiling eyes, now dark and serious.

"Hey, what's wrong?" I asked.

He wrapped his arms around me. "The *Roberts* is leaving on a six-month Mediterranean cruise next month," he said softly.

My heart, suddenly heavy as a bowling ball, tumbled into my belly. "Oh, no," I whimpered. "Not with another baby on the way."

"I know," he said, his lips pinched. "I don't want to leave now, either."

Med cruises were prolonged excursions for practicing wartime maneuvers, we knew. Yet, with less than a year of enlistment left, we'd hoped to avoid the extended separation.

We ate our spaghetti, barely tasting the delicious sauce. Later, as we rinsed our plates, I said, "Why don't I call the chaplain tomorrow and talk with him?" With little enthusiasm, Cliff nodded.

How naive we were. When I asked the chaplain if Cliff could be exempted from the cruise, based on our fragile situation, the graying, soft-spoken man replied kindly but firmly, "I'm sorry, Mary Jo." We were learning that the navy was a stern parent: we were there to serve, not be served.

When the *Roberts* deployed to the Mediterranean Sea, I reflected on the irony that I'd moved to Rhode Island to be with Cliff, and now he'd be away for all but several weeks before his discharge. Yet the *Thresher* loss cast our situation in quite a different light. I knew any *Thresher* family would happily accept a six-month deployment if their husband could return home. Once again, we embraced at the pier. Cliff patted my belly, smiled, and said, "Take care of Junior while I'm away," as we parted.

After the lonely early weeks, we adjusted into new routines. We wrote nearly every day, and Cliff called whenever he was ashore. My days at work passed quickly, and on weekends I cleaned, enjoyed knitting or sewing, or spent time with another navy wife, Melissa, whose husband was also deployed on the *Roberts*. I missed Cliff the most at night, when I snapped off the bedside lamp and settled beneath the covers alone, and in the morning, when I woke to remember he was gone. At those times, I reminded myself he'd be home shortly before our baby's due date: December 15.

Autumn leaves peaked bright gold when the *Roberts* slid into port in early October. I stood alone in the throng of waiting families, my waistline much expanded, watching sailors hurriedly disembark. Suddenly, there he was, slim, eyes dancing, jogging toward me. I was overjoyed, for although we'd been married nearly a year and a half, we'd lived together less than two months. *Now* we could finally be together.

Yet this reunion was also brief. Within days of the *Roberts*'s return, Cliff called from the ship, his voice tense. "We're deploying immediately, destination unknown. I'll let you know where we go when I can." I froze as we said another uncertain goodbye.

The next day, I drove to the base, simply to be near the place where Cliff had been the previous day, and was shocked to see just one ship at the dock, where dozens were usually sprawled all over the harbor like toy boats in a bathtub. Chilled with apprehension, I wondered, *What is happening in the world that we don't yet know about?*

That evening, President Kennedy addressed the nation and told us about the Cuban Missile Crisis. Recent spy-plane photos showed that, on Cuba, the Russians had placed nuclear missiles that were now aimed directly at the United States. President Kennedy and his advisers decided to order a blockade of ships around Cuba to prevent Russia from bringing in more supplies. On October 22, Kennedy told the world he had demanded that Nikita Khrushchev remove the missiles and dismantle the sites.

For a harrowing thirteen days, I prayed with our nation that the standoff would not result in nuclear war. I was terrified that a missile might blow up the USS *Roberts* or the Newport base, so near our home. My security in a world that I had always taken for granted was shattered. Soon we learned that all naval ships had been deployed to open seas to reduce US vulnerability if the Russians should fire missiles at bases. Many ships went to Cuba to form the barricade, while others were sent in multiple directions around the world. The *Roberts* docked in Newfoundland until the crisis ended.

Shortly, as we all held our collective breath, we learned that the leaders had made a pact: Russia would dismantle the weapon sites if the United States agreed not to invade Cuba. Khrushchev and President Kennedy publicly agreed. We all breathed again and believed the crisis was over. However, twenty-five years later we'd learn that, while the United States also pledged to remove its nuclear missiles from Turkey, the Soviets kept building a military arsenal, covertly continuing the arms race.

Cliff and I were shopping for a baby crib at the Newport base commissary on November 22, 1963, wandering among several choices. Suddenly, a clerk cried out, "My God, the president's been shot!" Staggered by the news, we hurried home and watched television as events unfolded that marked the end of John F. Kennedy's life. It seemed only yesterday that

I'd fervently campaigned for him in college, then joyfully celebrated his election, and now he was gone. Like Jocelyn. Like the *Thresher* crew. The world could change in a minute, I was reminded yet again.

Riveted to the television for days, we stared at the blood on Jacqueline Kennedy's pink suit ("Let them see what they have done to my husband," she reportedly said). We witnessed Lee Harvey Oswald's shocking murder by Jack Ruby, watched the president's final, solitary journey, felt the family's anguish at the funeral, cried as the dear small boy John Jr. saluted his father's casket, heard the haunting sound of Taps. These moments are embedded in my being as vividly today, half a century later, as the eternal flame that still burns in Arlington National Cemetery.

Yet, slowly, as a nation, we reconnected to our lives again, although none of us ever forgot where we were on that day of profound loss.

A few weeks later, I awoke early on December 15, 1963, and knew our child would arrive that day. At 7:49 p.m., my heart's deepest desire was placed in my arms: a precious, healthy son, sandy-haired and blue-eyed, eight pounds, fourteen ounces, with all his fingers and toes. He was perfect. We named him Clifford Stephen III, after his father, and called him Chip.

I kept him so close. A stay-at-home mom, I nursed him for several months, sang to him, took him for endless walks, and talked about everything we saw. I played and cuddled with him and vowed his life would be happy and perfect.

He soon slept through the night, and then one day he belly-laughed, the most wonderful sound I'd heard in my entire life. He was a happy, contented baby with a soft, gentle voice I loved to hear. He soon rolled over, cut his first tooth, and sat up, and by ten months he was walking—just as Cliff was discharged from the navy. We packed up our belongings and prepared to move back to Long Island, where our families still lived.

"We can't wait to get home, Mom!" I wrote. "Except for the few months of being together here between deployments, I feel like our real marriage will finally start when Cliff is discharged. We'll be together and we'll be a *real* family. It will be heaven!"

Chapter 12:

TUMBLING BABY BLOCKS—KEITH

Center Moriches, New York, 1964–66

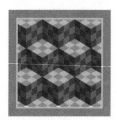

W e shipped our possessions back to Long Island, where
Cliff's military communications training easily qualified him for employment with Bell Telephone Company. We
rented an apartment in Eastport, New York, and soon I was
expecting another child. We hadn't planned to have two children eighteen months apart, but I was pleased and had no reason
to believe Cliff felt differently.

One evening when we visited my in-laws, I smiled and
embraced my belly as I talked with Cliff's mother. "Look, I'm
getting so big already."

She puffed on her cigarette, then exhaled. "You sure are,"
she replied, her blue eyes seeming to smile, yet the moment felt
artificial to me and I sensed she was not happy. *Why?* I wondered.
Because her twenty-two-year-old son will soon be a father of two?

Everyone called her Kay, the firstborn of twelve children to first-generation Irish parents. She often talked about how her father drank heavily all his life and spent his sporadic income mostly on bar bills, and how her overwhelmed mother handed Kay a new baby each year to care for. Was our joy for our new baby stirring up old, unhappy memories? Or something else? I recalled her reluctance to sign permission for Cliff to marry me. Did she really not like me? They'd visited in Newport after Chip was born, and I had seen only their glowing happiness about their new grandson. Now we were expecting our second child. Surely nothing could be very wrong.

In her teens, Kay married a sailor, Cliff Sr., who proved to be a stable husband and a modest, steady provider for his family. Their first child was a son, Chauncey. When Kay became pregnant a few years later, she and Cliff longed for a daughter.

"I was so upset when Cliffie [her nickname for my husband] wasn't a girl, I had a breakdown," Kay told me many times. "I was hospitalized for months and had to give him to relatives to raise." Long before I understood the importance of maternal bonding or developed my lifelong curiosity about human behavior, I thought this must have been a difficult beginning for my spouse. Did this have anything to do with Kay's less-than-enthusiastic response to my happy remarks about my pregnancy? Might she be thinking that because her second pregnancy had created a crisis, mine could, too? Time would answer those questions.

Needing a larger home, we rented a two-story house from Chip's godparents. It had been abandoned for a while and bordered on substandard, but we planned to stay there just long enough to save up a down payment for our own home. Cliff and his brother cleaned and painted throughout, and I enjoyed making cross-stitched gingham café curtains for the kitchen windows.

The month before my due date, we asked my sister Bonnie, then thirteen, to babysit for Chip while we went to Cliff's parents' home to play pinochle. Bonnie, who loved caring for Chip, easily agreed. When we returned home around midnight, Chip was sound asleep in his crib and Bonnie was sleeping on the couch, staying over, as we'd planned.

I woke in the night when Cliff went downstairs—to use the bathroom, I thought. Horrified, I heard my sister say forcefully, "Stop that, Cliff. Get away from me."

I froze. A few minutes later, he returned and I asked coldly, "Did you touch my sister?"

He dropped his head. "I drank too much tonight. I'm sorry."

Nausea stirred in my stomach as I heavily walked downstairs to my sweet, innocent sister, but she was gone. I stared at the empty couch, sickened. *This doesn't happen in my family! I cannot believe this!* I felt surreal, detached, as I trudged upstairs and said angrily, "You have to apologize to Bonnie."

First thing the next morning, we drove to my mother's. She came outside to meet us, looking grimly at Cliff.

"Mom, Cliff wants to talk to you and Bonnie," I said. I shudder now when I realize I spoke for him.

My mother looked icily at Cliff. "You can talk to me."

Standing beneath clouds in her backyard on that chilly March morning, Cliff apologized, sounding sincere. Bonnie, slender, her blond hair shoulder-length, stepped outside guardedly to stand by Mom and clung to her arm. My arms were wrapped around my sweet baby boy as I stood several feet behind Cliff like a spectator, tears welling in my eyes for what he had done to my little sister. With the same sincerity he'd shown toward my mother, Cliff said, "I'm sorry, Bonnie." She stared disdainfully at him and said nothing. Once again, as on so many occasions in my family, deep anger lay beneath the surface of brief spoken words. Decades would pass before I could talk with my sister about the awful incident.

"Mom, Bonnie, I'll see you soon," I said, my voice shaking, my self enveloped in shame and not knowing what else to say. Cliff, Chip, and I left quickly. Bonnie never came to our house to babysit again, nor did I want her to; I took Chip to her home instead.

Naive and intellectually immature, I knew this incident was serious, but not why. I'd never heard of "sexual abuse" or of the catastrophic effects it could have on a young girl. After several days of chilly conversation with Cliff, the event slid away to reside with other things I had "forgotten." But it, like all the others, would return.

After that incident, I remembered a summer day when I was eleven. Mom asked me to take some food to Aunt Phoebe and Uncle Gus, in their seventies, who lived next door. After visiting a while, I said goodbye and started to walk home, when Gus beckoned me to follow him into the backyard. He stepped into a small outbuilding and smiled. "Come here."

Oblivious, I followed. Suddenly, he pulled me to him, kissed me, pushed his tongue into my mouth, and slid his hand inside my shorts. My brain spun wildly, but I stood there passively until he removed his hand. Then I ran away and pushed through the high hedge between our houses. Later, I told my mother what Gus had done. Furious, she said, "He shouldn't have done that to you. Don't ever go over there alone again."

I could not appreciate then, as I do now, the gift of her response. When I was older, I learned that many mothers refuse to believe daughters who tell them someone had violated them. What would it be like to feel so confused and upset about the abuse and then not be believed? What would my reality have been if my own mother had denied it?

I'd wonder, too: Why didn't I run away when Gus touched me? In time, I'd understand.

Chip was a happy toddler when, on April 24, 1965, his new brother, Keith Gregory, arrived. I'd smile and cry in later decades as I stitched their endearing patchwork hearts onto my quilt. With his mop of dark hair, deep blue eyes that quickly turned brown, and striking olive skin, Keith was also a contented baby who soon slept all night. With two wonderful sons now, I felt our family was complete.

Within a year, Cliff and I saved enough to qualify for a mortgage. We found a gray-shingled, three-bedroom, two-bath Cape Cod on a half-acre parcel in a mixed neighborhood of young and middle-aged parents and retirees. Planning on happily ever after, we moved excitedly to Cedar Street, about a mile from town and around the corner from my mother's home on Adelaide Park.

By our third anniversary, I felt well-settled into life with my husband, my home, our two sons, and our black Lab, Sable. I loved cooking, had learned to make bread, and also sewed much of my family's clothing. While Cliff worked, I cared for the children, house, and yard.

Some incidents between us were troubling, though. If Cliff found dirty lunch dishes in the sink, he said nastily, "My mother's sink never had dirty dishes in it," as he banged them aside to wash his hands. I knew I was a less meticulous housekeeper than Kay, yet I also knew I traded off housekeeping time for things, like sewing, that Kay wasn't interested in. Cliff's periodic cranky comparisons between Kay and me, in which I never measured up, degraded me and pulled loose threads from the joyful fabric I wanted our life to be.

Then one night, after work and a few drinks, Cliff came home to find toys scattered on the living room rug. Pitching them into the toy box, he ranted, "Our house never looked like this when I lived at home. Why did I *ever* buy the cow when the milk was so cheap?"

This hateful phrase was often said in the 1960s by men who regretted marrying a woman they'd had sex with before marriage. He knew I'd never been intimate with anyone but him; his words slashed me like knives. Dazed and speechless, I watched him stomp out the back door.

A few nights later, he didn't come home. Ignorant as I was, some of my fog lifted as I surmised he might be seeing another woman. The following night, I met him in the hallway when he arrived after midnight. "Cliff, where have you been?"

His eyes narrowed. "Does it matter? I'm going to leave you."

I stared at him, disbelief diluted by belief, then returned to bed and curled into a fetal position. In the days that followed, I mentally prepared myself for Cliff to leave, but then he started coming home again each night. *He's decided not to go*, I thought, but we didn't talk about it.

When his brother, Steve, bought a glitzy nightclub in the Hamptons, Cliff began working there several nights and weekends. While he brought home a nice supplementary income for our growing family needs, we rarely saw each other anymore. The trade-off for the extra income was pricey. Did he prefer to be away from home?

Later, Cliff would tell me that his father had encouraged him to stay with us, to be a responsible husband and father. His dad had obviously been influential, and I was grateful to him for that. But I'd also learn that Cliff's mother supported his wish to leave me.

When friends of ours bought a cute new compact car, a Buick Opel, we liked it so much, we bought one, too. The weekend after purchasing the car, we attended a retirement party in the Hamptons for Cliff's coworker. It was a pleasant evening of dining, dancing, and honoring the retiree, John. Around midnight, the party broke up and we stepped outside, greeted by night air filled with fog rolling in from Great South Bay. We lap-belted into the cold, damp car—shoulder belts would be invented the following year—and started our twenty-mile trip home.

As we drove in what Long Islanders called pea-soup fog, our windshield quickly frosted over. We'd both had several drinks over several hours, and Cliff was unfamiliar with the control knobs. He tried one, then another, searching for the defroster. I was frightened as we forged blindly into the void. "Cliff, pull over, for God's sake. I can't see a thing," I yelled. He said something angrily and jerked the steering wheel hard to the right. Instantly, our compact car collided with a full-size, parked sedan. I heard the horrific crunch of metal and the tinkling of shattering glass. My upper body was thrust forward into darkness, and then I knew nothing.

In time—I have no idea how long—I heard a voice calling my name over and over. It was Cliff, talking strangely. "May-wee Jo, May-wee Jo . . ." He sounded like he was sobbing. We were inside the silent tomb of our car, but I was far away, unable to respond. I had a vague memory that he'd been angry with me just before this happened . . . so it probably served him right that I couldn't reassure him I was okay . . . I faded away again . . .

When I regained consciousness, I lay wrapped in something heavy on a hard sidewalk. Low voices murmured in the darkness. A man's voice near me said, "She doesn't look good. She might not make it . . ." Intuitively, I knew he spoke of me and that his words were true, yet I was peacefully so deep within myself, his comment neither startled nor frightened me; I simply noted it and slid away again.

When I next awoke, I was being lifted onto a table in a hospital emergency room, screaming with the worst pain I'd ever known. A voice said, "You've chipped your pelvis. I know it hurts, but try to stay calm . . ."

I tried. Then I felt injections on my chin, and I struggled to get away. A stern male voice said, "I'm numbing your face so I can stitch you back together. You *must* stay still."

The needles hurt. I sobbed. Then the pain stopped, but not the needles . . . I lay still and quiet, eyes squeezed tight, feeling a needle go into my chin, then out, then pulled tight, knotted and snipped, over and over . . . I slipped back into unconsciousness.

The next time I opened my eyes, I was in an intensive care unit, enveloped by white walls and beeping monitors. My bed had sides on it, and my mother gazed down at me tearfully.

"Hi," I said, turning woozily toward her. She stared, her face crumpled, her voice thick. "I can stay only five minutes, Mary Jo. What happened tonight?"

I talked rapidly, telling her about the alcohol, the fog, and the argument that led to the accident. A nurse tapped softly on the glass window, beckoning Mom to leave.

"I'll be back in an hour," she said quietly, gently touching my shoulder. I slid back into blessed darkness.

When Mom returned, I asked, "Is Cliff okay?"

"Yes," she replied flatly. "He'll be all right."

"Thank God. Are my boys okay?"

She nodded. "Bonnie's with them tonight. We'll get things worked out tomorrow. Don't worry, okay?"

Tears filled my eyes. *My babies . . .*

Two days later, I was moved from intensive care to a room near Cliff's. He soon stood silently in my doorway, his eyes sorrowful. *I guess I don't look very good*, I remember thinking. I don't recall feeling any emotions and believe I was dissociated—except when I thought achingly of my sons. Cliff had nearly severed his tongue when his chin hit the steering wheel on impact, and he, too, had multiple stitches.

After he left, in a quiet moment, I cautiously asked a nurse what my face looked like. Gazing at me, she replied, "You'll be okay in time." I gratefully accepted her words. When she left, though, I timidly touched my hand to my chin. It felt prickly, like whiskers sticking out all over. Stitches. I quickly removed my hand and "forgot" that feeling.

Daily, Cliff and I walked in the hallway—at first taking short trips, which progressed to an entire trip around the floor, then two trips. A week after the accident, Cliff was discharged. Cliff's parents had moved in to care for Chip and Keith, and, though I ached to see them, hospital rules forbade child visits.

Three weeks later, my doctor told me, "I think you're ready to go home." I'd longed to hear those words and, since I'd soon be discharged, decided I'd look at my face. As a friendly nurse gave me medication, I asked, "Can you give me a mirror? I want to look at my face."

She hesitated briefly, then handed me a small, round mirror. I sat upright in my bed and slowly raised it to my face, prepared for anything, I believed. I knew my front teeth were broken but had not asked for any information beyond knowing I had more than a hundred stitches in my face.

I looked into the mirror and, instantly staggered, heard fairy-tale words burst into my head: *Mirror, mirror on the wall. Who is the ugliest one of all? I am.*

I closed my eyes in a long blink; when I opened them again, I stared hard at my face, paralyzed because I didn't know the person I saw. The moment became surreal as I contrasted my innate knowledge that it was me inside my body with the reality of someone else's face. I recognized the now haunted brown eyes and forehead, covered with straggly chestnut bangs long overdue for a shampoo. But below them was a shattered face all tied together with black stitches that crisscrossed my face in little red lines like a road map.

My chin comprised a large, round circle of stitches that included part of my bottom lip. Between my nose and my upper lip were two rows of stitches. My nose was swollen and misshapen, and I already knew I couldn't breathe through one nostril. Circling my eyes were broad rings of color that included yellow, green, purple, and brown. It was not a face I could live with in this world. I was a *freak*!

Silently, I struggled to cope. The next morning, when my doctor came to discharge me, I wailed, "What *really* happened to me in that car? Why do I look like this?"

He pulled a chair next to my bed, sat down, and gently explained, "You pitched forward on impact, and the glove-compartment door flew open. The metal door sliced off your chin and part of your bottom lip, broke away your front teeth, and lifted your nose from your face." He touched my hand.

I shuddered as tears filled my eyes.

He gently continued, "I sent someone back to the accident scene to get the piece of chin and lip that was severed and reattached it. I'm hoping that will save it. Time will tell."

I nodded, until a paralyzing fear filled me. "What if . . . ?"

"If it doesn't reattach, I'll refer you to an excellent plastic surgeon."

"Oh." I had no idea what that would entail but felt comfort in knowing there was a backup plan.

"Thank you for what you've done," I said numbly yet gratefully.

He smiled briefly. "We'll see . . ." His voice trailed off.

As this silent earthquake moved through Cliff's and my marriage, so far away that we didn't even notice, the United States, USSR, China, and France were all conducting underground nuclear testing.

Chapter 13: HANDS OF FRIENDSHIP

Center Moriches, New York, 1966–68

I knelt down and gently extended my arms to my toddlers. "Hi, guys. I have missed you *so* much." My voice shook; my smile quavered.

Chip's wise, three-year-old eyes were round and serious; Keith, a year old, stared. They slowly moved away from me until they backed into Cliff's mother, Kay, standing behind them.

Kay encouraged them, "Say hi to Mommy, boys. I'll bet she'd love a hug." The silence as they didn't speak or move was awful. *Better get used to this,* I thought. *This is just the beginning of the stares you'll be getting.*

A new awareness swelled within: my house felt strange, wrong, almost like it wasn't home anymore. I sat on my haunches, talking softly to my sons, saying familiar words, seeking to ease their fear. Slowly, I inched a little closer, knowing they recognized my voice and perhaps my eyes, but also hyperaware that their shock about my face must have resembled mine the first time I saw it. In time Chip let me hug him, but his body was tense. I held him gently and extended my other arm to Keith, who hustled into my embrace. As I hugged Keith, he pulled his head back and touched my chin. "Boo-boo, Mommy?" he asked hoarsely.

If anyone had told my sons what had happened to me, they certainly hadn't understood. "It's getting better," I said.

"Oh, good," he said.

"Is anyone hungry?" Kay asked. We gathered at the table for egg salad and tuna sandwiches, but I had no appetite and ate little. When I looked around the table, I saw nearly everyone else picking at their food, too. Just Cliff's father ate hungrily and told Kay the sandwiches tasted great. *Does he really mean that, or is he just trying to fill in this awkwardness?* I wondered.

During the ensuing weeks, I slowly resumed being a mother and wife. Cliff's parents moved back home, but, not wanting to go out in public, I refused to leave the house. For several weeks, Cliff and my family did the food shopping, until one day my mother said firmly, "You've got to start doing this, Mary Jo." I knew she was right.

The next day, I stared in the mirror at the face the public would soon see. I noticed the reattached part of my chin looked slightly gray. *Is the reattachment dying? Will I soon have no chin and a broken lower lip?* Nauseated with fear, I called my doctor.

My surgeon confirmed the severed flesh hadn't "taken" and referred me to an "outstanding" plastic surgeon, Thomas Rees. Two weeks later, Cliff and I rode the Long Island Railroad into Manhattan for my consult. We walked from Penn Station to elite Park Avenue, walking on sidewalks filled with impeccably groomed, stylishly dressed New York women who caused me to become keenly aware of my handmade skirt and blouse, loafers, and ho-hum, shoulder-length, straight hair. When we reached Dr. Rees's office ten minutes later, I felt as if I'd emerged from an Appalachian pumpkin patch.

Inside the spacious waiting room, terrifying questions

swirled through my mind. *Suppose he says he can't fix my broken face? How can our insurance possibly cover the fees of a Fifth Avenue surgeon and a New York City hospital? What if he's not the excellent doctor I was told he is? Suppose my face looks worse afterward than it does now?*

My worries were interrupted, as I heard my name, "Mary Jo?"

I smiled nervously at the assistant as she led us to an exam room. In a few minutes, a tall, slender, dark-haired man opened the door and extended his hand in warm greeting. Dr. Rees's handshake was firm, yet conveyed a subtle, gentle regard, which I silently acknowledged in my smile to him. He shook hands with Cliff, and as we sat back down, my shoulders dropped slightly.

Dr. Rees sat on his mobile stool and wheeled in front of me, studying my face. "Tell me what happened to your face in the accident," he said. I quietly described how the glove compartment had flown open upon impact. He touched the dying flap on my chin and pinched places on my nose, all so tenderly that I felt no discomfort. He said "ah" a few times, and then, finally, "Okay, I can fix this." I raised my eyebrows expectantly.

He photographed my face from several angles, then put the camera down and said, "I'm going to do four surgeries." He described each in a calm, low-key tone that soothed my worries, then added that he'd take photographs during each procedure.

I sat quietly, attentively, nodding when appropriate.

"I may write a journal article about how we did this," he continued. *A journal article?* I was awed. *Is what happened to not-very-important-me significant enough to warrant an article in a medical journal?* I doubted that.

By the time we said goodbye, I could not conceptualize exactly what was coming, yet I knew, without doubt, that I trusted this doctor.

Four months later, I had my first reconstructive surgery at New York City's University Hospital. Dr. Rees cut a flap from my upper lip and grafted it to my lower lip and down onto my chin where the original tissue had died. My lips were joined in the center so that blood could nourish the new flap on my lower lip. For two weeks, I ingested only what I could sip through a straw.

After I returned home, my mother visited one afternoon. Our conversation circled around to the night of the accident, and I suddenly said, "I wish I could remember what happened before the accident. It's a complete blank."

She looked at me quizzically. "Don't you remember what you told me that night?"

I thought hard. "No, I don't remember a thing. What did I tell you?"

"You and Cliff were arguing. You wanted him to pull over until he got the defroster working."

Instantly, the moments flooded back. I wondered how I could have "forgotten" this until Mom's few words had triggered it. *Is that amnesia?* If so, it felt surreal.

When Mom left, I pondered. Cliff had never mentioned the events prior to the accident. Had he, too, "forgotten?"

Several evenings later, Cliff sat at our desk in the dining room, looking through bills while I cleared the dinner table. He picked up the hospital bill, unfolded the invoice, and exhaled loudly.

Walking toward him, I said, "We're lucky we have good insurance. What would we do without it?"

He said softly, "We'd go bankrupt is what we'd do. I wish that night had never happened."

I felt a beautiful segue into my question. "Do you remember the moments just before we hit the other car?"

"Yes. We were fighting," he replied, his back to me, his voice irritated.

I moved to his side and sat on my haunches. "I want you to know something," I said gently, placing my hand on his arm. "I love you. I hold nothing against you."

We locked eyes. What he was thinking, I will never know. Did he understand for the first time that his temper—along with our drinking—was a critical factor in changing my face forever? Or did he believe the words my heart spoke aloud? Did he already believe he could not live with a wife who would always have facial scars? Whatever his thoughts, that brief moment transformed into a turning point in our lives. Cliff began coming home very late again. One night, I waited for him downstairs to ask where he'd been.

"Never mind," he spewed. But I pushed him to tell me, until we were both yelling furiously. Without warning, he lunged at me and hit me so hard, I fell to the floor. I lay on my back, panting, listening to him stomp up the stairs. *My God, he hit me.*

A few nights later, when he came home at 1:30 a.m., I cut to the chase. "Cliff, is there another woman?"

"Yes," he said grimly, and strode into our room to begin packing. Hazily, I watched from the doorway, safe in my cocoon, until he snapped the suitcase shut.

"I'll bring you money every Friday," he said, and drove away without looking in on our sleeping sons. For several weeks, he did bring cash. When he failed to arrive one Friday, I panicked, for the boys and I now lived hand to mouth. I called the telephone company to talk with Cliff, but his supervisor said, "Cliff resigned. He's moved away."

Staggered, I asked where he'd gone. "I don't know," the supervisor said.

I called Cliff's parents. My voice shook. "Kay, do you know where Cliff is?"

With saccharine sweetness, she replied, "Yes, but I can't tell *you*."

Kay hadn't been overt about her dislike for me until that moment. "I have no money and little food. If you won't tell me where Cliff is, can you and Cliff Sr. please help us?" They could not, she said firmly. I ended the fruitless conversation and hung up angrily. *Now what?*

As I sat on my bed, Chip, face pale and eyes serious, walked through the doorway and quietly asked, "Where's Daddy?"

I gazed at him. *Lord, what do I say?* "Daddy's gone away, Chip. He's a bad boy."

I still see him standing there and hear his frightened words. My heart was sick for him. Later, I'd read *Old Black Witch* to my boys after their baths and tuck them in with a big hug. I'd descend the stairs, drop onto the couch, and mentally list my dilemmas: I was a twenty-five-year-old college dropout with two small, fatherless sons, a mortgage, no income, no savings, and no car. Soon I'd learn that, despite the three reconstructive surgeries ahead, I no longer had medical insurance, either. When I told Dr. Rees I could no longer see him and why, he said, "Don't you worry. I'll take care of that problem"—words that staggered me with gratitude. I never received a doctor or hospital bill for my next three surgeries. Later, I ached with profound appreciation when I tenderly stitched a heart for Dr. Rees into my quilt.

While I remained in a semi-stupor of fear and anxiety, my mother was furious and exploded with the dislike for Cliff she'd swallowed for years. My father simply said, "I always knew he was a bum!" *Why did they never tell me their feelings?* I wondered, yet then asked myself, *Would it have made a difference in my decision to marry him?* Honestly? I didn't think so.

Thus, necessity forced me out of the house, despite my scars. I was pleased to accept a part-time checker opening at the corner supermarket, yet soon saw that those earnings could not cover our food and mortgage. Worse, I knew the approaching holiday season of 1968 would be the bleakest we had ever experienced.

One late December afternoon, I left my sons with Bonnie and borrowed my mother's car to drive to a doctor's appointment. Two hours later, I returned home with the boys. As I opened our never-locked back door, I saw that someone had entered our home during our absence. I whisked my sons to the living room to engage them with toys, then returned to the kitchen and stared at Keith's feeding table. When we'd left, the Formica surface had been clear; now two large boxes sat atop it. My hands unsteady, I removed items from the first box: two fresh roasting chickens, a bag of stuffing, fresh celery, two onions, a can of cranberry sauce, a can of peas. I stared with wonder. *A Christmas dinner. Where on earth did this food come from?*

In the second box I found two bright red and yellow plastic dump trucks and two generic Matchbox cars. As I stared at these gifts, tears streamed down my cheeks, not as much for the tangible gifts from unknown strangers as for the knowledge that somewhere in my community, from which I felt so isolated, were people aware of my lonely plight, people who cared and had reached out to us. Their kindness cut through my brave exterior of courage and penetrated the loneliness and worry I lived with daily, wondering how, alone, I would care for my boys as they deserved. I sobbed as I refrigerated the food and hid the toys.

Later that evening, as my sons slept, I wondered, *If I hadn't had a doctor's appointment, would I have met my giver so I could say the thank you I ache to give?* Perhaps, yet I found the anonymity very powerful. I had learned in church that we must do our good deeds in secret and not speak of them to others. Now, I realized that anonymity made these offerings more sacred, and I grasped the richer, deeper meaning of gifts for the first time in my life. And something that I would not understand for a few more years shifted inside me: the priceless gift of human kindness and caring we received that evening had planted a seed within me that would forever be a fundamental part of the woman I was becoming.

In later years, as I added a patchwork heart to my quilt for the people I would never know who had extended a helping hand, I sent profound gratitude into the universe to each.

Weeks rolled into months, and I lost any hope that Cliff would be located or would help me. I fell further behind in my monthly bills, despite working, which led to an agonizing question: Should I apply for welfare assistance for my children? Everyone I knew, including my own family, thought of welfare recipients as societal leeches. *I will never be that person,* I affirmed when I decided I had no choice. My mother drove me to the Department of Social Services, where, shrouded in shame, I struggled to open the heavy door, walked in, and checked in at the wooden counter.

"Please have a seat until one of our intake workers calls you," the buxom woman behind the counter told me. I sat down in the corner of a long row of wooden chairs.

Shortly, a gray-haired woman wearing a tweed skirt and jacket walked to the counter and said, "Mary Jo?" I nodded, rose, and walked toward her as my throat closed over the words I'd need to say. I silently followed her to an office, where she turned, smiled, and said, in a soft voice, "Here, sit here by my desk."

I sat as she walked around the desk to her chair. "I'm Anna Franklin. How can I help you?"

I swallowed hard to push away the lump in my throat, then croaked out my story. Mrs. Franklin gazed at me kindly as she listened to my words, then said, "Do you have any idea where Cliff is?"

I tried to clear my throat, with partial success. "His former employer and his mother both said they couldn't tell me."

She pulled out a form, asked me several questions, noted the responses, then asked me to sign it to confirm the truth of my answers.

"I think we can help you," she said pleasantly as she nodded.

"Thank you. It was so hard to ask, but . . ." I paused, as she said gently, "Yes, I can see that."

Several minutes later, the paperwork completed, I thanked her and left, dazed by Mrs. Franklin's respect and understanding for my predicament. The assistance I would receive was minimal, yet with it I could just get by each month. I would later fasten Mrs. Franklin's so-unexpected compassion onto a quilted heart with small stitches.

My financial problem narrowly resolved, the days slid into a directionless haze. I worked part-time, prepared meals, did laundry, played with my boys, worked at housekeeping, and cared for the yard. In the evening, after I tucked my sons into bed, I began filling the quiet with a few drinks. Two single former high school acquaintances started dropping by a few nights each week. We played rummy and drank from the vodka bottle one or the other brought, while I contributed small snacks.

Not many weeks later, Keith started head-banging before he drifted off to sleep. Chip became quieter; his wonderful belly laugh grew rarer. Uneducated as I was then about childhood behavior, I knew these were concerns but not what to do about them. I kept wandering through my days and drinking at night, the alcohol blurring the shattered fairy tale.

One evening I opened the refrigerator and found no beer. In truth, I didn't even like beer and could barely afford it. *I've got to get to the store before it closes at six*, I thought, panicking as I saw five thirty on the clock. I looked out into what I knew was a bitterly cold night. I had no car. How could I drag my boys a mile to the store so I could buy beer?

Right then, in a sizzling moment of clarity, I understood I was becoming addicted to alcohol. I sank into a kitchen chair, clasped my hands together, prayer-like, laid them on the small table, and dropped my head. *What on earth am I doing?* I asked myself. My tender answer today to my then-hopeless self would have been, *You are becoming the stereotypical woman you think welfare moms are.*

The next words rang out as clearly as church bells: *I don't know where the future will lead, but I know I don't want it to be the road to alcoholism, the road to bloody hell.* That night, I knew I had to stop drinking and begin building a better future for the three of us. Aimless day-to-day existence was not the life I wanted for us. I didn't go to town that night, or any other nights.

"I can't do this anymore," I told the two friends when they called next.

"Why not?" they asked. Amid some discomfort on both sides during the conversation, the card games ceased.

Multicolored tulips had broken through the ground outside my kitchen window when my phone rang one afternoon. "Hi, Mary Jo. This is Bob. Remember me?" Several months earlier, Cliff had arranged a double date with Bob and his wife, Margaret, a woman he worked with at Bell Telephone. I'd thought it odd at the time, because Cliff never initiated social get-togethers outside his family, but I'd agreed. And we'd had a good enough time together.

"I remember," I said cautiously. *What does he want?* I wondered. Bob, a thirty-ish, slightly overweight teacher in the

Hamptons, told me that Margaret had left him and she was living with Cliff. In California, he believed.

I was stunned to hear this fact, yet it soon transformed into a *yes, of course* moment.

"Can we meet and talk?" he asked. I agreed.

Despite our curious tie, we developed a friendship, born initially of our need to share information, but I also sensed Bob wanted to help me find a path out of my poverty trap. One night he invited me out for dinner and, over our shrimp entrée, offered me a challenge. "You know," he said, "you do have a problem. I always like to interchange the word *problem* with the word *opportunity*. So if your problem—needing to support your family now—is really an opportunity, how can you turn it into something good for you and your children?"

I stared at him, fascinated by his question. "I don't know," I said weakly, and soon the topic faded into another. Yet this was a new kind of thinking that I was ripe to engage in after my recent moment of truth about alcohol. I considered Bob's powerful concept all the next week, absorbing the challenge like my tulips soaked up a rainfall. But one idea after another fell flat, because each circled back to the fact that I had no resources. I liked Bob's words but felt hopeless about their application to me.

He invited me to dinner again. That evening, Bob said, "Why don't you go back to college?"

"Well," I said slowly, squaring off my mashed potatoes, "no money, no car, no childcare, no time, no . . ." We dropped it.

Yet again, he'd planted a seed, and during the next few weeks I tentatively sought information. I talked with my case-workers, two men who alternated home visits with me every few weeks. In their fifties and always respectful of me, they became both enthusiastic about and committed to helping me return to college.

Encouraged, I called the admissions office at nearby Southampton College to inquire about transferring there. They told me I would lose nearly a year of credits. Barriers, discouragement, and failure, I was learning, were frequent visitors to a person on welfare, and I was no exception. I gave up the idea as hopeless.

The next time Bob took me out to dinner, I told him about my efforts and failures. But he, whose world was much broader and deeper than my contracted one, simply threw out another idea. "Why don't we try to get you back to Oneonta so you can pick up right where you left off? Three more semesters, and you'll have that degree."

I stared at him. "My God, what an idea," I said. Yet within seconds the brick walls rose again and I started my long litany: "But there's no money, no—"

"Look," Bob interrupted, "call the admissions office in Oneonta and see if they'll accept you back without docking you any credits. Let's hear what they say before we talk anymore, okay?"

I got right on it the next morning and quickly learned I could return to Oneonta without losing a single credit. I started to get excited, yet my practical challenges kept my enthusiasm in check. *Where will I live? Who will watch my sons? Where will I get tuition money? What about a car? What will I do with my house?*

Two things happened next. First, answers started arriving for each challenge: I was awarded financial aid; I was able to buy a used 1965 Chevy Bel Air; I found a tenant for my house. Second, my feelings toward Bob, given his kindness and caring, easily moved beyond platonic. We took a weekend trip to Oneonta to look at rentals and within a day found a four-room apartment close to campus where Chip, Keith, and I could live comfortably. My caseworkers transferred my case to my new county, Otsego County, where my caseworker, a recent graduate named Susan Hust, who remains a friend to this day, would be immensely supportive. Every detail had fallen into place.

Then came the day when my sons and I watched movers slide our belongings into their van; we would meet them in

Oneonta the next afternoon. The house on Cedar Street became an empty tomb that echoed every sound I made. By dusk, the rugs were vacuumed, the floors mopped, and the last trash bag removed. I stood at my kitchen sink—sparkling white and towel-dried—and stared into the darkness. My neighbors' windows were brightly lit, and I pictured those good people having an ordinary evening, while mine was about to change our lives forever.

I recalled some of the sounds—laughter, tears, the gentle snores of small boys, the reading of so many books together— of our ordinary days here. Tears stung my eyes for what could have been and for what would never be. In time, I brushed the backs of my hands across the tears, breathed deeply, and walked through each room to say farewell. I returned to the kitchen, stepped out the back door, clicked the lock for the last time, and walked into the dark night.

As I started my car's engine and drove to my mother's house for my final night as a Long Islander, I looked up and saw faraway stars. I thought of Martin Luther King and Robert Kennedy, both cruelly taken forever from our lives that past April and June, respectively. Now, life was taking Chip, Keith, and me somewhere new. We would never live here again. Kind people, many strangers just months before, had brought us to this moment, and I would always remember them, even though I would never know some of them. Years later, I'd fasten a heart onto my quilt for my Long Island caseworkers and my new one, Susan Hust.

Chapter 14: CROSSROADS

Oneonta, New York, 1968

Kernels of grief (*it's hard to leave my family*), excitement (*will this truly work out?*), fear (*can I really drive 250 miles safely alone with two toddlers?*), and anticipation (*I'm going to college!*) bobbled around in my belly like corn in a popper when I got up that morning. Our country had successfully launched *Apollo 5* to the moon and *Solar Explorer 2* to study the sun that year, and now we were moving to complete my degree.

Several hours later, after lots of stops and the repeated question "Are we there yet, Mommy?" we reached the top of Franklin Mountain, overlooking Oneonta. I pulled over, we got out and stretched, and I pointed below. "There's our new town, boys," I said, with deep pleasure.

I thought back to early morning: tucking my sons, their books, and activities in the backseat; saying goodbye to family and neighborhood friends; driving slowly down Lake Avenue to Main; savoring sights and memories. Main Street led us to the tense, dense, fast-moving morning traffic on the Long Island Expressway for seventy miles to the Throgs Neck Bridge, which carried us from the Bronx over the East River and onto the New England Thruway.

As we approached the bridge, Chip pointed excitedly, "There's the Frog's Neck Bridge!"

Smiling at his sweet innocence, I relaxed as the easier part of our journey approached: through the Hudson Valley and over the Tappanzee Bridge, which transformed our flat landscape into the gently rolling, lower Catskill Mountain range. Continuing north, we'd exited at Kingston and eased onto Route 28, a scenic state highway that led to Oneonta. We'd passed through West Hurley (a small town close to Bethel, famous the following year for its legendary Woodstock Music Festival), then Shandaken and Phoenicia. We'd stopped near a gorgeous, clear stream that flowed briskly over rocks and boulders. The bank had been too steep to descend, so we'd enjoyed watching from above.

Now here we were, after traversing two miles of S curves to the top of Franklin Mountain, looking down at our new community, which sprawled and filled the beautiful valley below.

"Take us to our new house, Mommy!"

"Okay, let's go!" I agreed, and we jumped back into the car. We slowly descended the mountain, behind a long, winding line of cars, until we reached the bridge over the Susquehanna River leading into town. On Spruce Street, I picked up my key from my landlord, then drove uphill to East Street. It was about 4:30 p.m. on the first day of September 1968—the first day of my lease, the first day of our new lives, the first day of the more than two decades I would live in these timeless mountains.

Home, at 61 East Street, was a three-story, dark chocolate–colored, wood-shingled house with four white pillars supporting the broad front porch roof. Two apartments occupied the first and second floors; another was on the top floor.

We parked, got out, and hurried happily to our front door. I unlocked it, and we stepped inside to explore the four rooms: living room, bedroom, kitchen, and, downstairs, a recreation room. "Here's your room, boys," I told them. They chortled as we planned how to arrange their beds, bureaus, and play area when the movers arrived. Uneasily, I noted it was nearly 6:00 p.m. Where *were* the movers? An hour later, I suspected they weren't coming until the next day. I had no phone yet, so they couldn't contact me.

We were hard-pressed to devise a comfortable sleeping area on the floor until we found enough clothing and other soft articles in the car to create a "camping-out" bed. When we were finished, I asked, "Anybody hungry?"

"I'm starving," Keith said. "Me, too," Chip agreed.

My college budget would not support eating out for a while, so we searched the town until we discovered the Victory Grocery Store near West Street. Chip sat in the shopping cart and Keith in the child seat behind the handle as we walked each aisle of this strange new shop. We gathered milk, bread, cereal, eggs, cold cuts, cheese, mayonnaise, peanut butter, jelly, condiments, and paper products.

I started to walk by the beer case, then stopped, engaging in a silent debate. I hadn't been drinking at all in those past several weeks, but that night I suddenly felt a deep loneliness. We were complete strangers here; I didn't know one single person in this entire town.

Should I buy a six-pack? *Yes. No. Yes! No!*

In a strange little hokey-pokey, I pushed the cart forward, stopped, stepped back, stopped, moved forward, before I hoisted a six-pack of Millers into the cart. I told myself it was just a symbol to keep in my refrigerator to remind me of an almost-addiction I had left behind. We checked out, went home, unpacked our purchases, and ate sandwiches, then tumbled onto our makeshift beds and slept soundly.

The Millers remained untouched in the refrigerator until months later, when company came one weekend and we broke them out to drink with a meal.

The moving van arrived at nine the next morning, followed by the telephone man to connect our phone. Chip, Keith, and I set up their beds in the recreation room. The arrangement they liked best was positioning the twin beds in an L shape, with their heads at the outside edges.

Hungrily, we paused for peanut butter and jelly sandwiches and a glass of milk. After we ate, we left to enroll Chip in kindergarten. Center Street School was a modern, one-story brick building, where Mr. Piccolla, the guidance counselor, greeted us professionally as we entered his office. Chip sat next to me and Keith on my lap as I told him of our move. "I'd like to enroll Chip in kindergarten."

Mr. Piccolla asked, "Chip, your birthday is December fifteenth?"

When Chip nodded, Mr. Piccolla told me Chip was too young to enroll that year. "You could check with the Head Start program," he advised, and gave me the contact information.

The following day, Mrs. B., the Head Start nurse, said that she didn't have two openings in the Oneonta program but that there were several openings in the Laurens program, about ten miles away. If I could transport Chip and Keith there, she said, the Laurens program would accept both boys.

I trusted I'd find a way to do it. "Yes, thank you!"

That afternoon, my sons and I drove to the Laurens center to meet the teacher, register, and get acclimated.

The following Monday, a sunny September morning, we rose early, dressed, ate a quick breakfast, and drove out on Route 205 for Chip and Keith's first day of Head Start. Inside the center, they both cried and said, "Don't leave, Mommy." I stayed a while longer, and when I tried to leave again, both boys clung to me. The teacher scooped Chip up into her ample arms, took hold of Keith's hand, and said reassuringly, "They'll be fine; don't worry. Chip, Keith, say goodbye to your mom. She'll be back in a little while."

I hugged them and left with a heavy heart. I thought of the mothers in my old neighborhood who stayed home with their children. Sadly, I wouldn't be able to give my sons that gift.

Back on campus, I went to Financial Aid and learned I was eligible for a work-study job. My eyes widened when I saw that the Laurens Head Start center had just such an opening. In a pinch-me moment, I signed up with delight. Maybe I couldn't stay home with my sons, but I *could* work in their day care program.

As I drove to pick them up that first day, I recalled how frightened and isolated I'd felt at nursery school. I prayed my boys had had a better experience this day. When I opened the front door and saw them both happily engaged in play with others, my heart sang.

Late that evening, I slipped out onto the front porch, sat on the rail, embraced my knees with my arms, and looked up at the stars. It was not a quiet street we lived on, yet as I stared at the bright lights above, my body filled with peace. I recalled telling Bob about all those seemingly impossible barriers to this move and reflected how each had worked out. We'd safely moved 250 miles to a town where I hadn't known a soul one week earlier, we'd settled into our little apartment, we'd found good day care, I had a part-time job, we'd met some nice people, and I was going to get my degree. Tears of gratitude streamed down my cheeks.

Later, I went inside and wrote Bob a letter describing how well things were going and thanking him for all his help and support. We'd never talked about love, yet I believed I loved him and hoped he felt the same toward me. I signed the letter "with love" and looked forward with some apprehension to how he'd respond.

Then classes started and I became immersed in college life. I watched my classrooms fill with young, carefree students and recalled when I was one of them, with no children or job except to be a good student. I briefly wished I'd had the maturity to appreciate and take fuller advantage of that earlier time. Yet, at age twenty-six, still a quiet and now serious student, I had grown: I listened more closely, took better notes, studied harder, and would earn higher grades than before. I had two strong motivators now: my sons.

Our days settled into a regular rhythm: I rose early, drove the boys to Laurens, worked, attended classes, and returned to Laurens to pick up my sons. Often, weather permitting, we went to a nearby park for some free-spirited play for all of us. Home again, we ate dinner, I bathed the boys and read to them, then kissed them soundly and tucked them in. Upstairs, I pulled out my books and studied for a few hours before I slept.

I liked my job at Head Start, where I worked directly with the children, sometimes with gross motor activities on the playground, other times indoors with fine motor skills, such as coloring or puzzles. I especially loved reading to small groups, hoping books would become their best friends, as they were for me.

On weekends, we did basic chores and then sought the outdoors. Oneonta had two great parks, Wilber Park and Neahwa Park, and we loved them both. Wilber was a two-level park close to our house. The lower level held tennis courts and a swimming pool that opened each summer. The upper level had a huge play area and a picnic area, both backdropped by a dense pine forest, where the boys and I learned to see the world in new ways as we lay on soft pine needles and looked up through the trees to the sky above.

I loved the swings as much as Chip and Keith did and alternated between pushing them and teaching them how to pump. Then I swung, feeling happy and free, as I held on tight, leaned far back, and pointed my toes toward the sky, each repetition reaching higher to the heavens. Soon the boys could pump their swings, safely propel up and down the seesaw, and whiz down the slides. We also loved climbing a huge, stately old maple tree.

I smiled at other parents and their children in the park, and they smiled back. The red, Y-shaped scar on my chin and the line on my upper lip had both faded. One day I realized people didn't stare at my face or ask questions anymore. I began to forget about my injuries.

One warm morning in spring, my neighbor Marji, with whom my sons and I had become close over the past year, joined me on my front porch while the boys played.

"I want to tell you something," she said in a soft voice.

"Sure," I said, curious about her furtive tone.

"The last time I took care of Keith, somehow we began talking about God and Keith said, 'I remember when I lived with God before I was born.'"

Stunned, she'd said to him, "Really? What was that like, Keith?"

He'd said, "It was bright there. It was happy. Fun, too. Jesus was there, and I liked it." Marji added that his eyes had been wide and his voice blissful as he'd spoken.

"I've never heard this before," I told her. Later that evening, I sat with the boys after their baths and story. "Keith, do you remember what you told Marji the other day?"

"I was with Jesus before I was born." His compelling eye contact and earnest tone lent his words a sacred depth that I could not disbelieve.

I said something like, "That's an amazing memory. I'm so happy to know that." We talked a bit more, about what I have now forgotten. Alone later, I reflected on my son's revelation and, in doing so, opened a deeper awareness for myself: that the vague spiritual world I thought I knew did truly exist and had just intensely touched our lives.

Chapter 15: SUNSHINE AND SHADOW

Oneonta, New York, 1969–70

During the winter of 1969, seven years after leaving the Catholic Church, I found myself longing to return to my rich Catholic roots, to kneel before my Creator and express thankfulness for all that had transformed our lives.

I took Chip and Keith to visit St. Mary's on a Saturday afternoon to see our new church home. "We'll start coming here every week," I told them. "I want to thank God for our new life." The next day, we walked in and sat near the front. As we quietly waited for Mass to start, Keith leaned over and whispered, "Mommy, when's God coming?"

In that precious moment, I smiled at him. "He's already here, Keith. We just can't see Him."

"Oh, okay," he said, satisfied, and leaned back into the pew as the priest walked to the altar and opened the Mass. I hoped my sons would feel embraced by the same spirit I was. An hour later, we exited the church and discovered that two inches of snow had quietly covered the ground as we'd worshipped. The exquisitely changed world, so hushed and unexpected, seemed a reflection of my stirring deeper faith, a mysterious event sent from above.

At semester's end, I was pleased with my five A's and a B. It was time for a welcome break, a holiday visit to Long Island with my family. I well remember that Christmas morning, my mom, two sisters, and I sitting on the floor near the tree, sharing Chip's and Keith's joy as they opened their gifts. I looked forward to all I believed our new life held ahead.

I was disappointed that Bob hadn't gotten back in touch with me, so I called him one evening. Always hypersensitive to a person's reaction to me, I immediately felt his discomfort upon hearing my voice. When he asked how I was doing, I answered vaguely, then said, "What about you?"

"I'm dating a district teacher." He paused, then added, "She's such a happy person."

"Bob, I'm happy for you both," I said, trying to feel glad for them, without success. I had not admitted to myself yet, but saw clearly in time, that I was not mature enough for a relationship with Bob, something he was wise enough to know. He had been incredibly kind to help me, and that would remain his singular, richly valued role in my life.

A few years later, I heard that Bob had married his girl-friend, that they had a son who was almost a year old and were a happy unit. That was the last I heard of them. Long afterward, as I stitched Bob's heart patch onto my quilt, I felt deep and genuine joy for him and his family.

My father invited Bonnie and me to spend that New Year's Eve with him at a small local tavern he frequented. He proudly introduced us to his friends, and we mingled a while, until I discovered a very tall man behind me, smiling down at me.

"Oh. Hi, Fred," I said, surprised, then smiled. "How are you?"

We'd gone to school together. He'd been a year behind me, and we hadn't socialized much, but I knew he was a good person. I liked, as we talked, that he was friendly and sincere without being flirtatious. We found a table and ordered drinks, and I asked teasingly how everything was in the wilds of Manorville, where he lived. He chuckled, his pale blue eyes twinkling beneath dark curly hair. "Oh, not much has changed." Then he asked, "You got married, right? What happened to your husband?"

I nodded. "Yes, he left and then disappeared last year. I've heard a rumor he might be in California." I didn't mention that the Department of Social Services was looking for Cliff.

"What kind of person does something like that?" he wondered.

"It's not been easy," I said, then described the months I floundered around and my eventual realization that I needed to find direction. "I couldn't earn enough to support us on minimum wage," I said. "I decided to go back to college to finish my degree."

"You moved two hundred and fifty miles away with two little kids to go to college?" His tone was incredulous.

I chuckled. "I did."

"And you work part-time, too? You are really something," he said. I valued the look of pride in his eyes and respect in his words. I'd not heard those words—*you are really something*—in my entire life, I believed, and they sounded awfully nice. I sipped my rum and Coke. "Thank you. What are you doing these days?"

He took a sip, too. "I'm taking the test for Suffolk County patrolman soon," he said, anticipation in his eyes.

"An Irish cop! Imagine that!" I teased.

He laughed.

Then I added, more seriously, "I think you'll make a great cop." I could easily picture this even-tempered, humorous, very tall Irishman in uniform, carrying out the work.

"You think so?" he said, eyes thoughtful.

I nodded. His eyes told me he liked those words.

For the rest of the evening, we shared interesting conversation and danced to some popular songs from that year by the Temptations, Johnny Rivers, the Turtles, and to "Ob-La-Di, Ob-La-Da," from the Beatles' newly released *White Album*. By evening's end of the dawning of the new decade, the 1970s, Fred and I clearly looked forward to the fresh directions we were crafting in our lives. We also felt drawn to each other.

He took me home and enveloped me in a gentle bear hug at the door. He did not kiss me, and that felt just fine. Inside the house, I slid between crisp, clean sheets and into sweet dreams.

The next day, I drove back to Oneonta with Chip, Keith, and Fred's promise to call. One day, I would understand how my insecurities had so constricted my own world and how attracted I was to Fred's vast capacity for living fully.

He visited us every few weekends, when winter weather allowed. The activities we did were simple yet deeply felt pleasures: a midnight stroll up the East Street hill in the hushed world of a silent snowstorm, flakes falling on our eyelashes; walking with Chip and Keith on Sunday mornings to Mass at St. Mary's Church; ice-skating at Neahwa Park; sleigh rides down the upper East Street hillside with the boys, the four of us rosy-faced, laughing all the way to the bottom, our hands always joined. With each visit, as I witnessed the affection flowing between Fred and my sons and the sincerity of his actions and words with them, I grew to know my boys truly mattered to him.

A lifelong habit of mine was to fear a problem that might likely never happen. Today, I call it "awfulizing." On a Sunday in March, Fred tossed his travel bag in his car as I looked over-head at the gray sky. The forecast predicted no precipitation, yet worry churned in my belly. "Fred, what will you do if a snowstorm starts on your way home?"

He turned to me. "Hey, listen to me, okay?"

I stared into his clear eyes as he tilted his head sideways and said, "A problem is only as big as a person lets it become, and it always has a solution." He bent down to kiss me, a kiss so tender that ignited the rich affection flowing between us.

After he drove away, I drew his words into my heart. That act of trust, in turn, freed me to believe that our growing rela-tionship could be what it appeared: a healthy, growing bond. I didn't awfulize with Fred again.

One day when I arrived at the Head Start center, Mrs. B. grinned at me and said, "So, who's Fred?"

"How do you know about Fred?" I asked.

"We had a dentist come in this morning to give oral edu-cation. He brought one of those oversize toothbrushes, about a foot long, you know, and a set of large teeth to demonstrate how to brush properly. Before he started, he asked the kids, 'Does anyone know someone big enough to use this toothbrush?'"

"Fred!" Keith had called out without hesitation. When asked who Fred was, Keith described our gentle, six-foot-four friend, giving insight into the perceptions of a small, four-year-old boy.

In late winter, we drove to the top of Franklin Mountain one afternoon, got out of Fred's green Pontiac, and stood quietly on the lookout over the town. I glanced up at Fred as the bitter wind sliced through his curly hair, and saw the deep peace in his eyes when he looked into the valley where I lived.

"This is one of my favorite places, up here on the mountain," he said quietly. "When I get here on Friday nights and see all those lights shining down there, I know one of them is yours, waiting for me." His arm around my waist, he pulled me close. "I'm the happiest man in the world up here because this mountain brings me to you."

We looked forward to the end of the spring semester, when the boys and I would stay with my mother for the summer, one town away from his home.

In his last letter to me, he wrote toward the end:

I have talked with my Friend [his Creator] and He said to have patience, that there would be another short spell of winter and then spring would arrive. He said, though, that when it comes, to remember that it is coming for you and me.

Then:

Well, Beautiful, I'm going to dream some wonderful dreams tonight, so if you should hear someone knocking on your door in your dreams, you'll know who it is. I love you and miss you terribly, but I guess those two feelings will go hand in hand until springtime.
All my love,
Fred

I hold that aged letter in my hand today after recording it above and remember how treasured my feelings of caring for and being cared for by Fred were. Our affection was richer and deeper than any I'd experienced, and I felt happier, I believed then and know now, than I ever had before.

A few days later, on St. Patrick's Day, the boys and I moved through our usual evening routine while Fred decided to go out with his lifelong best friend for a brief celebration a few miles from home. Jim told me later that Fred wanted to celebrate something related to me—something that Fred would tell me about when he called Saturday morning.

The accident happened less than half a mile from his home. Fred, in the passenger's seat, died instantly, while Jim walked away physically unhurt.

He returned to me several weeks afterward. I awoke and felt an elusive yet powerful presence surround me in the silent, dark room. I was confused at first, then sensed Fred was near. He stayed until he filled my shattered heart with the sure knowledge that he was at peace and lovingly waited for me.

I treasured that final gift and in time discerned a powerful message in my young life: while I'd lost Fred's presence, his love remained. When spring arrived that year, it was far from the springtime we'd anticipated. *That* springtime, I realized, would be somewhere far in the future.

When my sons and I returned to Oneonta after Fred's funeral, I plodded numbly through mothering, studying, and working in a now-gray world. One cool afternoon, when I saw new leaves opening on Franklin Mountain's trees, my tears flowed, at last breaking through my stoicism. Springtime color was absent in my world that year. Instead, I buried myself in studies. I canceled my plan to spend the summer on Long Island. Fred wasn't there, so I remained in Oneonta, enrolled in summer school, accelerated my studies, and received an unexpected benefit for my intense studying by making the Dean's List for the first time. Then—suddenly, it seemed—I had completed student teaching and had more than enough credits for my bachelor of science degree in English education. In November, I was finished. I noticed, but did not celebrate, the event.

In my mind, I returned to Franklin Mountain many times, standing next to Fred as I had all those years earlier, seeing his peace-filled eyes and hearing his loving words again. I ached for his presence. Then one day when I looked into the valley of the Seven Hills, I discovered my grief had softened enough that I could smile and feel filled with sweet memories of our brief time.

One summer, experimenting with a healing writing exercise, I wrote the story of how I envisioned our life would have been. It was a blissful story: Ours was a strong marriage. We raised Chip and Keith, along with a son and daughter of our own. Fred achieved his dream of becoming a state trooper while I taught English in our local school. Our well-nurtured children grew up to be well-rounded adults with contented marriages and had eight grandchildren we adored. Our homes were filled with lovingly hand-crafted quilts I made through the years for each child and grandchild and for Fred and me. He and I lived long, healthy lives and even met some of our great-grandchildren. We were gifted with living happily ever after.

Fred's heart-shaped fabric leaf on my vibrant patchwork plant is one of the largest fastened lovingly to my quilt.

Chapter 16: COUNTRY ROADS

Oneonta, New York, 1970–72

With my brand-new degree and temporary certification as an English teacher in hand, I realized my recent life experiences now tugged me more toward a human services career than teaching. Just as I'd been helped, I wanted to help others rise up from challenging times. I applied to the social services agency that had assisted my family and was offered a foster-care caseworker position for fifty children, from newborns to late teens. I began my new career on January 2, 1971, celebrating that I could fully care financially for my family and believing our gray world of poverty was forever behind us.

My feelings about my work were passionate and my goal noble yet naive, I realized in time. I wanted to help every disenfranchised person in my county work his or her way out of poverty, as I had been so graced to do. Each day brought different challenges: visits to my foster children, foster parents, or the child's natural parents; transporting my caseload kids to medical, therapy, or dental appointments; family court appearances to review a child's situation. Sometimes the court released the child for adoption and I facilitated the adoption process between the child and the new family.

Personally, I was learning better parenting skills, making new friends, and paying all my bills, retaining a modest balance at month's end. To celebrate our financial independence, I traded in my gray, crinkle-roofed 1965 Bel Air for a brand-new baby blue 1969 Chevy Malibu.

My coworker Marge lived in a camp on nearby Goodyear Lake with her friend Deni, a legal secretary. They invited me to their occasional parties at the camp, where I met new people. Thus, two years after Fred's death, my social world began to expand beyond reading books. I planned to remain single; I had adjusted to being solitary, going places and doing things alone, and felt content with the life I was building for my family. I saw married couples who seemed deeply happy together, yet an enduring marriage was so far beyond my life experience, I doubted one existed for me.

One summer day, our secretary, Eleanor Bennett, said, "Ed and I want to have a party at the lake. You're all invited to the camp this Saturday!"

The boys and I loved secluded Arnold Lake, where we enjoyed a great afternoon of swimming, eating, and, later on, something I'd never done: waterskiing. While I had grown up on Long Island and often went to the beach, I'd always feared water and was a poor swimmer. Ed and my coworkers encouraged me to try, and soon an orange life jacket hugged me as I crouched in clear, gently lapping lake water, my bottom touching the end of the skis, a boulder of apprehension in my gut, watching Ed and his idling motor. Looking back at me, he gently accelerated as I rose to stand and immediately fell, slapping down hard into the water.

"No problem," Ed called out. "You're getting it!"

We repeated this scenario several more times, as Ed cheered me on, until I remained standing and he pulled me in a wide circle around the entire lake three times. It was the most exhilarating water experience I'd ever had.

Ed took me around the lake as many times as I asked, until I called out, "I'm pretty tired, Ed. Let's go back."

"You sure?" he asked. He'd been so patient, kind, and willing to work with me as long as I wanted; tears spilled from my eyes as I thanked him. My excited sons met us on the dock. "We saw you water-ski, Mommy! You did good!"

We embraced with big, happy hugs.

Why those tears for Ed Bennett's kindness? I pondered after my sons were asleep that evening. I thought of my father. *What if he'd driven the boat?* The first time I'd fallen, he would have called me stupid and returned to the dock. I felt sad. *And Mom?* Well, stressed and worried about so much, she wouldn't have had patience or time to keep trying until I got it. But I knew all this; it was no big deal. What I didn't understand then was how profoundly their attitudes—his of dislike and degradation, and hers of continual unavailability—stripped me of all sense of self-worth. These reflections were early moments of glancing back to my childhood experiences and seeing threads that linked to the present.

Yet new thoughts were pushing away these old, unsettling ones. That evening, back home, I decided I'd buy a parcel of land on Arnold Lake and build a log cabin for my small family. I smiled as I visualized it in detail: small-paned windows and doors, a wide front porch, trees surrounding us in a woodland embrace, a rustic interior with a simple kitchen and other necessary rooms. I saw my sons playing for countless happy hours indoors and out, as they grew contentedly through the years.

Yes, the cabin would become our true home, and my first real home—within a year, I hoped.

Marge and Deni invited me to an autumn party at the camp, and Ed brought a friend. Ed beckoned to me when I walked through the door and introduced me to Don. "Hi," I said to the tall, sandy-haired guy. "Nice to meet you."

"You, too," Don said, grasping my hand in a firm shake as I looked into his hazel eyes. He was soft-spoken, trim, and muscled, and possessed a strong yet quiet presence with which I felt at ease.

Deni walked over, brown eyes sparkling, and I sensed an invisible Cupid's arrow in her hand. "Hi, Don, glad you came over tonight." She'd met Don when she'd visited Ed in Bovina Center, where Ed lived and owned the tiny town's garage. "Anyone for wine?" she asked us.

Soon, glasses in hand, Don and I walked onto the screened-in front porch that overlooked Goodyear Lake, ten feet below. The evening was warm, with sweet fresh air meandering through the screens. As we looked down at the shimmering, gently moving water, I said, "Deni tells me you're a dairy farmer."

"Yep, the farm's small," Don replied quietly. "But I'm building my herd numbers because my folks want to retire soon. I plan to buy the farm. I've lived there all my life . . . well, except when I went to college."

What would it be like to live in the same place all my life? I wondered. I couldn't imagine, let alone even remember some of the houses I'd lived in when I was young.

I told Don I was a single mom with two young sons. He nodded and said, "What happened to your husband?" The words felt like a chilly breeze rising off the water, and I shuddered inwardly.

"Let's just say I'm cured of marriage," I replied vaguely, not wanting to recount the story. "What else can we talk about?"

He nodded, so I explained that I was a foster care case-worker. "Some of my foster parents own and operate small dairy farms," I said. "On Long Island, where I grew up, we had duck farms and potato farms, but I'd never been on a dairy farm until I met these foster parents."

He smiled. "What do you think of dairy farming?"

I said, "What I like best is that everyone works together and the kids are an important part of the family."

He nodded. "We have lots of long days and work seven days a week. It's not always easy, but working together is one of the best parts of it all."

"Do you raise your own meat? Have a vegetable garden?"

"Yep," he said. "Pop and I raise beef and veal. Mom plants a garden, then cans and freezes what we don't eat right away. Since she got asthma, though, the garden's a lot smaller."

"I'm sorry she has asthma," I told him, and was silent for several seconds to give my genuine sympathy time to fill the space as more than idle words.

Then I went on, "You have such a healthy lifestyle. You raise your own milk and meat and vegetables. It's such a balanced, wholesome way to be."

"I guess it is," Don said, as I reflected that nothing in my childhood experience exposed me to a tiny vegetable or flower garden, let alone to a father who was home, spending quality time playing or working with his children. What would that have been like?

At evening's end, I drove home, reflecting that our conversation had been interesting but that I didn't expect to see Don again. Monday morning, I returned to work, the memory of the party already faded.

Three weeks later, my phone rang one evening. "Hi, Mary Jo." I recognized Don's deep voice.

"Oh. Hi," I said. This was my first phone call from any man since my last conversation with Fred, more than two years earlier. I'd always felt my decision to remain single after his death was clear to others, through either my words or my actions.

We talked briefly about the weather, and then he asked, "Would you like to go to a movie this Saturday?"

I stammered, "Oh, I don't think so . . ."

"*The French Connection* is playing. You mentioned you'd like to see it when we talked at the camp."

"Oh . . . yes, I did . . ." I stalled for time to answer. My reply should have been easy: *no, thanks.* Those words didn't come, though. Instead, I felt curious to know more about this farmer. "Well, okay, yes, I'd like to go." We made our plan.

When Don knocked on the door that Saturday evening, I suddenly thought longingly of Fred as I gazed at this new man who seemed interested in me.

After the movie, which I thoroughly enjoyed, I asked Don what he thought of it. "It was okay, but different from what I usually see."

"What do you like?"

He replied, "John Wayne and other westerns, historical movies, and comedies."

"Well, thanks for putting up with my love of suspense and mystery," I said, smiling.

"No problem," he said, then invited me to a nearby cocktail lounge, where we sipped rum and Cokes as we talked, engrossed in all sorts of topics, until early hours. As I lit a cigarette, Don glanced at his watch. "I better be going soon. Morning milking gets here early." We drove home, and as I unlocked my door, I turned to give him a hug. He bent down and kissed the top of my head. I thanked him for a pleasant evening, and he left.

A few evenings into the next week, Don invited me to go dancing at another nearby lounge. Again I hesitated, but only briefly. Again we enjoyed another nice evening, which ended in a lingering good-night kiss.

When Don met Chip and Keith soon after that, he asked, "Have you boys ever seen a cow?"

"No," they replied in unison.

"Would you like to?"

"Yes!" they enthused.

We visited the farm, where we stepped into a new world and learned how cows were milked, where the blackberry patches grew, how to safely ride a hay wagon, and how Don chopped corn, then blew it into the silo.

Don's mother, Gladys, short and buxom, with cornflower-blue eyes and curly gray hair, was warm and affectionate with my sons and me. I noticed that in Don's family, there was no manipulation or power struggle, and nobody was "stupid." Our time together was happy, pleasure-filled, and respectful. Don's family gave me unconditional acceptance, a heady freedom I'd never experienced until I'd met Fred. I'd thought that very rare.

Gladys enjoyed feeding people sumptuous country food in her large old farm kitchen. Shortly after Thanksgiving, she taught me how to make the only holiday fruitcake I've ever loved. In late winter, the family tapped maple trees and boiled down the sap to make pure maple syrup in the old sap house near the stone wall. My sons and I witnessed the birth of a Holstein calf inside the weathered barn. The boys watched with awe when the calf silently slid into the world.

Chip softly said, "Wow." Keith was speechless. The moment felt sacred to me. With the exception of birthing my own children, that moment was as close to a miracle as I'd ever been, yet here it happened regularly. My children were discovering a world they'd never witnessed, while I was uncovering my deeper self: loving the four of us working and being together, drawn to this lifestyle as a moth to light in a dark night.

One late-summer weekend as my sons were absorbed in playing in the stream and Don's mother watched them, Don said, "Let's go pick some blackberries" as the time for us to return home drew near.

I loved gathering any kind of food the farm gifted us with and said, "Sure, let's!" We got a large bucket and hiked up the hill behind the barn, over to the secluded property line, where a huge patch of thumb-size blackberries silently offered generous bounty. Eagerly, I started picking, but before many berries had thumped into my pail, Don slipped his arm around my waist and tipped my chin up for a kiss. Soon the bucket sat on the grassy ground as I awoke to a new experience. We shared our love and desire outdoors, embraced not only in each other's arms but also by Mother Nature—by soft, grassy-covered earth beneath us, fresh, sweet air enveloping us, and warmth and light shining down upon us. I felt uneasy that we might be discovered, but Don reassured me that wouldn't happen. How I wish today that I could have fully experienced the sheer perfection and, yes, sacredness of those lovely moments, as I write about that gorgeous encounter. The beautiful experience of opening abundantly to the present moment would come, but not for decades.

Later, we gathered a few more blackberries, then walked back to the farmhouse, where Don's father peeked into the bucket and said wryly, "You didn't go to pick berries."

I bit my lips together so I wouldn't laugh, yet felt embarrassed, too, that he knew we'd made love. I liked Don's dad a lot; he was similar to Don in many ways: quiet, with a dry sense of humor. He was also hard of hearing and often quipped that when he answered his ringing phone and couldn't hear anyone at the other end, he'd call out to Don, "Jo's on the phone."

I giggled, thinking about that soft-spoken voice of mine, which, to this day, remains much quieter than an average person's.

Don called me Jo and told me that my return to college to carve out a better life reminded him of his relative named Jo, whose husband died and left her with eight children. She was a hard worker in the face of adversity, he said, just like I was.

At home one Friday afternoon, the phone rang. I answered, and a male voice said, "Hi." Though I'd not heard the voice in years, I knew it instantly.

"Cliff," I said, in a voice so chilly it could have made ice cubes. Just before I'd graduated from college, I'd learned that Social Services had found him in California and taken him to court for child support. The judge awarded me a pittance, which did not nearly cover the assistance I was receiving. Happy, however, that Cliff had been made somewhat accountable, I gave his support checks to Social Services. I'd never considered I'd hear from him again and had never sought a divorce, because I naively believed that since I'd never marry again, it didn't matter.

"How are the boys?" he asked, speaking as familiarly as if we'd talked just yesterday.

"They're fine. What do you want?" I asked shortly, stunned and wondering why he'd called.

Cliff told me he'd moved back to New York and obtained a divorce in Mexico from me (which I'd known nothing about); he and Margaret had married; he missed his sons and wanted to reunite with them. Somewhere during his monologue, I dropped into a chair, unable to take it all in at once. I suddenly felt horrified.

"I'm in town now. Can I see the boys?" he asked.

I couldn't believe he was physically in Oneonta. Every cell in my being wanted to prevent this unreliable man from seeing my innocent boys ever again. If I'd spoken from my abandoned-parent self, I would have said, *No, you dumb jerk, there's no way I'm going to let you see my sons, the children you walked away from years ago.* Instead, I swallowed and shifted to my professional self, the one that allowed me to function with calm, with grace.

"Cliff, I have no idea if the boys want to see you, so my answer is no, not today, not until I talk with them," I said.

To my surprise, he agreed. We left it that I'd talk with Chip and Keith that evening and Cliff would call back tomorrow. I hung up the receiver feeling as if I'd just entered a carnival house of horrors. *What now?* I wondered, as I agonized about what I'd say to my boys.

After dinner, I washed dishes with my radio for company. Simon and Garfunkel crooned the soothing words to "Bridge over Troubled Water," but tonight they did not dispel my dread. Dishes done, I went into the living room, lowered the volume on *The Dick Van Dyke Show*, and said, "I have something to tell you. Your father called today."

They both stared at me. "My daddy called?" Chip said.

"Yes," I said. "He's been in California but has moved back to New York, not too far from here. He has a new wife, and he'd like to see you."

My eight- and six-year-olds instantly shouted, "Yes! I want to see Daddy."

I talked about choices—that they might, for example, feel angry with him for leaving and could say no. But they cut me off and reaffirmed, "We want to see him."

"You're sure?" They didn't budge. I acquiesced and told them I'd work it out the next day.

Keith had no memory of Cliff, and Chip's was scanty at best, yet I knew from my work with children in foster care that preventing a child from having parental contact, no matter how hurtful the parent might have been, often resulted in the child creating a romanticized, unrealistic image of that parent. So the next day, with a heavy heart, I told Cliff he could visit the boys at the house, and that I would be present the entire time. Once again, he agreed amiably.

When he rang the doorbell the following Saturday, I opened the door and froze as I stared at the dark-haired man who was a stranger. *How did I ever think he was cute or nice?* I wondered. And what was I doing, letting him into our new life? Was I still that little girl trying to please everyone, hoping they would love me? Well, no, not this time, not *him*. I reminded myself I was a professional now, with skills in how to help children from broken families.

I forced myself to say a polite "Hello, Cliff," as I held my sons' hands. He said an equally civil hello to me and then looked down at Chip and Keith. His eyes seemed to fill with emotion as he bent and said, "You've both gotten so big. And so handsome. Do you remember me?"

Chip stared at him and nodded solemnly, while Keith said quietly, "No."

"I hope we can make up for lost time," Cliff said softly, and then, "I've brought you a present. Would you like to have it?"

The boys nodded. Keith said shyly, "I like presents."

Cliff smiled and handed them each a wrapped gift the size of a deck of cards. Within seconds, the boys each held a small Matchbox car.

"Thank you?" I prompted Chip and Keith.

"Thank you," they said in sweet voices.

"You're welcome," Cliff said, reaching into his shirt pocket, then handing them each a Three Musketeers candy bar.

"Thank you!" they said again, their faces more relaxed and smiling. I invited them all to sit on the porch chairs, as Cliff talked with the boys. I said little, seeking to fade into the background and observe. I saw the initial tension begin to lessen in my sons as Cliff asked them about school, what sports they liked, and other questions. In about half an hour, he ran out of things to say and looked at me. "Hey, boys, is it okay with you if I talk with your mom for a few minutes?"

"That's okay, Daddy," Chip said, trying out the intimate word for *father* a little uncertainly. Keith echoed, "Okay, Daddy."

I heard in their voices and saw on their faces how much it meant to say that word. I asked them to play inside for a little while so Cliff and I could talk. They agreed and went inside, where they stood at the living room window, about five feet from where Cliff and I sat, quietly watching us.

Cliff handed me a thick package, saying, "You asked for the divorce papers."

"Thanks," I said. "I'll take them to my attorney. If this is legal, I will be so glad to be divorced."

Soon I beckoned the boys to come outside and asked if they'd like to play a game of Chutes and Ladders. All three liked the idea and they were soon at play, sliding up and down the ladders and chutes, laughing. When they finished the game, Cliff stood and stretched, then said, "That was fun, guys, and I'd like to play again sometime, if that's okay with your mother."

I looked at my sons' hopeful faces and heard sincerity in Cliff's voice. I hated to admit that the visit had gone better than I'd expected; I had seen nothing that upset Chip or Keith. Just the opposite, in fact—they obviously felt quite happy.

"I need to think about this," I said to Cliff. "Call in a few weeks, and we can talk more," I said tentatively.

He agreed, then bent down to tell Chip and Keith it was time for him to go. Keith looked at him, wide-eyed and serious. "Are you coming back, Daddy?" he asked, while Chip watched Cliff closely.

"I hope so. Your mom and I will talk about it," he said, looking over at me. They hugged, and the visit ended. I watched Cliff walk to the red Pontiac Firebird we had purchased together just before he'd left us and felt anger surge through my body as I thought of his decision to get into that car and disappear from our lives, tossing us aside like roadside litter. *What a rotten thing to do!*

Some years later, a therapist gave me a different perspective: "Mary Jo, many people solve their problems by running away from them." I didn't like his comment; I felt as if he was siding with Cliff. Today, I understand better. It's still a rotten thing to do, though.

I sat on the porch with Chip and Keith after Cliff left, and asked if they really wanted to visit with their father again. It was a silly question. "Well, we'll see," I told them, then watched their behavior and sleep patterns for the next several days. I saw no signs of disturbance. Not pleased, I concluded that the situation seemed clear; they wanted more time with their dad.

I took the divorce papers to my attorney the day after the visit. He reviewed them and advised that the divorce was legal, unless I wanted to contest it. I stared at him. *Does a hummingbird refuse nectar?*

So I was officially divorced and had been, in fact, for over a year. Well, that was easy, albeit underhanded and covert. I made a copy of the divorce papers, handed the original to Cliff the next time I saw him, and said a sincere thank-you.

Cliff returned monthly several times after that first visit, then one day asked if he could take Chip and Keith to his home for a weekend. The phenomenon of parents kidnapping their children from a former spouse would not begin for another few years; if it had, I probably wouldn't have risked such a visit. Much as I hated the idea, my basic nature was to trust what seemed right to me, and, in fact, I'd seen no problems thus far. In truth, my sons loved having Cliff back in their lives, and, although I certainly didn't, I knew I must respect their feelings.

I could never have imagined that Cliff would disappear a second time in the not-too-distant future.

One Friday afternoon, I drove the twenty miles of back roads between my house and Don's farm, singing along to "Take Me Home, Country Roads" as John Denver's joyful voice emanated from my tape deck. This exquisite song had always connected with my deep longing for home. The summer day was warm, my windows wide open, and fresh air blasted through the car. I felt at one with the universe as I traversed through rich, varied shades of green covering the rolling hills on the winding Catskill road. I sang the song over and over for the entire trip with all the volume I could muster.

I thought of Sunday mornings, sitting in St. Mary's Church, a child on each side. I recalled the overwhelming number of times I'd felt abandoned by my Creator. Yet on this day I knew we had never been alone on our journey. We had weathered the hard parts, and our future ahead was bright.

This day, I was unabashedly blissful at the end of my week. An hour earlier, I'd met Cliff and Margaret fifty miles away, where I'd hugged my boys tightly and said our pre-visit litany: "Be good boys, now. Have a wonderful time." They'd replied happily, in a duet, "Yes, Mommy, we will." The visits at Cliff's house seemed to be going well, I mused as I'd watched Cliff's taillights fade toward Route 17 for the one-hundred-mile trip to Westchester County.

In one aspect, I resented the boys' visits with Cliff and Margaret because they were always fun vacations, while our lives were filled primarily with the routines of daily living. I was also sensitive to the fact that their seeming affluence contrasted starkly with our modest lifestyle and hoped that fact would never become a problem for my sons. I resented that Cliff was behind in his absurdly low child support payments, yet despite the fact that I worked in the social services system and had custody of my sons, a vague but deep-rooted terror held me back from confronting Cliff. In fact, crazily, I often felt guilty about the support and believed I needed to explain to Cliff how I spent it.

The decades ahead would bring me an understanding of the root of this seemingly bizarre behavior. In school I had been labeled "emotionally immature," but, as the truths of my life unfolded in later years, I would learn that in the deepest part of my soul, I had always believed I had no more value than a piece of roadside trash.

Yet that day I felt no resentment whatsoever, for our lives were about to change and I was ecstatic.

Don and I had been dating for three years when he invited me to dinner at the upscale Homestead Restaurant in Colliersville. After a sumptuous steak dinner, he pulled a small box from his jacket pocket and raised the black velvet lid to reveal a modest diamond sparkling in a simple setting.

"It's beautiful," I murmured, raising my eyes to Don's solemn hazel gaze. He smiled as he said, "Jo, will you marry me?"

We'd tentatively talked about the idea of marriage in recent months, and I'd thought a lot about this question, as I'd reconsidered my earlier vow that I'd never marry again after the wreckage of my first marriage. Now, I smiled shyly at him. "Yes, I will." I was never more serious about anything in my life than I was about those words of commitment to Don. Likewise, the raw emotion in his eyes conveyed the deepest feelings I'd experienced with him until that moment.

I looked down at my left hand wrapped around the steering wheel so that my ring was fully visible whenever I looked. Sometimes it winked a rainbow of sparkling colors at me.

We planned to wed the following summer, 1973.

Chapter 17: GOD'S EYE

Oneonta, New York, 1972–73

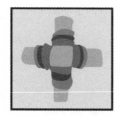

Winter circled around again, that gray season when we forgot about sunshine until a rare day surprised us with the golden orb. December 8, 1972, was a cloudy day much like any other wintry Catskill one. I rose and showered, then pulled on a black turtleneck and black tights, along with the warm black-and-red wraparound fleece jumper I'd recently made. Downstairs, I woke my sons, kneeling first by Chip's bed, tousling his hair and saying softly, "Morning, Chip. Rise and shine."

He opened his hazel eyes and said sleepily, "I'm awake." His ninth birthday, December 15, was one week away.

As I moved toward Keith, his eyes popped open. Grinning mischievously, he said, "Surprise! I'm awake."

"I see that." I chuckled and sat on his bed. "How do you feel this morning?" He'd stayed home from school the past few days with a stomach bug. When I'd picked him up the day before after work, the babysitter had said he'd seemed to feel well all day.

"I feel good," he said, his voice deep and eyes bright.

"Aw, he's okay. He can go to school," Chip said, grinning.

"Yup, I can go," Keith said, without hesitation.

"Okay, see you upstairs in ten minutes for breakfast," I said.

At eight thirty sharp, I pulled the car in front of Center Street School, wished my boys a great day, and kissed them. When they disappeared inside the school's heavy front door, I signaled left, shifted into first gear, and started my twenty-mile drive to Cooperstown. I felt no apprehension about the wet snow predicted for later. My little car had superb traction, even in the back hills.

The morning passed quickly as I caught up with paperwork. Near lunchtime, our secretary, Eleanor Bennett, rang my phone to say the school nurse was on the line. *Uh-oh.*

"Keith says he feels sick again," the nurse said, "and he looks quite pale." I explained he'd seemed okay that morning. Why had this illness returned?

I said, "I'll make an appointment with his doctor and be there in half an hour."

By 4:30 p.m., Keith and I had visited his pediatrician at Bassett Hospital, who advised, "He has a viral infection, but he should feel fine by the end of the weekend."

I thanked the doctor. As we walked to the car, I said, "Keith, I need to wrap up a few things before we go home for the weekend."

"Here, sit at my desk," I said to him at the office, and handed him a bright orange piece of paper with a happy face on it. "Want to practice your printing?" I asked, smiling. We both knew his teacher wanted him to write more neatly.

"Okay," he said, and reached for the paper. I pushed work papers aside to give him space, handed him a pen, and said, "I'll be right back." I went to my supervisor's office to review a situation I'd been working on, and we developed a follow-up plan.

Back at my desk, Keith looked up and said, "Look, Mommy. I did some writing."

He handed me his happy-face paper, which now said, "I love Mommy" in his unsteady printing. Below, he had written his name in cursive twice, as if practicing. This was precious, and I hugged him. "Thank you. I love you, too, Keith Gregory." He beamed.

"Shall we go get Chip?" He nodded and hopped off the chair while I tucked the orange paper into the corner of my desk blotter and slid other papers into my inbox. Keith zipped into his gold hooded jacket while I slipped on my coat. Holding mittened hands, we trotted down the stairwell and out into the darkness. The air was moist and heavy, the still-falling snow mushy beneath our boots.

We belted into our cold bucket seats, my shoulder belt across my chest and Keith's belt behind his back. (Conventional wisdom said children below age ten could sustain a broken neck on impact with a shoulder belt.) We eased into the moonless night and rode quietly as I drove slowly and carefully through the unplowed slush covering Route 205. We passed through Hartwick Township and headed toward Mt. Vision. Oncoming headlights slowly approached as I entered a dip in the road. The other car's lights disappeared momentarily and then emerged from the dip, its headlights full in front of us. Before I could think *head-on collision*, before I could reach over to protect Keith, before I could feel terror, I heard the gruesome smashing, crushing, pulverizing sound of metal, of glass breaking, tinkling, and spraying into the front seat, then felt my car spinning in circles, before finally coming to a standstill. Then I saw no lights and heard only the roar of dark, deadly silence.

"Keith?" I asked quietly, cautiously. He inhaled deeply but did not answer. I couldn't see him, so I reached over to touch him. He lay crumpled against the passenger door. I felt afraid to move him.

"Keith?" I said, more loudly. Silence.

Then I heard myself screaming his name over and over inside the twisted metal that had been our car, until, abruptly, I stopped, knowing instinctively he wouldn't answer. The sudden silence made me feel as if we were encased in the cold darkness and stillness of a tomb. I paused, dissociated from all feeling, and reached out my right hand in slow, controlled motion to turn off the ignition, remove the key, and release Keith's seat belt and then mine, as if we had just arrived home.

Someone approached my broken window. "Are you okay?"

I replied calmly, as if I had only stubbed my toe, instead of just having had a head-on collision. "My little boy is hurt. Please help him."

People pulled Keith's door open and lifted him onto the ground and bent over him, and, God, it was so wet and cold for him to be on the ground, I didn't want him to be there, but they were helping him and I guess they had to do that on the ground so it was okay because then he would be okay and could talk to me again and tell me he was fine, but it was terribly quiet outside my car, so I sat still like such a good girl, staring ahead into nothingness, because if I was very good then everything would be okay again, and if I couldn't hear anything they were saying about Keith they might be saying he was conscious again, so I just sat there very still and silent so they could make Keith all better.

Someone broke through my bubble to say that two ambulances were on their way. "We're sending your son and the girl from the other car in the first ambulance."

"Is Keith okay?" I asked.

"He's alive," they told me. *Oh, thank God. He's alive.*

I remained still in my seat as metal started screeching in grinding, crunching resistance, until the Jaws of Life finally forced my door open. My eyes remained riveted on the rearview mirror, on the flashing lights that carried my son away from me in the silent ambulance. I stared until I could see the light no longer. Soon I was strapped to a board that slid into an empty ambulance. When the wheels started turning, I stared out at the reflections of the red flashing lights on our roof, swinging in endless, soundless circles on the white snow, as my son and I returned to Bassett Hospital.

When the ER nurse asked whom she could notify about the accident, I said, "No one. I can't burden my mother with this."

She took my hand and looked gently into my tears. "If you were my daughter, I'd want to know," she said, with so much kindness that I started to sob and then gave her my mother's phone number.

A nightmarish jumble of days and nights followed. I learned Keith was in intensive care, on life support, with critical head injuries; my physical injuries were painful but would heal. From fragments of conversations with others, I slowly pieced together the story. My son had stopped breathing at the accident scene. The deep breath I heard him inhale right after the impact was apparently the last independent breath he took. Good Samaritans, whom I'd never know, performed artificial respiration until the ambulance arrived. No one knew how long Keith had been without oxygen; it became the critical question.

A policeman told me that the young woman who'd hit us told him she'd steered to the right as she approached our car and suddenly dropped four inches off the pavement. Trying to get back on pavement quickly, she'd turned her steering wheel too hard, overcorrected, and slid head-on into our car.

My mother could not come be with me because she had no respite care for Jackie. Bonnie and her husband made weekly weekend visits when they could safely drive the 250-mile trip in our unpredictable winter weather. Don and his family, my friends, and my coworkers made everything else happen.

A week later, I was discharged on crutches from the hospital. Unable to drive, I visited Keith whenever someone could give me a ride. When I returned to work, I walked into our huge caseworker room and said, "Hi, everybody," as if there had been no pause in my attendance. I could not yet articulate words to these incredible people who had poured out their generous hearts to my son and me, although I had thanked each one with cards.

My workplace was close to the hospital, so I visited Keith during every lunch hour. Hospital staff counseled me about the importance of communicating with a comatose person, as did Elisabeth Kübler-Ross in her book *On Death and Dying*. Every day I told Keith what Chip and I were doing, what was happening in our family, his school, and the world. I read him his favorite books and introduced new ones. I touched him, hugged him, kissed him hello and goodbye, and bathed and shampooed him when I was allowed. Over his bed I hung the God's eye he'd brought home from school for Christmas. If God's eye was watching over my son, surely all would be well, I reasoned.

"I've never heard of a God's eye. Tell me about it," I'd said to Keith when he'd brought it home, my fingers softly rubbing the pretty yarn. Two narrow pieces of cardboard were placed in a cross formation; Keith had woven red (symbolizing life), blue (sky and water), and green (vegetation) yarns on the outer edge.

"It's to hang on our Christmas tree," he'd said.

"Shall we hang it on the window here until we get our tree up?" I'd asked.

"Sure," he'd said, and we had, never imagining there would be no Christmas tree that year.

Keith's God's eye is always near me on my desk. I pick it up, rub the soft yarn that still holds his DNA, and remember. I eventually researched and learned a God's eye was an ancient symbol that originated in Jalisco, Mexico, with the Huichol Indian tribe. When his child was born, a Huichol father wove the central eye in the God's eye, or *ojo de Dios*. Each year until the child was five, the father wove another round of yarn, another "eye." On a deeper level, this Christian symbol represented a spiritual covenant with God, to watch over and grant the child good health, good fortune, longevity, and auspiciousness. The four ends of the cross symbolized the four life elements: earth, air, fire, and water. Whether a God's eye was hung on a wall, on the end of an arrow, or in the child's hair, the Huichol believed it had the power to heal, protect, and ensure the child a long and healthy life.

Keith's eyes always stared, never blinked. On a rare day he'd turn his head and make eye contact with me; I would get excited, but the nurses cautioned that I keep my expectations low. I minimized the fact that he was on complete life support and, if the doctor was right, that he couldn't see, hear, or even breathe without his respirator. I believed he could not heal if I didn't think positively.

Cliff and his now-pregnant wife visited a few times. Cliff told me he was initiating a lawsuit against the driver of the other car. I was appalled. "That's crazy. No. We have no idea yet what the extent of Keith's injuries is and no idea of costs." Nevertheless, his New York City lawyer called me one evening and tried to convince me to start a lawsuit.

I refused.

My father did not visit; did he even know about the accident? I can say only that I didn't think to call him. My mother visited a few times during those months when she could arrange care for Jackie. On Mom's last visit, I looked closely at her face when she left Keith's room—at her gravity, her shaking head, her tears. When she saw me watching, she stilled herself and tried unsuccessfully to smile.

Three agonizing months later, Keith's condition had not changed. I tried to accept what his medical team had hinted all along: Keith's coma was, in reality, severe brain damage. Then Dr. Mackey, Keith's primary doctor, summoned me to his office. I was apprehensive as the highly esteemed physician gently invited me to sit down.

Quietly he said, "Mrs. B., I believe Keith has experienced brain death, but there's no way to know for sure without an autopsy."

I wrapped my arms around myself and bent forward, staring at him.

He continued, "I've tried everything I know to do for your son. If he has suffered brain death, Keith will never experience life again as we know it. We can keep him alive for years, but I'm not sure that's the right thing to do."

I swallowed. "What are you saying?" I asked, my voice a monotone.

"Here's my suggestion," he said. "I propose a new treatment plan in which we extend the intervals between suctioning Keith's lungs."

I stared at him, instantly grasping where this plan would lead. Suctioning prevented pneumonia.

"We need to make a decision, I'm afraid," he said gently. I had known for a while that the hospital wanted to transfer Keith to a long-term nursing facility but had been unable to find one willing to accept a child on a respirator.

"If you agree with my recommendation, we'll proceed. Now, if we proceed, please know you can change your mind and I will honor your wishes, but I will withdraw as Keith's primary doctor. Another physician will take my place."

He stood up. "Think about this, and let me know by tomorrow. Okay?"

I nodded, wide-eyed. He walked around his desk to me and extended his hand. We shook wordlessly; then I trudged numbly through the parking lot to my car. While I drove home, I trembled as I allowed the full implication of Dr. Mackey's words to assemble in my head: *If we decrease suctioning Keith's lungs, he will develop pneumonia. And then he will die. Dr. Mackey is offering a plan to allow Keith to die. The decision is mine. My child's life is literally in my hands.*

I did not speak of this to anyone. Right or wrong—probably wrong—I behaved as usual when Chip and I shared our evening. We said his prayers together and added an extra blessing for Keith. I kissed him, tucked him in, and left his room to enter a solitary night unlike any I had experienced. Curled into a fetal position in my bed, through the night I prayed, cried, and occasionally ranted silently at my Creator. I slipped in and out of restless sleep, woke from bad dreams feeling nauseated. Sometime before dawn, I pushed myself out of bed and sat by my living room's picture window. The night held no star or moon to catch my eye or give my heart hope. Instead, it was a void into which I slid, stared, and stayed until, utterly depleted, just before dawn, I whispered, "Thy will be done."

I returned to bed with one request for my Creator: to show me clearly if I should not agree with this new plan. When, by the middle of the next day, I could discern no sign from Him, I called Dr. Mackey and told him I agreed to his proposition.

Now I knew that my son's beautiful spirit would soon leave his hopelessly broken body to go home to that place that he remembered from before his birth. Silently, my precious Keith Gregory slipped away on the morning of April 2, 1973, twenty-two days before his eighth birthday. I believed there was nothing in life that would ever hurt more than his death.

I would learn those are words a person should never say.

Chapter 18: TINY STAR

Oneonta, New York, April 5, 1973

I needed new shoes, dark ones, to match my winter coat with the faux fur around the hem and sleeves. Chip and I drove to Bresee's Department Store, where, holding his hand, I wandered numbly around the shoe department until I found a pair of low navy heels. As I paid the cashier, she looked kindly at Chip. "Would you like a balloon?"

He smiled shyly. "Yes, thank you."

When she handed him three helium-filled balloons, one red and two blue, he smiled with more happiness than I'd observed in many days. Back home, Chip released his balloons and we watched them bobble around the ceiling, much as he and I had done these recent days.

We prepared for Keith's funeral that morning at St. Mary's Church, the church I had attended as a college student, the church I had returned to with my sons five years later, the church we'd attended with Fred. This day it would enfold us yet again as we said goodbye to my third-born child.

Chip and I met Don at the church entrance. We were ushered to our seats, where Mom, Bonnie, and her husband all sat somberly, while Don's parents sat behind us. Jackie remained home, knowing she couldn't cope.

Centered below the altar was the small, gleaming mahogany casket, awash with flowers. Chip's and my white-roses-with-baby's-breath spray embraced the precious child within. The profuse beauty of abundant flowers and the presence of so many people from my community overwhelmed yet soothed me. *Do they have any idea how much comfort their presence gives?* I wondered. Still, I felt utterly alone.

Then Mary Ann Ross's exquisite soprano voice rose to fill the church as she opened the Mass of the Angels. The spiritual service lasted an hour, a lovely fusion of music, comforting words, scripture, and the sacrament of communion. As Mary Ann sang her final song, I envisioned angels filling the space in the church above and around us, their support and love embracing our souls.

When I thought of Keith, I could feel peace that he had been freed from the prison of his broken body. When I faced the truth, I knew my son hadn't died three days earlier; his life as we knew it had ended four months ago. Yet I ached, beyond the greatest pain I'd ever endured until then, to embrace him just one more time.

The mass ended. I walked unsteadily from the church, holding Chip's hand tightly, aware of eyes watching me as I stared at something unseen ahead. We slid into a black limousine and rode nearly an hour to the Bovina cemetery, where the stark, snow-covered ground waited. As I stood by Keith's final resting place in my crazily inappropriate shoes, I dissociated from the pastor's words as I stared at the miniature casket, aching to push away this final cut of the umbilical cord. Later

I would envision Keith in his casket much as my mother's marquise diamond lay inside her jewelry box, both sparkling lights now hidden by darkness.

The ladies of the Bovina United Presbyterian Church, Don's church, had prepared a reception in the church basement, with finger food and beverages to nourish our bodies and people to nurture our souls. I was deep inside my childhood cocoon as I carefully smiled and thanked each kind person for their "I'm so sorrys" and their hugs. I had reverted to the little girl who felt she had to take care of others, and so I comforted my comforters. I paid a high price for dissociating, though; it rendered me unable to let in the tender consolation others expressed to placate my grief.

As the afternoon passed, their low voices shifted into conversations about events in their own lives. Suddenly, I wanted to go home. Once more, people said heartfelt words and goodbyes and then returned to their unchanged lives. As for Chip and me? I knew life would go on, but I simply couldn't imagine how.

Later that night, when he and I were alone, Chip walked to his room and returned to the living room, clasping his three balloon strings.

"Mommy, if I let these go, will they float up to Keith in heaven?" he asked, with innocence so pure that my throat closed momentarily. I smiled at my precious son and said, "Yes. What a wonderful idea, Chip." My tears welled as I looked into his large eyes and strained, pale face.

I reached for his hand and pushed open the door, and we stepped into the quiet night and walked slowly to the end of the road. As we gazed silently up into the darkening sky, I found myself mourning as much for my living son as I did for Keith. *I'm shattered that you have to endure this, Chip.* I remembered my fierce determination at his birth that his life would be happy—and perfect. I'd naively believed I could shield my child from traumatic events that I was certain happened only to other people.

"Can I let the balloons go now?" he asked softly. The night was still; the stars twinkled above us.

"Whenever you want to," I said softly, squeezing his hand and releasing it. He raised his small right arm toward heaven as I stood behind him, one arm wrapped around his chest. He slowly opened his hand and we watched silently as the three balloons rose to meet air currents that carried them sideways and upward. Suddenly, one balloon moved swiftly away from the other two, in the opposite direction.

We watched closely, pointing and speaking in hushed voices, until we couldn't see any of the balloons anymore. We remained silent, still looking up for a long time.

"Keith sees your balloons—I just know it," I said, as my voice broke. In fact, I could almost see Keith's sparkling, mischievous eyes and hear his husky voice saying, *I love the balloons, Chip. Thanks.*

I wanted to say more to comfort my son, so I swallowed hard. "And Keith is smiling at us, so happy, probably even clapping his hands. He's there, Chip—I know that without a doubt."

I thought again of Keith's disclosure to Marji about his blissful remembrance of having been with Jesus before he was born into our family. Later, I read Dr. Wayne Dyer's final book, *Memories of Heaven*, in which Dyer shares numerous stories of children who remember having been in heaven before they joined their earthly families. I'd never heard another story like Keith's until I read Dyer's book, and I treasured knowing them.

Standing in the darkness with Chip and remembering Keith's story, I felt serenity wash over my body. I asked Chip if he remembered the story.

"Sure, Mom. I'll never forget it." As I rested my hands on Chip's young shoulders, I felt them relax as we talked quietly about Keith being with Jesus again.

Chip became silent then and stared upward again. In the stillness of my heart, I realized that, among the staggering abundance of kind and compassionate gestures that people had offered Chip and me during the weeks and months following the accident, Chip's simple, loving act that night had moved me more deeply than any other.

Chapter 19: ALTAR STEPS

Bovina Center, New York, 1973–77

Years later, my mother said, "You changed so much after Keith died."

Having little self-awareness, I asked, "What do you mean?"

"You were slower, more serious. You rarely laughed anymore." This, then, was the woman who prepared for our wedding. I felt happy as I stitched my wedding dress and looked ahead to my life with Don, yet I see now that my buried grief for Keith had largely diluted my earlier joy. We decided to keep our original wedding date of June 29, yet downsized to a small, immediate-family reception, instead of the large one we'd planned. A big celebration felt like a betrayal to Keith.

I wanted to remain Catholic, and Don, Presbyterian, agreed. We engaged in three prenuptial counseling sessions with my Catholic priest, conversations about the importance of faith, our commitment to supporting each other, and the challenges that life would bring us. We agreed we would raise any children we might have as Catholics, glibly, perhaps, since I didn't foresee having more kids.

At the end of our final session, the priest said, "I'm impressed with your maturity as a couple. You've been open and realistic in our conversations; I wish more of my couples were like you."

We thanked him and parted, feeling positive about our future. Given all I know today, I wonder how the priest could have felt I was mature. Did I speak words I thought he wanted and needed to hear? Or am I being too hard on myself?

Coincidentally, the weather on June 29, 1973, resembled that of my first wedding day, bucketing rain so hard that flooding prevented several of Don's relatives from crossing a bridge to attend our evening ceremony. Fortunately, weather was the only similarity. My son and I both welcomed the new stage we were entering with Don, my in-laws, and country living.

At 7:00 p.m., I entered St. Mary's Church for my second life-changing event there in two months. The powerful silence enhanced the holiness of our impending sacrament. The dimly lit church was filled with candelabras elevating tall candles that lifted our eyes upward. My white dotted-Swiss dress was floor-length, embroidered with tiny pale pink hearts and green leaves, with a rounded neckline and puffed short sleeves. Three daisies plucked from my bouquet were tucked into my upswept hair. My sister Bonnie and friend Sandy were my attendants, their multicolored floral dresses matching my dress. Sandy had made her dress, while I'd made Bonnie's and mine.

Chip glowed with happy smiles and radiant eyes. He sat with my mother as the organist played "Here Comes the Bride." I walked in slow, measured steps down the aisle, my father holding my arm, savoring St. Mary's majestic ambience, and then met Don—looking handsome in his white jacket, black slacks, and black bow tie, vulnerable yet steadfast—at the altar. Before family and friends, we exchanged traditional vows in the presence of my priest and Don's minister. When Don slid my ring on and looked deeply into my eyes, saying, "Until death do us part," I knew in my heart how profound his commitment was. Similarly, when I slid Don's ring onto his finger and said, "I do," my words reflected the deepest commitment I would make in my life.

The priest introduced us as husband and wife, then said, "You may kiss the bride now." We happily embraced and followed his directive as the organ exploded into joyful music that reflected the moment. Don was twenty-eight; I was thirty-one.

Glowing, we moved through a long reception line of family, friends, and coworkers who blessed us with love and good wishes. When the photographer finished snapping his pictures, we drove to Sandy's apartment overlooking Wilber Park for our small reception. Our parents, our siblings and their children, and dear Aunt Madeline—eighty-five and widowed then—celebrated quietly in simple, time-honored ways: a bubbly champagne toast that tickled our mouths; a small, silky-frosted wedding cake that supported a semi-happy-looking miniature bride and groom; and the sweet sounds of child and adult conversation and laughter that flowed warmly through the spaces between us. Later, Don and I left for a long weekend in Lancaster County, Pennsylvania. The end of June gave us a brief space between harvesting our hay and corn, dictating a short honeymoon.

I was as drawn to Amish simplicity as Don was. We loved the beautifully groomed farms, breathtaking countryside, and savory German food. Although our four days passed quickly, we looked forward to returning to the farm.

Home. Already I felt more grounded in the tiny rural town tucked well off the two-lane Catskill Mountain highways in

Delaware County than anywhere I'd ever lived. The century-old Greek revival farmhouse, built on a knoll, surrounded by a stone wall crafted by early Scot settlers, had won my heart even though the stone wall was the most attractive part of the setting. Unlike the house, it had weathered the decades well, retaining its timeless beauty.

Don's parents had purchased a modular home, placed it on a nearby meadow, and recently moved. Undaunted by our needy old house, I committed my energy, abundant ideas, and resourcefulness to re-creating it. Outside, the white asbestos-shingled residence appeared small, yet it was surprisingly roomy inside—not even including three unusable, unheated back rooms with crumbling plaster.

The large kitchen, containing a small woodstove vented to an old chimney, was the humble center that had embraced family and friends through the decades with country bounty and warm fellowship. If those uneven plaster walls beneath the beige wallpaper could have told stories, they would have described decades of everyday meals, seasonal conversations, and countless holiday and birthday celebrations.

I envisioned the original, gorgeous oak wainscoting, ornate oak doors and window framing, and a huge oak floor-to-ceiling kitchen hutch with tiny window panes beneath the white paint. When my in-laws had purchased the farm decades earlier, soot and wood smoke had covered the walls. My mother-in-law had papered the walls and painted the wood to cover the mess. Now I wanted to restore the oak, my favorite wood.

The kitchen opened into the living room, where, when I placed my tropical-fish aquarium against a wall, the water level on one side was two inches higher than on the other. Finding a level section of floor took several attempts.

I questioned Don about a curious feature of the farmhouse I'd noticed. "Do you know how many doors are in our down-stairs?" I asked one day, after counting them.

He looked surprised. "Well . . . no."

I laughed out loud. "There are five rooms with twenty-two doors, Don." Invoking the Scots' reputation for thrift, I joked, "There must have been a sale on doors the year the house was built."

He chuckled. "Probably!"

Few doors matched each other. Though I never measured, I felt certain the doors took up more square footage than the walls. Upstairs contained the bathroom and three bedrooms. Some doors were as primitive as three wide boards fastened together with three horizontal boards on the back, opening with a black antique latch. Imperfect as it all was, this was home.

I soon learned many new skills: stripping off old wallpaper and carefully matching each new sheet I pasted on, no small feat with uneven walls; stripping paint from wainscoting, something I never enjoyed; putting up sheetrock; and precisely spackling. My longing was simple: to create the nicest home possible for us. I didn't realize yet that Don had little interest in the house or in the care it desperately needed; rather, his interests lay across the dirt road, where the gray-brown, sagging barn stood, testimony to decades of harsh winters.

The world beyond our town felt surreal: females were disappearing in alarming numbers, though we didn't yet know Ted Bundy's name, and our government voted to impeach a president clearly involved in covering up criminal activity. Exciting things happened, too: A few hundred miles away, the tallest building in the country, the World Trade Center, opened. And our new president, Gerald Ford, told us the Vietnam era was over. Yet we remained far removed from it all.

On our secluded 170 acres, Don and I rose at 6:00 a.m., pulled on barn clothes, and entered each silent new dawn. He walked to the barn to prepare for milking, while I hiked uphill on the sixty-acre pasture until I found the forty-five loosely clustered cows, looped around behind them, then followed them to the metal gate, where they circled the aged maple that turned fire-red each autumn. Don met us at the gate, and we guided the cows across the road and into the barn, where they took their places. We quickly fastened each cow into her stanchion as she munched hay and crunched grain. Barn cats, nestled on a hay pile near the silo, stirred, knowing that warm bowls of milk would soon reward them for catching mice.

I'd learned to milk cows while we'd dated. Now, as we moved through our morning work together, I felt enveloped in a cozy womb where life was renewed each day. I loved the earthy barn smell and the quiet *shush* of the milking machines as they *whooshed* milk from the cow through the pipeline into the bulk tank, and I treasured working with my husband. I had never lived so close to the land or to the direct sources of food, and I'd fallen head over heels in love not only with Don but also with country life.

On weekdays, Don's father helped him milk as Chip boarded the school bus and chugged away; then I drove to Cooperstown, fifty miles away. I kept my job, reluctant to give up my entire identity all at once, and planned to work until year's end. My days were long, though, and once, I fell asleep at the wheel for a few seconds. I knew then it was time to resign. Yet I dreaded leaving those who had shared so much with me during my four years at DSS.

One Friday night, Don and I were sleeping soundly when an earsplitting racket, like a helicopter thwacking its blades against our bedroom walls, woke us. "What on earth is happening?" I asked him.

He chuckled. "This is a horning, Jo. The neighbors are outside our window, holding a chain saw against the house."

I'd heard of hornings and thought them a cute idea. But this appalling noise was surely the worst way to be awakened. We threw back the covers, flipped on the light, and dressed quickly. Don called through the screened window, "We'll be down in a minute." Bill Inman, always a prankster, was laughing as hard as I'd ever heard him. Thumping down the stairs, I lamented that I had no baked goodies to offer our mischievous neighbors.

"Wish I'd known you were coming," I said. "I'd've baked a cake."

"Oh, pooh! We came to have fun." *At two in the morning? Hmm.* We talked, kibitzed, and laughed for a while, then said good night.

After they left, I asked Don, "Do farm people have more than one horning per family?"

He chuckled. "Not that I've ever heard."

Six o'clock came very early the next morning, yet I smiled as I walked up the hill to get the cows. That horning was fun.

I was incredibly busy, on the move every minute, every day, in part because my life was very demanding—and for other reasons I could not yet discern.

After Keith's death, I decided to emulate Jackie Kennedy's stoic, graceful grieving following her husband's tragic murder. I failed to realize that, behind public scenes, she must have had a strong support system: family, friends, priests, therapists. I knew nothing about grieving, and the notion of a process was foreign to me. Nor did I have a support system. I simply acted like I was okay.

One day I stared at Keith's adorable second-grade school picture, his last, centered on a small, quilt-covered table in the living room. No one talked about Keith anymore. He was gone. I carried his photo upstairs and put it on my bureau, thus unintentionally removing him from my family's sight. I can only guess now what this silence must have conveyed to Chip.

Chip had been daydreaming in school and underachieving after Keith's death; while not surprised, I was concerned. The school psychologist saw him weekly, and we kept in close touch, until several weeks later he reported that Chip appeared to be doing better. After Don's and my marriage, Chip started fifth grade in a new school. He seemed happy on the farm and with his school friends. When Don and I met with his teacher, he confirmed that Chip was having a very good year. I breathed more easily.

Our neighbors across the road, Pete and Linda, who lived in a restored schoolhouse on a small parcel carved from our sixty-acre meadow, had three children: Kathy, Doug, and Jeff. Their boys and Chip were close in age and enjoyed playing together. One of their favorite activities—pushing their big Tonka trucks around the road with a long stick, one behind the other, making *vroom-vroom* sounds—reminded me of Chip, on his small knees, pushing his trucks around our living room floor in our previous lifetime on Long Island.

Near the end of December 1973, I tearfully said goodbye to my coworkers and then cried, until, close to home, I remembered an immense challenge waiting ahead. My New Year's resolution was to quit smoking, to get through the tough process of withdrawal that I knew so well. Six months later, I'd not smoked one cigarette, after a fifteen-year habit, and knew I'd stopped for good.

Meanwhile, Cliff continued to take Chip to his home for monthly visits. He and Margaret had a new son, Kevin—another life-changing event for Chip. I watched my son closely. At first, he seemed happy to visit his dad, but over time I noticed an uneasiness when he returned home.

"Was your visit okay?" I asked one afternoon after a visit.

"Dad and Margaret don't like the farm. They say it's smelly; they don't like me being here," he said, reluctantly.

Incensed that they did not keep their snarky feelings to themselves, I shifted to my social-worker self. "I'm sorry they feel that way. How do you feel about the farm?"

"I like the farm," he said quickly, his eyes rising from the carpet to mine.

Yes, he did; I knew. It had been his idea to name it Hobbit Hills Farm, after his love of J. R. R. Tolkien's *Hobbit* series. "There are natural smells that our animals have, and that's not bad," I continued, "but some people do feel the way Cliff and Margaret do about farms."

"I know," he said.

"Do their feelings get in the way of your having a nice time at their house?" I asked.

"Maybe," he said sadly, his expression, body language, and words telling me his true answer.

The next time I talked with Cliff, I said, "Please stop saying negative things about the farm to Chip." He made an irritated sound. "Also, you are over two thousand dollars in arrears with child support. When can I expect some?"

"I'll try," he mumbled. But, in fact, he hadn't tried in the past and didn't then, and from that time on, the fragile relationship between Cliff and Chip again spiraled downward. When spring arrived and Cliff had rarely called, Chip did not appear unhappy. I silently let the situation unfold as it would, as life geared up for our second summer on the farm.

I learned to drive the huge Case tractor that summer, then to mow hay and side-rake the rows of mown hay to roll them over to dry. I helped throw off bales into the haymow and stack them neatly away for winter. Chip was too young to drive, but he watched closely, knowing his day would arrive. He often rode the wagon or tractor while Don or I worked, as well as helping in the haymow.

Don plowed a large area for my first garden—the extent of his gardening interest. I eagerly ordered vegetable seeds, bought onion sets and seed potatoes, planted them carefully in neat rows, and weeded fairly regularly. I *loved* the magic of watching the vegetables grow weekly until I could pick them. In fall, I taught myself to can and freeze the produce from that first, successful garden.

When the season for preserving ended, I trotted down the basement steps one afternoon to gaze with deep pride at the now-sagging, heavy wood shelves of fragrant cinnamon applesauce from our heirloom apple tree; relishes (beet, zucchini, and cucumber); pickles (bread-and-butter, sweet elongated, dill, and zucchini); nearly two hundred quarts of canned tomatoes, peaches, and pears; sauerkraut brined in an antique crock; and three bushels of potatoes and onions on the dirt floor. My gratitude overflowed, and, though I could not have verbalized this then, I see now that I was breaking through my cocoon as I learned what I loved creating and how I wanted to live in my new life. Truly, I felt home at last.

Along with our harvest rewards, I learned three vital gardening lessons: never plant an entire package of zucchini seeds; the Bovina growing season was so short that I could harvest few ripe tomatoes before frost, then had to take the rest indoors; and, most important, a garden, like a healthy relationship, requires daily time and attention.

When canning season was over, I explored what I could create from the fresh milk in our bulk tank. I purchased a small booklet that taught me to make yogurt, butter, and cottage cheese, as well as mozzarella and cheddar. Cheddar needed to be aged several months, but we usually held out only a few weeks before eating it. I decided I'd buy the sharp aged cheddar at Russell's General Store in town. We may have been modest farmers, but the rich harvest from our land allowed us to eat like royalty. While I was filled with awe, Don took it all for granted; this was the only lifestyle he'd ever known.

I discovered that March brought a day where, when you stepped outside, you felt a subtle change in the air—slight warmth, forty to forty-five degrees, and dryness—that whispered, *Maple syrup season is here.* Don's father would announce, "Time to tap the trees"; then he and Don would gather taps and buckets from the sap house and ride out on the John Deere to do their task. In the following days and weeks, we'd collect the sap and boil it down to pure maple syrup in the old sap house. Cold nights and warm days produced the best-quality sap, I learned, as well as the astonishing fact that forty gallons of sap was needed for each gallon of syrup. In our best year, we made about fifty gallons of pure amber syrup, adding another precious resource to our abundant larder.

When spring arrived the following year, 1976—my fourth summer on the farm—I planted a larger vegetable garden and a nearby raspberry patch to add to our apple and wild-blackberry resources. I purchased bushels of peaches, pears, and tomatoes at our farmers' market and made dozens of pint jars of fruit syrup, jams, jellies, and marmalades from every imaginable fruit or wine, including champagne, for us and for holiday gifts.

That year when we raised and butchered a pig, I taught myself to render the lard and made scented bars of soap and laundry soap from it. I also attempted wine making, with fair success, and candle making, with good results.

This abundant creativity and curiosity kept surging within me, gifting me with riches I couldn't have known inside my bubble. I was a partner in a loving, healthy, working-together marriage, with a happy child and an ever-deepening relationship with Mother Nature. I was also forging a connection with my tiny community that would have stronger threads than anywhere else I'd ever live. I no longer had to make myself invisible to feel safe. I was energetic, awed, and excited to be alive in this, one of the most profoundly happy times of my life.

Unfortunately, and unbeknownst to me, I had more of my

cocoon to shed. I am grateful now that I did not know then what lay ahead for us.

Near the heartbeat of this intensely creative time in my life was my love of fabric and thread—the art of quilting—that I grew to treasure most. Quilting had always been part of the rhythms of daily life in the pioneer dairy town of Bovina since its establishment in 1820. When I, a city girl who had never seen a handmade quilt, arrived in 1973, I felt as if I'd stepped into another century as I came to know my approximately five hundred eclectic, endearing rural neighbors and townspeople. I cherished my opportunity to learn a craft that women had been doing long before they settled in the new world.

My friendship with Marilyn Gallant began in Bovina when we discovered our common love of sewing and crafts. Marilyn and her family moved to Bovina about the same time I did, and I soon learned that previous generations of women in her family had taught her to make quilts. I asked if she'd teach me, and she generously showed me how.

Our families belonged to the one church in town, the Bovina United Presbyterian Church, whose roots traced back to the early 1800s, when the first ministers arrived through the Scottish missionary movement to America. Marilyn and I brought lots of enthusiasm and energy to the projects the Women's Missionary Society did, which were generally activities we both loved. One of my favorites was gathering clothing and hygiene supplies at the end of each year to send to poverty-stricken locations the larger church recommended.

On occasion, one of the longtime members—all were three decades or more older than we were—rejected an idea Marilyn or I suggested, such as when we proposed creating a town quilt to raffle in a fund-raiser. Unknown to either Marilyn or me, those deep Scottish roots included a long-held protocol that raffles were taboo. Our idea was quickly squashed. I still recall the member trying to be tactful in her rejection of the idea, but old scars caused me to feel stupid. After that, I kept quiet about my ideas so I wouldn't shame myself. Yet I remained keenly committed to supporting our service mission and worked energetically on the projects we undertook.

Thus, I was surprised and humbled when, a few years after I joined the Missionary Society, the women nominated me to become the next president. I accepted the one-year commitment, and we soon decided to make the town quilt, without mention of the word *raffle*. Marilyn and I took on that project enthusiastically: we bought yards of muslin, preshrunk it, cut it into squares, and gave a square to any present or former Bovina resident wanting to participate.

The Bovina quilt became the longest project either of us had ever been involved in. Cranky at times, I felt as if we were pushing an elephant up a mountain, yet Marilyn's sweet nature never allowed her to become discouraged. Slowly, people returned their lovely squares. More than a year later, when I was no longer president of the society, Marilyn called me to say excitedly, "I've just received the last square! We have a total of sixty-three. Isn't that wonderful? We can start making the quilt now."

Indeed, the news was superb. Missionary members who had made quilts all their lives helped organize the project at the community center. On a large folding table, we planned the layout of the squares, cut strips to join the squares, and gave stacked rows to each woman who wanted to stitch a row together. Soon the quilt top was assembled and the final step arrived: setting up the quilting frame in the community center. One quilter brought in her aged frame and assembled it with others who had done this numerous times. Then Missionary Society members attached the pinned, layered quilt—quilt top, batting, and backing—to the frame.

We soon sat together around the quilt frame in afternoon quilting bees when we could join in, a small circle of unsophisticated yet skilled rural women. We talked about all sorts of topics as we made our small, even stitches with short needles that bound the quilt's three layers together. A cloth sandwich, someone called it. I smiled at the description as I sat silently while the older women told stories of other quilting bees and of the women who had quilted before us but who were no longer present.

Although I was too shy to talk about myself or my life then, whenever another woman told a story about herself that I could relate to, I felt something new: a small, quiet connection with her. I didn't realize yet that her story had affirmed a part of mine, that I was no longer alone with my experience, as I had previously thought. These silent seeds of knowledge nudged me awake to a new way of relating to people of my gender, who had heretofore been mostly competitive, controlling, or judgmental, thus severing the possibility of any connecting threads I might have stitched with them.

With these Bovina women, though, I felt a growing closeness as we sat around the quilt frame and stitched. While I did not yet understand the deeper significance of our tender work, the others likely realized it: we were creating a tangible, tactile portrait of our way of life in Bovina Center in the 1970s. Today the quilt remains, as it has through the decades, silently and beautifully on display in the Bovina Museum in the heart of town. And each of those women are tenderly stitched, along with Marilyn, into my patchwork quilt.

These were sweet beginnings—of quilting bees, of a rich attachment to my community, of women gathering, working, sharing stories, and nurturing together. My early years spilled over with intense creativity and deep harmony with Mother Nature and our community. I was thriving as never before, working in partnership with Don, learning farm-woman skills, and seeking to nurture a healthy and happy new family. Like a starved bear emerging from a lifelong hibernation, I was gobbling up every bit of creativity I was drawn to, especially quilting, in order to satisfy my seemingly insatiable longing to express myself. My soul sang, often with my favorite John Denver song, "Thank God I'm a Country Boy"—although I sang "Country Gal."

Chapter 20: HOUSE ON THE HILL

Bovina Center, New York, 1977–83

As the seasons of our early years blended one into another, a surprising new feeling took root in my heart—one that was alternatively terrifying and exhilarating. After pondering each side for several weeks, one evening after Don turned out our bedside lamp, I said, "How would you feel about having a baby?" adding, "I didn't think I'd ever feel this way again, but lately I've felt an ache to have our child."

He inhaled deeply, remaining silent for a seemingly long time. "I, uh, think our life is going along pretty nice as it is," he drawled.

My heart started to hurt. I remained silent.

"Well," he said, slowly, "if you want to have a baby, then I think we should."

"Are you sure?" I asked hesitantly.

"I'm pretty sure," he replied, wrapping his arms around me. "Besides, think how much fun we'll have trying to make one."

"Will you be *serious*? This is important!" I said, playfully punching his shoulder.

"I am," he said, chuckling. I conceded and kissed him. And so I began to daydream about the person our son or daughter might become.

The following months, though, brought two early-term miscarriages, one fetus that self-aborted at seven weeks, and, several months later, another who died in utero at eleven weeks. I slid into a dark place both times and, after the second loss, told Don, "I'm not sure I want to have another baby now." Unspoken was my fear that my body was covertly rejecting the risk of another child, and perhaps—unlikely as the odds might be—avoiding another loss.

"Whatever you want," he said softly.

As I write today, I think of all that remained ahead for me to uncover about my personal history. Perhaps my grieving psyche was telling my body, *No, not another baby*. In the following months, my dreams of our child slipped sadly away.

I understand now that another manifestation of my terror of losing a child was how overprotective of Chip I'd become. I held a covert belief that if I wasn't super-vigilant about my only child, I would lose him, just as I'd lost Jocelyn and Keith.

Sometimes, for example, Chip got to the barn late for evening chores. When Don was young, arriving late for chores was absolutely unacceptable. Don would say with annoyance something like, "You should have been here half an hour ago."

I would say, "Don, it's not his fault. I lost track of time."

Still irritated, Don would shake his head and say nothing, until, some years later, he shouted at me, "When will you stop making excuses for Chip?"

"I am *not* making excuses," I asserted, refusing to see that I often did exactly that. Many years later, I'd understand the roots of why I didn't trust Don. I'd also come to see the harm I had inadvertently done to our three relationships.

In late fall 1976, I was stunned that I had become pregnant. Bracing for another miscarriage, I visited my obstetrician, Dr. Dorsey, who assured me that all appeared fine. As anxious weeks passed, somewhere during my sixth month, I dared to believe I might bring this child to term. I hired a local carpenter to install new walls and subflooring for a nursery in the midsize bedroom upstairs. With pleasure, I sized those new, smooth walls, then papered them with pastel-colored wallpaper overflowing with baby toys. Then I purchased wall-to-wall carpeting. Huge in my eighth month, knowing that Don had little interest in the house, I installed the tan tweed carpet without asking for his help. I remembered, not long after our marriage, having asked him to help me wallpaper the kitchen.

"Jo, my work is in the barn. Mom always did the paint and papering in the house," he'd said. I'd asked for assistance a few more times after that, but he'd always declined. I grew lonely and resentful because he wouldn't work with me in the house when I shared barn chores with him each day. My resentment grew through the years from mild to, on this day, deep frustration.

"Don, my back is killing me from kneeling on the floor all afternoon. Why can't you help me sometimes?"

"I'm not going to fight with you," he said tersely, and the conversation ended. If I pushed further, as I had on other occasions, he'd say, "Stop trying to control me."

His words transformed our conversation into an instant dead end, resulting in our never solving a conflict when it was small. So I would shut down, too, and sulk awhile. This became our problem-solving pattern and resulted in our never resolving our differences. Yet silent change approached . . .

One day while Chip ate cookies and drank milk after

school, he said, "Mom, I wish I had the same last name as you and Don."

"That means Don would adopt you. We'll have to talk with Don and then ask your dad if he would agree to that; if so, it's likely you wouldn't see him or Margaret or Kevin anymore."

"It's okay," he said. "I just wish *we* could be a family."

Wow, I thought, *so do I!* I knew these were tricky waters and felt pessimistic that Cliff would agree but kept that to myself. "I'll see what I can find out, Chip. It's great you feel that way."

That night I talked with Don about adoption. He smiled, "Two kids in one year? Sure, why not?"

I called my attorney and asked him to explore Cliff's releasing Chip for adoption, adding that, if he needed a negotiating point, I'd forgive the back child support. We waited uneasily for two weeks. Would Cliff actually release Chip? I didn't think so. How does a parent legally let go of his son? And, despite Chip's wish for us to become one family, how would he accept that his father had terminated their relationship? I knew I could never let Chip go. I didn't think Cliff would agree.

I was wrong. Cliff agreed to sign the adoption consent, with the support-forgiveness contingency. We were stunned. Chip was thrilled. Did I explore Chip's surely mixed feelings with him? I wish I could say yes. *Where did my former social-worker self go?* I wonder today. So happy in our moment, I didn't consider what his later reaction might be.

The adoption process moved along quickly: papers were drawn, signed, and returned, and we were scheduled to appear in court to finalize Chip's adoption. Later in my life, when I crafted heart-shaped leaves onto my patchwork quilt, I debated whether to appliqué a heart for Cliff. I thought about the brief time we'd shared, filled with our separation, his disappearance and reappearance, and his final disappearance, when he released Chip to Don. I tried to be generous in my consideration but found it difficult to include him on the quilt. Then I recalled

Mary Catherine Bateson's words in the first pages of this book: "Part of the task of composing a life is the artist's need to find a way to take what is simply ugly and, instead of trying to deny it, to use it in the broader design."

He *was* part of our life, I acknowledged then, and pondered how best to represent him on the tree. I came to see him as a leaf bud, blown off the stem in a powerful nor'easter and withered on the ground beneath the tree.

Meanwhile, my neighbor Louise Barnhart, hoping for a baby herself, held a baby shower for me. This caring act by my neighbors moved me deeply as I appreciated yet again the warm community I had joined: Viola, Helen, and her daughter-in-law, Connie; Diane; Mary; and my sweet mother-in-law, Gladys. When we said our goodbyes at the end of that afternoon, just a few days remained before the baby arrived.

Early on June 21, 1977, as on every day, I did morning milking with Don. Later that afternoon, our daughter, Polly Anne, was born. She was a big, healthy baby—nine pounds, six ounces, and twenty-one inches long—with wispy brown hair and huge, deep-blue eyes that gazed around her new world with intense interest. I was so thrilled to hold my daughter in my arms, I could barely speak. When Polly's pediatrician, Dr. Preiser, visited me after her postbirth examination, tears spilled from my eyes as he said, "Your daughter's in perfect health."

"Are those tears of joy?" he asked gently, eyebrows lifted. I didn't know. *Are they tears for babies lost or joy for this brand-new life?* I thought perhaps both.

Polly was content and so easy to care for. I carried her everywhere with me in a cloth baby carrier on my chest. Chip was ill at ease holding her. I wondered if he'd ever held his new half-brother. I knew he'd wished for a brother, and hoped in time he'd have a good relationship with his new sister.

Polly slept between feedings in my great-grandmother's maple cradle in the living room. For longer naps, I took her up to her nursery, where she was delightfully content. Often when I peeked into her room to see if she was awake, I found her quietly looking around with wonder in her big, now-brown eyes.

One evening as we sat at the kitchen table after milking, Don said, "The minister stopped by to talk about Polly's baptism."

I nodded, as reminders of my discontent with our religious observances tapped at my conscience. After we married, Don attended his Presbyterian church while Chip and I drove down the mountain to the Catholic church. I soon felt discouraged because we were separated in a spiritual sense. We compromised by attending Don's church together one Sunday and mine the next. This proved unsatisfactory, too, when, for example, we'd attend Don's church, discover it was Food Bank Sunday, and, because we hadn't been present the previous week to get the bulletin reminder, have no donation.

I'd been wrestling with possible solutions as I ached for us all to belong full-time to one church, especially now that we had a child to baptize.

When I said this to Don, he readily agreed. "Would you join my church?" I asked.

"I'd rather not, Jo. I've been a member here my whole life," he said.

"I thought you'd say that," I said, my voice quavering. "You know I swore I'd never leave my church again."

"I know," he said.

My throat constricted as I choked out, "But I don't know what else we can do to be united about this unless I join the Bovina church." His eyes widened as I went on, "I know God is present in both churches, and since Louise had the baby shower for me, I've come to see that the people in Bovina are my Christian community. So, if your church will have me," I said through my tears, "I'll join."

He embraced me. "That's wonderful!"

Uneasily—because Don and I would be rescinding our commitment to raise our children as Catholics and would probably be condemned to the furies of hell for all eternity—I contacted my priest to tell him our decision. He soon visited and, to my amazement, kindly gave us his blessing.

I told Chip about my decision. "I want to join, too, Mom," he said. "My friends all go to Don's church."

And so, one sunny, late-summer Sunday morning, Chip and I joined the Bovina United Presbyterian Church. Several Sundays later, Polly was baptized there. Two weeks after that, we appeared in family court, where Chip's adoption was finalized as I held Polly in my arms. We were now a family of four with the same last name, who attended the same church. Surely now we would all live happily ever after.

Polly was ten months old on the Saturday afternoon Don's mother had a fatal stroke as she and her husband drove home from our neighbors' Farmer of the Year award celebration. Gladys' sudden death devastated us all. The family, from Maine, Colorado, and New York, gathered to grieve together as Gladys was laid to rest in the Bovina cemetery, not far from Keith's grave. I had treasured Gladys, knowing I couldn't have had a kinder mother-in-law, nor could I have had a better father-in-law in Ed. I cut out two fabric hearts for them when I made my quilt in later years, and lovingly stitched them so that one heart overlay the other.

A few months later, on election night 1978, I sat cross-legged on the gold living room rug, watching television. The polls had just closed. Don was at the firehouse, the town's voting place, closing down the antiquated ballot machine that creaked and struggled to serve our tiny community yet another year, while Chip, fifteen, and Polly, one, slept upstairs.

Scattered across the rug were tissue-paper pattern pieces, scissors, a pincushion so dense with straight pins it resembled a porcupine, and a swatch of soft, floral-printed combed cotton. I was cutting out a T-shirt for Polly, treasuring the moments, as I always did, when I could work with textiles to create something for my family or our home.

As I worked, something triggered the thought that I was feeling different, unusual. I mused lazily, *Hmm, what's this about? Well, flutters in my belly, heaviness, some queasiness . . . Queasiness?* I jumped, as if startled awake from a nap, as I realized what those collective symptoms had meant in the past. Pregnant? No! I'd had an IUD in place since Polly's birth and hadn't kept track of my cycles, so I could not remember my last menstruation. I put my palms on my breasts and inhaled sharply: they were tender. Suddenly, my delighted absorption in my fun little sewing project ended, as I whispered with awe, "I think I'm pregnant!"

I wrapped my arms around my belly and smiled, picturing a new being silently growing, a brand-new little boy or girl probably no larger than a kidney bean. My heart swelled with this miracle. I knew Don thought our family was complete with a healthy, fine son and a lovely daughter. Yet, had anyone asked, I would have said that since Polly's birth I had longed for one more child. I stared out the window at a star in the sky, wondering if my yearning had been powerful enough to bring about the creation of this precious new life, despite the presence of a preventive device. *Yes, possible,* I thought.

I stared at that faraway star and crooned "Twinkle, Twinkle, Little Star" to my baby, until the final stanza:

As your bright and tiny spark,
Lights the traveler in the dark,
Though I know not what you are,
Twinkle, twinkle, little star.

So I'd not been alone that evening after all—or, in fact, for several weeks. Overjoyed and perhaps selfishly, I hugged my delicious secret close to my heart for several days. When I told Don that we were expecting again, he was silent, then said, "I think you stole that baby from me."

I'd never heard words like those but understood he wasn't happy. I also felt blamed, which silenced me from talking about the baby with Don. Yet, although I tried not to let him diminish my deep joy about another child, I felt lonely in my pregnancy.

She arrived on July 3, 1979, my beautiful, blue-eyed, blond baby girl, weighing in at nine pounds, nine and a half ounces, and twenty-two inches long. She was rosy-cheeked and a perfect armful to hold and hug, dear Susan Emily. Now our family was complete, I knew in my heart; I also requested minor surgery to assure it.

Busier than ever now, we began to slide into a fiscal downturn. Financially, we had done well our first year while I worked, and into the next. During the past few years, though, when bimonthly milk checks arrived, they looked lush, yet every dollar and more had to feed the cows, repair the aging, high-cost machinery that often broke down, pay vet bills, and more. At tax time, I saw our income was far below federal poverty guidelines.

Using my passion for sewing, I contentedly filled a creative as well as practical need by making many of our clothes: T-shirts for Don and Chip; tiny, patterned, fitted flannel diapers; and dresses, overalls, flowered shirts, jumpsuits, and jackets for the girls. I budgeted $20 per week for our basic food staples, like flour and sugar, and prepared from scratch everything we ate, including bread.

Despite the poverty cloud above our farm, when I placed dinner on our pine table, I paused to appreciate that nearly everything we were about to eat—the meat, vegetables, fruit, milk, and dessert—had been homegrown or raised by us. Susan ate food I puréed for her from our meal, and she loved my creamy homemade vanilla yogurt. Nutritionally, we were incredibly healthy.

I pondered other ways to supplement our income as a stay-at-home mom. Bovina had no day care, so I decided to start a program. I talked with mothers in our playschool group at church and began to care for three preschoolers with working mothers: Heather, Kendra, and Kellen. Then Chris and Danny joined our group part-time.

My goal was to provide a well-rounded day for each child: an hour of *Sesame Street*, a morning activity outdoors when weather permitted (walking, exploring the farm and surrounding area), a midmorning snack, some interactive play, lunch, story time, a nap or quiet time, and a return outdoors when possible. For three years, the children and I thrived on simple, enriching activities in and around the farm through the seasons.

We often walked up the secluded dirt road to the pine forest where we'd created a small play area: our balance beam was a fallen tree; our swing was a rubber tire fastened to a tree with thick rope. In autumn, the forest floor revealed brilliantly colored red and yellow mushrooms. In springtime, the pond further up the dirt road hosted an abundant polliwog population. Throughout the seasons, we packed lunch and walked to the pine-secluded lake for a picnic. Or we crossed the narrow stream that trickled down the hill above the barn, then carefully stepped across rocks to pick autumn's large, sweet blackberries. Below the stone wall in front of the house, we'd lean over the bridge, hoping to see minnows swimming upstream. Sometimes the stream trickled gently; other times it rushed high and torrential after a heavy rain. Endlessly, the farm gave us simple, natural beauty and physical challenges that created days of fascination.

When our longtime town clerk, Margaret Hoy, retired, the town supervisor stunned me by asking if I'd run for the position. Margaret, gentle and respectful of all, was a person I'd admired since I'd moved to Bovina. I saw her as a role model and would feel fortunate to follow in her footsteps.

Bovina was a one-political-party town: Republican. I doubted anyone knew I was liberal, yet my frail self-esteem convinced me to change my party affiliation if I wanted to win. The point was moot, for I ran unopposed and won the highest number of votes on the ticket. I was shocked by this positive affirmation, yet, just as with receiving my Balfour medal for excellence in the eighth grade, I could not let these pleasures in. Another decade would pass before events would reveal why I closed myself off to any positive declarations of my worth.

My office would be located in our house, so Don hired a contractor friend to restore the crumbling back room, which had a private entrance into what became the town clerk's office. I used my first year's salary for the restoration and loved serving our community from my home.

My mother was delighted to have two more grandchildren and spent her vacation time from work visiting us. Jackie had been accepted into a residential home for dual-diagnosed adults, and Mom was freed to travel and do other activities she'd long postponed. In time, she grew to love our small town and considered retiring to Bovina. She dreamed of building a log cabin on a small parcel of land on our farm.

As Mom happily considered these ideas, I experienced a new, silent interior drama whenever she visited. When I heard her impatiently or negatively interact with my small daughters, her words stirred memories of long-forgotten, similar exchanges with me when I was young. I began to withdraw from her, hurting as decades-old pain and anger surfaced.

One morning, Mom and I sat at the kitchen table, sipping a second cup of coffee, chatting about the day ahead. Polly and Sue were playing with Legos in the living room.

Polly called out, "Mommy, come help me with my Lego tower."

My mother muttered, "Oh, for Pete's sake! Can't I ever have you all to myself?"

Instantly I felt sick inside. *Doesn't she understand these few minutes of nurturing are important? Why won't she join us for a little Lego time together? Why must she put me in a position of having to choose between her and my daughter's small request?*

I'd been away from home more than a decade and had forgotten my family's constant winner/loser setups. When I lived at home, it was Jackie or Bonnie; now it was Polly and me—one a winner, the other a loser. But I refused to let Polly become a loser simply because she was defenseless, as I had been as a child.

If anyone had asked me what my childhood was like, I would have said, "It was okay." And meant it. The fact was that anytime I thought back through the years, I found a smoggy unknown that I couldn't see into. Since I'd never discussed this fact with anyone, I assumed the same held true for everyone.

But now, during these visits with Mom, I was remembering slivers of times when she was similarly upset with me as a child. I did not know then that those moments were small early flashbacks.

I looked at my mother, her lips tight as she lifted her cooling coffee. I always tried, sometimes unsuccessfully, not to snap at her. I'd been strongly shaped as the family peacemaker, and I also had quietly chosen, at some point, to be the family role model for how to kindly nurture all three of my children, not just one.

"I'll be right back, Mom. Polly will be fine after I help her with a few blocks." I couldn't wait to get away.

She looked at me with defeated brown eyes. "Oh, go ahead," she said in a voice so wounded that it reminded me why I'd always felt guilty, why I'd always gotten angry when manipulated. Ironically, Mom had set up the win/lose situation herself, and now she felt like the loser. *Dammit!* I thought. *She's doing this to herself.*

I walked into the living room, where my daughters and I were easily visible to Mom, and breathed in the sweet company of my girls. We snapped some more Legos on Polly's colorful wall until she was satisfied; then I reached over and smoothed the dress of the baby doll in Susan's lap. "She's a good baby," I said, "and so are you."

Susan smiled and nodded. "I'm a good girl."

Polly chimed in, "But I'm better than Sue, right?" I chuckled and ruffled Polly's hair. She jerked her head away.

"You are *both* good girls. I love you," I said, and stood up to trudge back to the kitchen.

Subsequent years brought increased tension between my mother and me whenever we visited. While she and the girls shared many endearing activities that they loved, like reading or playing games, the painful moments persisted.

I couldn't talk with her about them, for if I had, one of us would be the winner and the other the loser—we knew no other way to dialogue. Gradual resolution came when Mom visited less often as she entered her eighth decade. We talked on the phone weekly and got together a few times a year, on a holiday or birthday. Mom no longer spoke of moving to Bovina.

It would be another decade before I learned productive, problem-solving skills so I could talk about and resolve hard topics in an open, respectful way with others, including my mom.

A few years earlier, my father had married his longtime girlfriend, Lil, and they had moved away to Jensen Beach, Florida. Dad's brother, Matt, and his wife also wintered there. Dad and Lil extended several invitations to Bonnie and me to visit, and in January 1980, we purchased Amtrak tickets out of New York's Penn Station to take Polly, three, and Susan, one, to visit for a week.

I hugged my uncle Matt tightly, then my father, when they met us at the train station. As Dad drove us to the trailer park, we were enthralled with the orange trees that dotted most small yards, including Dad and Lil's. Susan and I stayed with Dad and Lil, Bonnie and Polly with Diane and Matt. Happy hour began as soon as we got to my father and Lil's home and extended until well after midnight. Matt and Diane drank juice or tea, while Bonnie and I had mixed drinks. Since I'd given up drinking every day after I had returned to college and graduated, I drank rarely and only socially, as I had with Fred on that long-ago New Year's Eve.

Around six, my sister and I helped Lil serve a tasty dinner. After we ate, I bathed the girls and read them a story, and Bonnie left with Polly for Diane and Matt's house while I settled Susan down for the night.

Dad and Lil drank through the evening. Around 10:00 p.m., desperately needing a break from the tension I felt building between them, I said good night. Later, I was awoken by my father ranting ugly, abusive words at Lil. A feisty woman with the deep voice of a lifelong smoker, Lil flung nasty words right back at him. I lay paralyzed as I listened reluctantly, and was thankful Susan slept soundly.

The next morning, I felt uneasy about greeting my father and Lil. But their pleasant daytime home was apparently much different, at least on this day, from their malevolent night world.

When Bonnie and Polly returned, we sat down to breakfast, sweet juice dripping down our chins as we all laughed and munched our orange sections.

"Honestly, this is the best orange I've ever tasted," Bonnie said. We had fallen utterly in love with our oxymoronic winter embrace of warmth, bright sunshine, lush tropical plants, and fruit in the backyard.

My father and Lil were cheerful with us, as well as each other, that morning. This visit was the first they'd seen my daughters since their births, and they seemed to greatly enjoy the girls. Lil's eyes twinkled as she interacted with Polly and Sue, yet, to my sorrow, I quickly saw that my father's feelings were superficial and limited. ("They're so pretty." [*Smile*.] "Isn't that cute?" [*Smile*.]) He showed no ability to relate to them on any level beyond trite words he might express to a stranger.

"Dad, would you like to read the girls a story?" I asked, offering him Dr. Seuss's *Green Eggs and Ham*.

He looked at me, raised his hand, and dropped it toward me in a go-away motion. "Nah, I'm not good at that stuff." It was the same gesture he'd made toward me when I'd asked him years earlier if he'd help me with college costs, as if the notion were preposterous. *Was this how he interacted with me when I was little?* I wondered, as I filled with sadness for my daughters' loss. And probably my own.

When Lil mischievously suggested that Polly handcuff my father with some toy cuffs he'd received as a gag gift, Polly giggled as she snapped a cuff onto each of his wrists. He chuckled, too, his eyes alight with humor. Not more than a minute later, though, he said sternly, "Okay, that's long enough. Where's the key? Take the cuffs off."

Polly looked at me questioningly. I looked at Lil. "Do you have the key?" I asked.

Lil frowned. "It's here somewhere," she said, burrowing around in a basket on the counter, without immediate results. In another few minutes, my father's eyes darkened and hardened, and he shouted, "Someone get these goddamn handcuffs off me. *Right now!*"

What had been fun a few short moments earlier had shifted to scary for my daughter and, I realized, for me. Bonnie and I nervously transformed into our childhood selves—*we need to do anything to please him*—and hurried to help Lil find the key. Then Lil called out, with obvious relief, "Here it is, Polly!" Polly grabbed it and rushed to unlock the cuffs. They wouldn't budge.

"Hurry up!" my father growled at her. I took the key from Polly, then worked nervously at the stubborn, piece-of-junk cuffs that I tried to break apart but could not. When they finally released, a collective sigh of relief emanated from everyone in the room.

Overall, the visit was bittersweet. By the end, we'd enjoyed some beach time, sunshine, and good food, but my sister and I were relieved and happy to board our train and take the girls back to Bovina.

I returned home unaware that I had experienced small flashbacks to my childhood relationship with my father, during the same year that some from my mother had also returned. That they were significant, I couldn't have imagined, except for the deep pain I felt when either of my parents was present with my small girls and using words or actions that I experienced as very painful.

Chapter 21: KALEIDOSCOPE

Bovina Center, New York, 1979–86

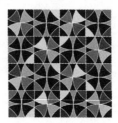

Chip entered high school in 1978. His first report card reflected average grades, except for one subject.

"What can we do so you pass algebra?" I asked, bracing for a firestorm. Chip was no longer the happy boy he'd been when we'd moved to Bovina, and I naively believed that was due to the onset of adolescence.

"I don't understand it," he said, "and I don't see why I have to take that stupid subject. I'll *never* use it."

Although Chip did fairly well in most other subjects, he needed math for college. We tried tutoring, but he missed passing by just a few points and repeated algebra the following semester. Again, he didn't pass. Happily, six weeks of summer school brought the charm.

One morning, Chip's guidance counselor called me to report that Chip had been found in possession of marijuana at school and the police had been called. I was stunned—until I thought of Chip's mood swings, slipping grades, and growing isolation from us. *Dammit, why didn't I see this?* I berated myself as I drove to the school. What would I say to my son? Words of anger? Of disappointment? Or something else?

A state trooper was talking with Chip in a small room when I arrived. He explained the charges he would press, then left us alone.

I looked at my son's eyes and saw no anger or surliness, but rather silent, wide-eyed trepidation. I knew I didn't need to lecture him; he was doing that to himself. I put my hand on his arm and felt him tense. "Chip," I said softly, "I love you. You're in a mess, but we'll get this figured out."

The coming weeks brought his local court appearance, a fine, and mandatory sealing of the documents. Meanwhile, we also started family counseling, sessions during which Chip, Don, and I talked together with increasing openness and I began to feel we were becoming healthier, communication-wise.

When the following summer, 1982, arrived, our local community college accepted Chip into its liberal arts program, where he would explore his interests to determine his major. As he entered college, Polly began kindergarten. I felt excited and happy for them both as each opened a new life chapter.

Our farm's financial struggles deepened to the point of terror for me; I decided to work harder to supplement our income. Along with my day care program and town clerk responsibilities, I started a small cottage industry of creating fabric Quiet Time Books to teach toddlers the fine motor skills of using zippers, Velcro, buttons, and tying shoe laces. I took them to outdoor markets and was pleased with buyers' responses, yet those modest dollars, like any others I generated, were gobbled up by the farm like minnows by a shark.

Soundlessly the farm economy slid into the deepest collapse since the 1930s. Farmers who just a few years earlier had been encouraged to expand their farms to increase production suddenly could not meet their debts. The costs of grain and fertilizer soared while the price of milk plummeted. We, like our peers, were busy working every minute, trying to make ends meet, and were often unaware of current events outside our immediate neighborhood.

Although Don and I didn't talk about money, as with most other areas of our life, the topic caused me ongoing anxiety. Early one afternoon, Don walked out to our mailbox, where the words Hobbit Hills Farm, which I'd painted so proudly years earlier, had faded to a weary, weathered green. As he returned to the kitchen, I slipped an apple pie into the oven, anticipating the sweet, cinnamon-nutmeg aroma it would soon breathe into the air. Don slid into his captain's chair and opened the mail. I carried my cup of Red Rose tea to the table.

"What do we have today?" I asked, sitting down.

He pushed the disorganized pile over to me. "Not much," he replied flatly.

I looked through the unopened envelopes and the three opened invoices, each a month overdue. I tore open the feed bill and saw that the amount due was three times greater than our checkbook balance ever was. A blade of fear sliced through my veins.

I looked at Don, staring out at the snow-covered hillside across the road, his hazel eyes so dark they appeared brown. The low hum of the overhead fluorescent light seemed to notch up its volume every few seconds, until it sounded nearly thunderous to my ears.

We were separated from the world by our rural isolation, and these years of hardship were grinding us down, just like the piece of nutmeg I'd rubbed back and forth on my miniature grater to spice the apple pie. Every part of our life was affected:

our sleep, contentment, well-being, peace, self-esteem, happiness, and, ultimately, faith.

I recalled the temporary taste of poverty I'd experienced with my small sons before I'd gotten my college degree. It had been tough, yet I'd known my graduation would bring a new beginning. On the farm, though—I can vividly feel it still—there was a much deeper level of poverty, a razor-sharp arrow that pierced not only our finances but also our souls. Financial poverty was devastating, but soul poverty stole our hope and emptied us.

Taut with tension now, I looked at the feed bill again. An idea had occupied my thoughts lately. I inhaled and decided I would say the words today.

"Don, I think it's time for me to work off the farm again." I hated the words, hated the idea of not being home as a partner, hated not being there when the kids got home from school and, much more, that those changes would impact the core of our family.

He looked at me over his dark-framed glasses, pursed his lips, and stared out the window again.

I watched him silently. Trancelike, he nodded slowly.

My heart plunged as I realized we had just agreed on this step. *I will be the only farm wife in Bovina to work off the farm*, I mourned, *but this is my only option.* We'd wrestled with selling the farm, but we knew farming was cyclical, that better days would return, and that all farmers were in this boat with us. I knew Don wanted nothing more from life than to be a farmer. I loved him and our lifestyle and told myself I still wanted to support his dream—our dream. But was that dream losing the rich colors I'd held in my mind for so many years? I wouldn't have admitted it then, but I know now that, for me, it was dimming.

We talked about transitions that would affect our routines when I went to work. "I can take the girls to the school bus in the morning before I leave for work, but you'll need to pick them up after school. The afternoon bus arrives when we're usually preparing for afternoon milking, so that will change your routine."

He nodded grimly. He'd be the only farmer working alone on the farm each afternoon, except on weekends. While my father-in-law still walked to the barn every morning, he helped less with each passing year as he ambulated through his eighth decade.

In that moment, we were innocents. Would we have chosen this plan had we known the long-term outcome? Either way, it was imperative that we generate more income, or we couldn't survive, and my returning to work seemed to be the best way.

I pored over the classifieds the next day. I was forty-two—removed from professional employment for thirteen years—and lacked confidence about reentering that world. I considered teaching English but needed postgraduate credits for licensure. I rejected taking my family into further debt by taking more academic courses, so I ruled out teaching.

I applied to a county not-for-profit agency that was expanding its services to disabled adults and advertising several positions. I interviewed there within a few days and was offered a teaching position that required no education beyond my bachelor's degree. The fact that I could now significantly supplement our income and provide health coverage, too, was the upside of returning to work.

The downside hit me hard when I dropped the girls at the bus stop the next Monday and drove to my first day of employment, my heart heavy as a cinder block. Within the hour, however, I became completely absorbed in observing the highly positive teaching technique this agency used to increase participants' positive behaviors. I shadowed an instructor, Nancy, as she taught daily living skills. When she worked with her lunch group, I quickly saw that the meal was more than a time to eat; it was also for learning good eating skills. Six moderately disabled adults sat around a table; Nancy sat in the center like an orchestra leader. As they opened their lunch boxes, she prompted, "Now, remember, let's chew our food with our mouths closed."

Some nodded, while others silently arranged their food on the table. Greg, a fair-haired man in his thirties, said, "Yes, Nancy." He unwrapped his tuna sandwich, raised it to take a huge bite, and smacked loudly, with his mouth wide open. Nancy said nothing as she reached into a pocket of her carpenter's apron and pulled out a bag of peanuts.

She smiled at Cindy, who sat next to Greg, chewing her food with her mouth closed. "Cindy," Nancy said, "here's a peanut; thank you for chewing with your mouth closed."

Cindy, nonverbal but possessing good receptive skills, smiled at Nancy and ate the peanut. Nancy then gave a peanut and praise to everyone at the table for eating with their mouths closed. She ignored Greg's behavior, giving him no eye contact, no attention, and no peanut, as she continued to praise and reinforce others.

Greg still chewed with his mouth open, and when I peeked unobtrusively at him, he was smiling, as if he well understood what was going on. After more minutes of Greg's noncompliance, Nancy again reinforced each compliant participant with praise and two peanuts.

I was fascinated. Although Greg was deliberately not complying, nothing negative was happening to him, except Nancy's lack of attention and edible reinforcement. As each of his tablemates received two peanuts for the expected behavior, I noticed Greg had stopped smiling, then closed his mouth as he chewed. Immediately, Nancy extended two peanuts to him, saying, "Good job chewing with your mouth closed, Greg. Would you like to have these peanuts?"

"Yes, I would," he said happily, and held out his hand. He popped them into his mouth, closed it, and chewed. "Thank you, Nancy," he said politely.

"You're welcome. Are those peanuts tasty, Greg?" Nancy asked.

"Mmm, they're delicious," he replied, rolling his eyes upward as he smiled. For the remainder of the meal, Greg chewed compliantly and was included in all the ensuing reinforcements given for that specified behavior.

Later, after the participants boarded their buses for home, Nancy and I debriefed. I told her I was especially impressed by the change in Greg's behavior without anything negative or shaming having happened to him.

She smiled, her blue eyes reflecting her pleasure in the outcome. "Greg's the highest-functioning participant in my group. He's been here for years now and understands how the reinforcement system works. He tests me at times, but I'm consistent with him. He loves peanuts, but one peanut wasn't meaningful enough. Two peanuts were the right motivator today. Could you see how happy he was to finally hear praise like the others?"

I nodded, beginning to understand the power of this teaching model. "There's no power struggle. The choice of how to behave is the participant's. If he chooses the negative behavior, he's simply left out of the positive rewards."

"Exactly," she agreed, her blond curls bobbing. "It creates a completely positive learning environment, the best setting for learning. And," she added, "we want our participants to grow; we aren't a babysitting service here."

"I experienced this teaching technique as both calming and nurturing, with clear expectations. I see why participants evolve."

"Me, too," she replied. "I've been here six years now, and if I have my way, I'll retire from this agency. I love working with these folks, and this is the best organization around for disabled individuals."

My thirteen-year career with the agency proved Nancy's words true.

As I drove home after work that afternoon, I mused that what I had seen at work showed me a less negative way to raise our children. Several evenings later, after Polly and Sue finished their baths, I walked into the bathroom and saw that Polly's towel was in the hamper, while Sue's lay in a soggy green mound on the floor. The girls were in their rooms, getting ready for bed. When I called out, "Polly, thanks for putting your towel in the hamper," she laughed, well familiar by then with behavior modification, and said, "Hey, Sue, better put your towel in the hamper."

Sue started giggling and walked back into the bathroom, grabbed her towel, and said, "Sorry, Mom. I meant to, but I forgot."

"No problem. Thanks, Sue," I said. The right things were happening; we were all positive and laughing.

Further, while we started having fun at home in moments like these, I began to discover that catching and reinforcing good behavior and downplaying negative behavior was great for all relationships: spouses, children, parents and other family members, friends, and, well, anyone. I became passionate about our little gem of an agency in the heart of sprawling, economically challenged, rural Delaware County.

I was soon promoted to case manager, overseeing my participants' individualized plans, assuring their growth, working with their instructors, and leading quarterly team meetings. I also became a member of the agency's administrative team, which, along with the board of directors, guided the development of our programs.

Six months later, I was promoted to associate director of day treatment for a satellite program two major mountains away from our farm, a position I held for a decade. Don and I divided our bills: he would cover farm expenses using the large business checkbook that lay on a clutter of mail on his desk, and I would pay everything else from my personal checking account. He assured me he could do his share, and I knew I could do mine, so, although neither of us ever happily adjusted to other transitions my absence demanded, the paralyzing cloud of poverty that had long hung over our lives disappeared. Now we knew that, with time, we could pay off all our bills. Don and I began to laugh more, as well as enjoy fun moments, like spontaneously playing ball with the kids or sitting on the stone wall to talk. During that period, if I'd been able to write the rest of our life story together, we would have deepened our bonds and lived happily ever after. Life, though, had plot twists in store, the kind found only in well-crafted mystery novels.

Chip graduated from our community college, where he discovered his passion in his second year and became an electrician. He moved to Otsego County, where he and I had lived before moving to the farm, and began work as an apprentice electrician.

For all the years I worked, I always ached to be home, especially in summer. While I did have two weeks of vacation for the first five years, it felt much too minimal for the time I wanted to give my children. The most troubling part of summer for me was coming home to find that Don, absorbed in his daily routine, rarely interacted with our daughters and left them alone nearly all day.

I encouraged ways he could include the girls in his activities, but, while things changed briefly, they always relapsed.

Sometimes I came home to find Polly and Sue in their rooms, angry after an argument that no one had been there to help resolve. I was sadly reminded of how I'd always felt as a child, that I was simply there in the house but not part of anything. I didn't want my daughters to feel that way. Don's mother had been home to fill that role while I was absent ten hours each weekday. We continued our cyclical conversation to include the girls.

But then, late one evening, Don came in from the barn, anger radiating from his dour expression.

"What's wrong?" I asked, standing at the sink, washing dishes.

"I'm disgusted with Polly."

"What happened?" I asked, always the peacemaker.

"Just leave me alone," he said, glaring. He didn't speak for the rest of the evening. I knew from earlier variations of this scenario that he would never tell me, and that whatever had happened would remain unresolved.

I wonder now: Did he ever feel the uneasiness that I did about the quality of our lives weakening, similar to the weathering-away of our barn siding? For all the hard work we'd put into our lives, I wanted us to do better.

Chapter 22: SHADOWS

Bovina Center, New York, 1987–91

Shortly before Christmas 1987, I arrived home from work late, tense and weary from driving over slippery, snowy mountains. The barn lights and humming generator told me Don was milking; two second-floor house lights told me my daughters were in their rooms. I carefully climbed the snow-covered steps, walked through the doorway, and slid off my L.L. Bean down-filled jacket. I wrapped it around a metal hanger, then shoved against Don's jacket to make room for mine. His jacket felt rough and unyielding, so I pushed harder and finally squeezed my jacket into the overcrowded closet. I tugged my boots off and tossed them onto the carpeted closet floor, littered with sneakers, shoes, and boots; as I did so, a sudden thought pierced my mind: *There's no room for me in this house.*

Where did that crazy thought come from? I wondered, as I finger-combed my snow-speckled hair back from my eyes and pushed the closet door to cover the disorganized mess inside.

In the kitchen, I ached once again because my once fra-grantly scented sanctum was now as odorless and sterile as an operating room. I wished the ground beef, Ragú chunky sauce, and package of spaghetti I'd brought home was ready to eat. I lamented my former love of preparing food for my family.

I called up the stairs, "Hi, girls. How was your day?"

In unison, they said, "Good." It sounded like a song note—a middle C.

"Come on down when you're done what you're doing, and we'll get spaghetti on the table," I said.

"Yum. I'll be down as soon as I finish this chapter, Mom," Susan said. I smiled; Sue reminded me of my adolescent self, always reading a book.

"I'm cleaning my guinea pig cage," Polly said. Her fourth-grade teacher had given her the class pet at the end of the school year, not knowing the animal was pregnant. Polly was thrilled with the three babies, as always, cherishing the arrival of every kitten, puppy, and other miracle of new life on the farm.

I pulled out my stainless-steel bowl and prepared meat-balls, then filled a large pot with water to boil the spaghetti. As I did so, I wondered how dangerous the roads would be during my morning commute to work. My hands began to shake and fear knotted in my belly as I thought of forcing myself to drive on slippery morning roads. Sometimes I fantasized about work-ing at home as a writer. Recently I'd rekindled my old hobby, applied to the Institute of Children's Literature's home-study program, and been accepted. I'd felt encouraged by my instruc-tor's comments on my early assignments, yet I knew a novice writer had to keep her day job. *Maybe someday*, I dreamed, as I drained the meatballs and smothered them with thick sauce that *glug-glugged* over them.

After dinner, I recalled my earlier, strange thought about there being no room for me in our house. *Why do I want solitary space?* I wondered, as I wandered through my home, looking for a niche that might work. Opening the creaky door to the two unused back rooms, I pulled the old chandelier chain. Dim illumination revealed the decades-old, torn brown wallpaper that resembled heavy grocery bags; some fallen plaster; and a floor that heaved years ago from winter frosts. In the tiny corner room, a bare lightbulb dangled from an old chain fixture. My bones, chilled now by lack of heat in this dismal part of the house, shivered as I gazed at the two windows, their antique glass panes rippled, set into an eight-inch sill. I suddenly thought, *Those windows would be attractive with some white enamel. And wouldn't some green plants look lovely on that sill?* I saw other possibilities, too: the beautiful view, through the windows, of the back forty acres up to the tree line. The total silence was also beguiling.

I left the room, knowing the sorely needed new walls, ceilings, and flooring were not possible. Don and I hadn't talked about money recently, but I'd noticed invoices on his desk and knew we'd slipped behind in the farm bills. I grieved about our opposing methods of money management: I wouldn't buy anything I couldn't pay for, while Don would charge whatever he felt he needed and figure out how to pay for it later. One day, I came home to find a door-to-door salesman had persuaded Don to purchase an accident insurance policy that, with our health coverage, we didn't need.

"I wish you'd talk with me before deciding things like this," I said. "Don, please cancel this policy."

He refused.

I shook my head and thumped the door shut, aching for space for myself.

Two years later, Lil died unexpectedly one afternoon when my father was away on a brief errand. He found her in the living room when he returned and ran to a neighbor, who called an ambulance. At the hospital, she was pronounced dead from a stroke.

Bonnie and I flew to Florida the next day and were greeted by the rage Dad felt toward Lil's doctor for her death, because her recent medical visit had not shown any problems. We hoped to convince him to return to New York, where he'd be closer to our assistance.

"I will never move back to New York," he said unequivocally. "I love Florida and want to live the rest of my life here. In fact," he continued passionately, his brown eyes watering, his voice cracking, "when I die, I want you to cremate me and scatter my ashes on Florida waters."

We were disappointed but honored his choice. After helping him for several days in his difficult transition, Bonnie and I returned home. Shortly after that, my father had a minor auto accident and we returned to talk with his doctor, who prescribed revoking Dad's driver's license. Dad had been drinking and driving for decades and, by God's grace, had never hurt another person. We also hired Marjorie, a soft-spoken widow who provided elder day care. We talked candidly about his alcoholism and the potential verbal-abuse challenges of working with him, but Marjorie said, "Don't worry about that. I can handle him."

We believed her and arranged that she would come to his home a few hours each day to assure the essentials of good food, health care, and cleanliness. The arrangement worked surprisingly well for a year, until Marjorie called to say she could no longer manage his needs. Generously, she gave us a flexible resignation to coordinate with his doctor's recommendation: a nursing home. We flew down and again encouraged him to return to New York. Again, he refused.

My dear sister and I researched acceptable options. In the third of three nearby facilities, we believed we'd found one and took Dad to visit. He was delighted and could not wait to move. "Such nice nurses—and I liked that patient Eleanor," he enthused.

Suddenly, his eyes narrowed. "But wait—can I drink my vodka there?"

We'd asked the nursing home that question. Failing to mention that it would impose limits on his daily alcohol intake, we said, "Yes, you can. Staff will keep your bottle but will bring you a drink when you ask."

Without hesitation, he said, "Okay! When do I move?"

"As soon as they have an opening," Bonnie told him.

Bonnie flew home while I stayed on to complete some final tasks. The next morning, I prepared eggs and toast while Dad sipped coffee and stared out the window. I said, "Let's go to the funeral home this afternoon to make your final arrangements," and we did. As we drove home, I asked, "Is there anything else you'd like to do before I go home?"

He nodded, "See my friends at the Moose Lodge one more time." Tears filled his eyes.

Cheerfully, I replied, "That's a great idea." I called one of his lodge buddies to tell him we'd visit the following day, hoping that most of his friends could gather.

I drove us to the lodge the next evening in my father's Crown Victoria, parked and removed his wheelchair from the trunk, then helped him into the seat. When I wheeled Dad inside, we saw eight or nine people near the smoky bar, some on high stools, others standing in shadow. I was surprised to see so few people, yet I had little sense of how many friends my father had.

"Hi, Joe," the burly bartender said heartily, as ice clanked noisily in the drink he shook. "Long time no see. What'll you have tonight?"

My father ordered a vodka tonic, and I asked for a rum and Coke. A plump woman whose dark roots extended below her cropped blond hair like upside-down matchstick tips said, "We heard you was coming tonight, Joe. How you doin'?"

He smiled weakly at her. "I'm moving to a nursing home, Patty, so tonight's my last time here." He pointed to me. "This is my daughter Mary Jo."

"Nice to meet you," she said to me, then asked him, "Which nursing home are you going to? That one in Port St. Lucie?"

I answered. "No, it's in Stuart, on Palm Beach Road."

She glanced briefly at me with an expression that seemed annoyed because I'd answered, not my father. She resumed talking with him as I kept quiet and observed. The patrons were all his audience now, and his eyes traveled sentimentally over each face. "I want you all to come visit me," he said, his voice cracking.

"Sure, Joe, we'll come," they all said. Someone else asked, "Did you hear Frank had a heart attack?" My father hadn't heard, so the friend relayed the details. Dad nodded, his eyes dropping to the floor, and then, one by one, the friends drifted back to the bar and resumed their loud talking and laughter. We'd been there only ten minutes. *Have they already forgotten about my father?* I wondered.

"Let's sit at a table," I said. He nodded, so I pushed his wheelchair to a small, round table in a cluster of empty ones. I placed our drinks on the table and sat across from him. As moments ticked away in the huge, soulless room, I glanced surreptitiously at him. His eyes were watery, staring off at the wall across the room. His mouth was pursed in a small, sentimental smile that caused laugh lines to appear around his eyes, a mixture of happiness and sadness, I thought.

Dad, what are you thinking? Such a brief few minutes these people gave you. Are you wondering, as I am, if they really are your friends? Are you wishing you might have spent more time with your family and less time in bars?

An enormous wave of sadness washed over me: for my dad's lack of depth and for the fact that in his lifelong quest for quick money, which he never did achieve, he'd overlooked his true wealth: a devoted wife and three fine daughters. Not the son he always wanted, no, but three daughters whose lives could have, would have, been so much different had he been a nurturing father.

But those chapters of his life were long behind him and he was closing yet another chapter that evening. I sat quietly, letting him be with his thoughts, until he looked at me through tears and said softly, "We can go now."

In some ironic way, the moment felt sacred. I stood and pulled his wheelchair back from the table, then pushed it toward the bar.

"You leaving now, Mary Jo?" someone asked.

I smiled and nodded. My father said, "Yeah, it was good to see you all." He opened his wallet and extended a $10 bill to the bartender.

"Put your money away, Joe. Tonight's on us," one of his friends said.

More tears sprang into his eyes as he nodded and slid the bill back into his worn brown wallet. His voice quavered as he said, "Thank you, everybody. So long, now."

The group said, "Take care, Joe. We'll miss you."

He nodded, then called out stridently as I turned the wheelchair, "And don't forget to come see me!"

"We won't. You'll be in Port St. Lucie, right?"

"No!" he shouted, frustration rising. "In Stuart, on Palm Beach Road."

"We'll visit, Joe. We promise . . ."

A few weeks later, the nursing home called to say they had Dad's opening. Bonnie and I planned our trip and included Polly and Sue, now nine and seven, who wanted to see their grandfather again. I weighed their wishes, eventually deciding that in a nursing home I could structure brief contact with him so that he'd have no opportunity to target them with his unpredictable disposition.

After we moved Dad into the nursing home and left him looking quite happy, we took the girls to Disney World. Our two hot and delightful Minnie and Mickey Mouse days became, for my daughters, the best memory of their Florida visit. A few days later, they flew, supervised, to my mother's home on Long Island to stay while Bonnie and I disbanded the possessions Dad hadn't taken with him. We sold his trailer to the park owner, drove home in his car, and sold it in New York.

A month later, I was working in my office, the morning of July 28, 1988, when Carol, our secretary, buzzed me to say I had a call from a Florida nursing home. My heart plummeted.

"Hello?" I said quietly, squaring off the papers on my desk.

"Hello, Mary Jo," the administrator said. "I'm sorry to tell you your father's body is starting to cease functioning. Our doctor just said he doesn't have much time left—perhaps until the end of today."

I slipped into a sort of fugue state that softened the message he had just given me. As when I was a child retreating to my cocoon, all emotion was cut off, too. In a few seconds I said, in a perfectly normal voice, as if I heard this news every day, "What happened?" He explained the details, emphasizing that my father was resting with a nurse nearby and was in good spirits. "We're keeping him comfortable."

"Thank you," I said. "Do I have time to get on a plane and come down?"

"It's possible you might get here in time to say goodbye," he replied. "That is, of course, your decision."

"I'll talk with Bonnie and let you know what we decide."

My world metamorphosed into slow motion: I replaced the receiver on the cradle, stood to close my office door, sat down again, and let the surreality envelop me. *A thousand miles away, my father is dying at this very moment.* I held my forehead with my right palm, staring at my desk. Questions flooded my mind: *Does he realize he's dying, is he truly comfortable, how close to death is he, what is he feeling, what am I feeling?* If I had allowed myself to feel, which I couldn't, I would have cried out to my Creator, *Please give us more time to have the caring relationship that could have been between us.* But now that could never be.

Then I thought, *Any normal person would go home. Yet what would I do there?* I'd missed so much work lately, I decided I'd stay in case my staff needed me. My agency might not get my usual 110 percent from me that day, but I felt no guilt about that.

I called Bonnie. We talked quietly, with heavy sadness.

"Should we fly down?" I asked, troubled by the thought of throwing together a frantic last-minute trip that had no guarantee of getting us there before Dad died.

"I'm at peace with staying home," Bonnie said softly. "I've been saying goodbye for a while now, and we were just there a few weeks ago." Our feelings matched.

"I'll let the administrator know," I said. "I'll ask him to tell Dad we called and both send all our love." And that's what we did. A few hours later, the call came to Bonnie: Dad had died, peacefully. She called me; I called my supervisor and drove home.

Bonnie received Dad's ashes a week later; we planned to return to Florida together to scatter them. I stayed home all that week, experiencing not grief so much as a profound longing for solitude. I often walked to the lake—where my daughters, day care children, and I had spent so many happy hours—yet could not sort out what I was feeling. All too soon, I was drawn back into my fast-paced life, yet before my confusion got completely buried, I contacted my employment assistance program. The representative encouraged me to do two things: attend some

Adult Children of Alcoholics (ACOA) meetings, and read Dr. Janet Woititz's book *Adult Children of Alcoholics*.

Chip accompanied me to my first ACOA meeting. I feared the experience, yet what I discovered were people who talked about topics I'd never thought about: loneliness, trust, intimacy, pain, and much more. I kept returning, listening carefully, catching glimmers of insight, and feeling some resonance with others' experiences. Occasionally I shared one of my own.

I read Woititz's book and was stunned to see myself in nearly all of the thirteen characteristics that adult children of alcoholics commonly exhibit. I identified most strongly with these five: I constantly sought approval and affirmation from others, felt I was much different than other people, judged myself without mercy, had difficulty having fun, and guessed at what normal behavior was. Beyond those awaited a profoundly painful awakening, two years ahead, that would also illuminate the roots of my difficulties with intimate relationships.

For the first time, I grasped the fact that my childhood family experience had been outside the ordinary and affected me in adverse ways. The painful response I felt was offset in part by a new understanding that when I watched popular kids in school and college and observed how different from me they seemed, that's because they were! They were happy, had lots of friends, did fun activities, and were entirely comfortable to be themselves. My new perspective was like finding an updated focus button on an antique Brownie camera that let me see old moments with new clarity.

In Woititz's later, 1990 edition of *Adult Children of Alcoholics*, she noted that after writing her earlier book, she'd learned that the same characteristics for children of alcoholics were also found in those who had lived in a dysfunctional family or system that included someone with compulsive behaviors—such as gambling or alcohol/drug abuse—or profound religious attitudes, or who grew up in foster care or were adopted. She concluded that "this understanding can help reduce the isolation of countless persons who also thought they were 'different' because of their life experience."

I began devouring self-help books from my Waldenbooks store, which, in 1988, amounted to half a bookshelf. Wayne Kritsberg, in *The Adult Children of Alcoholics Syndrome*, identified four general rules in an alcoholic family: rigidity, silence, denial, and isolation. This perfect description of my own family of origin stunned me.

And then life brought an unexpected twist.

With no warning, Chip arrived at the farm one morning as Don and I were rising for the day.

"Chip! Are you okay?" I asked.

He replied somberly, "I need to come home, Mom. I started using cocaine ten months ago, and now I'm addicted. I have to shake this habit, or it will be the end of me."

My heart dropped to my stomach floor, which churned as my old protective instincts erupted: *I cannot let anything happen to Chip. If I don't take care of him, he will die, too—and he* cannot *die!*

Outwardly, I said, "I'm glad you came home, Chip."

We sat down to talk after Don went to the barn, and by the end of the conversation, he'd agreed to join Narcotics Anonymous.

He attended regular meetings for several months, stayed home and worked with Don on the farm, and socialized mostly by visiting our neighbor on some evenings, where we knew he did consume some alcohol.

One weekend evening in late winter, as he and I sat talking in the kitchen, an idea struck me. "Chip, come look at the little back room and tell me what it would take to fix it up."

Interested, he developed a materials list for both rooms and said, "I could do this for not a lot of money, Mom." When he totaled his list, he smiled as he handed it to me. I decided that, despite the farm's financial needs, I would, after my bills, use some of my salary to honor my longing for this solitary space.

Over the following months, we ripped down cracked, lumpy plaster walls and Chip replaced them with smooth drywall. Chip installed new subflooring, ceiling tile, and an overhead light fixture. I painted my walls white and the woodwork around those two windows with deep sills a low-gloss enamel, then ordered Dresden-blue carpeting for both rooms. I purchased a love seat in pale mauves, blues, and grays and moved my former town-clerk desk against the window wall, where I could look out at quiet beauty. My final purchase was French doors for my privacy.

I called the room my sanctuary and never anticipated the journey I would take in that tiny space.

Two years after my father's death, in early April 1991, his brother, my dear uncle Matt, died. My clearest memory of his funeral was of my tears spilling onto the white rose I dropped onto his casket. Then one night, just a few days after we arrived home from Matt's funeral, something terrifying broke within me as Don and I prepared to go to a PTA meeting. I began experiencing inner turmoil that felt out of control.

"Don, please go without me. I feel sick," I told him.

"What's wrong, Jo?"

"I'm so nauseous."

After he left, I hurried to my sanctuary and curled into a fetal position on my love seat as mayhem churned in my dread-filled belly. From my inner chaos rose deep rage toward Uncle Matt. *I'm going crazy*, I thought. *I loved him; he was always so kind to me.* Although our families didn't often visit, I treasured any time with him, often wondering how it was possible that he and my father were siblings. They didn't even look alike; my father's face was long and angular, and he was bald, while Uncle Matt's face was as round as the rest of him, and he had a thick head of white hair. While Uncle Matt was compassionate and gentle, my father was dark, moody, and angry. My father drank; Uncle Matt rarely did.

So why am I feeling this rage toward Matt? I wondered.

During the following days in my sanctuary, my heart again ached for solitude, for time away from my family. Alone, I thought, I could figure out what was wrong with me. My feelings were similar to, yet much more intense than, my feelings after my father's death. So I told Don and my children of my desperate need to be by myself. They didn't understand the reason any more than I did, but they encouraged me to do what I needed.

I had no available vacation days, so I checked myself into a motel close to work for two weeks. My family and I agreed we'd contact each other only if something urgent happened. On Monday through Friday, I worked, avoiding any overtime, and nurtured myself at all other times: I exercised, rested well, ate good food, read, wrote, and journaled. As I read Joseph Campbell's *The Power of Myth*, I began recording my dreams and studying the symbols.

One night Bonnie called me, concerned that I'd gone away by myself.

"I think you should try some therapy," she said. "You've been through so much—and all of it alone." Her words startled me as would have a sudden lightning strike with thunder immediately following. Later, I decided to write a timeline of what I'd "been through," and was so shocked when I looked at the list of traumas that a cavernous pain erupted within me and ached nonstop for days. My sister, who was in therapy herself, was right—I would seek help when I got home.

One evening in my motel, I watched Bill Moyers television interview of Sam Keen about his book *Your Mythic Journey*. The questions Keen posed captivated me:

What do you have to offer the world?
What are your gifts?
What do you really want to do?
What is important to you?
Then, once you know these answers, how can you earn your living?

I was powerfully drawn to Keen's invitation to take a mythic journey into my self, despite his warning that it could be profoundly disturbing. *Crikey*, I thought, *how profoundly disturbing could it be? Look at what I've lived through already . . .* Such arrogance I had.

Then Keen said, "A person can either avoid the journey or take it and become aware. Most people choose to avoid the journey."

Those words consummated the challenge. An unknown-until-now part of me firmly asserted I must rise to this occasion and reject any notion that I was like "most people."

In my journal, I wrote, "I must be careful to follow where this quest leads me, rather than try to make this search go where I think it should." I chuckle now when I reread those words, amused by my naiveté in thinking I had any control over the journey ahead.

In July, Michael Landon died and I felt as if life at *Little House on the Prairie* had disappeared forever. I wondered what would happen to life at Hobbit Hills Farm.

And suddenly it started—in a way I could never have imagined.

Part II

Chapter 23: TANGLED COBWEBS

Bovina Center, New York, October 4, 1991

The early-October night outside my kitchen window was pitch-black. The children were in bed. Don was still milking. I loaded the dishwasher, pushed the START button, and listened to it softly burble, then drone. My chores accomplished, I picked up the October 7, 1991, issue of *Newsweek*, expecting to read about the rising Arkansas governor, Bill Clinton, who was seeking the Democratic presidential nomination.

Instead, I stared at the cover headline: "Surviving Incest: Can Memories Be Trusted?" Agitation stirred in my gut as my thumb urgently flipped through the thin pages until I reached a title that sizzled off the paper: "The Pain of the Last Taboo: For Many Survivors of Incest, Struggling with Suppressed Memories Is the Hardest Battle of All." A sidebar featured a picture of a weathered home with an elongated window that looked a lot like my kitchen window. A photo of a forty-something couple standing on rust-colored leaves crossed the page bottom. She—wiry, thin arms across her chest, dark circles beneath her eyes—leaned against a slender tree. He stood farther away, hands clasped behind his back. Their lips were pinched, their brown eyes haunted. Thick woods behind them showed a tiny sliver of light breaking through overhead.

My inner turmoil notched up, like my dishwasher beginning a new cycle. Abruptly I shoved my chair across our rust-colored carpeting, rose, and began to pace the length of the kitchen. *What is wrong with me?* I anguished. After multiple back-and-forth trips, I sat in my chair again, fear knotted in a heavy ball on my stomach floor. I gulped, taking a breath so deep, it broke as I exhaled and sounded like a sob. I forced myself to read on.

"My name is Roseanne Barr Arnold, and I am an incest survivor. That is the nasty little secret that has taken all my energy and all my courage to keep."

I read further claims of childhood sexual abuse by other prominent personalities: Oprah Winfrey; a former Miss America, Marilyn Van Derbur Atler; and La Toya Jackson.

The next paragraph described Harvard graduate Betsy Petersen's book, *Dancing with Daddy*, in which she related that her father, a highly respected community professional, sexually abused her, starting when she was only three and a half, until she was eighteen.

My body suddenly took on a life of its own. The fingers of my right hand formed a claw so constricted with strength and emotion, I thought I could snap off a digit as if it were a slender twig. I stared, shocked that I apparently could no longer control that part of my anatomy.

What is wrong with me? I cried silently. My rigid claw filled with a deep ache in each finger. *Maybe I can figure this out if I read more.* I forced my eyes back to the article.

No one knows how many children are sexually abused because it often happens within families and is kept absolutely secret. Arnold believes she must speak out. Two years ago, her husband, Tom Arnold, phoned her from his drug treatment rehabilitation program and told her that he had been sexually abused . . . when he was a child. After she hung up, Arnold began to shake and sweat. "I started to see little scenes or pictures. . . . [T]hey kept coming. . . . I knew I'd been physically and emotionally abused . . . but I didn't remember the sexual part until two years ago, when my head burst open."

My body started shaking as if I were outside in the cold night without a coat. My hands and arms stiffened and involuntarily slammed across my chest. I start rubbing my opposing arms hard and swiftly. Deeply agitated, my body rigid, during the next few minutes I clasped my hands together and curled them around my bowed head, then pressed them against my ears. My hands continued to move with an intensity of energy I'd never known. I surrendered to let my body do what it sought to do, and, after several minutes, it calmed. Dazed, I read more.

"Arnold said, 'Voices in my head say you're making this up. Maybe you took everything the wrong way. Maybe you imagined it . . . [were] just making it up for attention.'"

The article concluded with words Van Derbur Atler told fellow abuse victims in a speech the previous year: "If you violate your children, they may not speak today, but as we gather our strength and stand beside them, they will one day speak your name. They will speak every . . . single . . . name."

Well.

Thank God I remembered nothing like that in my background; I certainly was not one of the people in the article. Yet

I was deeply shaken as I became hyperaware that I was observing my actions as if I stood off to my side, a detached observer assessing a troubled person.

In a while, Don trudged upstairs. He walked to the kitchen sink and quietly washed up. Drying his hands, he sat down at the table and looked closely at me. "What's wrong, Jo?" he asked, his hazel eyes showing sudden concern.

I showed him the article, and, as I read parts of it in a monotone, my hand reformed into a claw. He watched me, eyes wide.

"I don't know what's wrong with me," I said, my voice agonized. "When my fingers go rigid like this, I could kill a person if I wrapped my hands around their throat."

He was, as he most often was, silent. He placed his roughened hand over mine and rubbed gently for several minutes, until it finally relaxed.

I close my eyes now and, with compassion, see us seated together at the table, knowing now that the end of our innocence—the most difficult chapter of our lives together—had just opened.

CHAPTER 24: NORTH WINDS

Bovina Center, New York, 1991–92

The next day, I glanced again at that *Newsweek* cover and my physical responses returned in full. During the days that followed, my work routine kept me grounded . . . until my mind would disengage from a task and I'd remember my hand's transformation into a claw. *Did that really happen?* I wondered dozens of times. *Of course not—that's crazy*, I would deny . . . until a rush of energy surged into my right hand and the claw returned. *So it did happen*, I was forced to acknowledge. *So I am going crazy.* Whichever way I tried to believe—either acceptance or denial—I had to conclude I was losing my sanity. I needed help.

A therapist recommended by our pastor gave me an appointment for the following week. *What will I say to her? How can I talk for a whole hour? I've never talked that long about anything to anybody. Will she tell me I'm crazy? That she's never heard of anything like what I'm describing?*

Nauseated with fear, I sat at my computer and wrote facts of my life she might want to know. I wrote for two reasons: first, I'd never spoken many of these events to anyone; second, I'd go blank and forget them when I sat in her office. I became aware of how impaired my expressive skills were, probably silenced by childhood mantras: "Children should be seen and not heard." "You are so stupid." "You don't know anything," and the subtle "You shouldn't feel that way!"

So the written word would be my pathway. I'd write my overview and read it to her when we met.

I wrote about marrying Cliff; Jocelyn's death; Chip's and Keith's births; our auto accident; my husband's abrupt disappearance. I detailed moving upstate to return to college, becoming financially independent, and building a better life; graduation; employment as a social worker. I described my dream to build a small log cabin near a stream, where I could raise my sons with nature at our doorstep. I noted meeting Don, our long courtship, Cliff's return to New York to see his sons again, our divorce, his remarriage.

I explained the accident with Keith and his death four months later; Don's and my quiet wedding; Chip's initial happiness on the farm and in his new school; the contented early years Don and I'd had working together on our farm; the births of Polly and Susan; the farm economy cave-in; the onset of my son's addictions; how I'd supplemented our income with day care by making Quiet Time Books and with my town clerk and Planning Board clerk positions; and then my return to professional work.

I recorded the onset of growing problems in our marriage, how they affected our children, and my then-present feeling that, since my father's and uncle's deaths, something was horribly wrong with me, though I didn't know what.

Meanwhile, the new issue of *Newsweek* arrived, containing a letter to the editor about the previous week's incest article.

I'm glad you addressed the fact that repressed memories can take years to surface. I was 36 . . . when my memories awakened. I thought I was going crazy. It was as though I had lived a false life from birth and had to relearn my . . . history. Your article helps empower all incest survivors by putting our experiences in the mainstream of American discussion.

—L.D., Batavia, NY

I wept as I read that L.D., also a fellow New Yorker, had experienced what I was experiencing; maybe I wasn't crazy after all.

The night before my therapy appointment, I packed my three-page, single-spaced narrative into my black briefcase, along with the prior week's *Newsweek*. The next day, holding the case in a death grip, I climbed a long stairway and cautiously opened the door to the therapist's office. I stepped into a pale green waiting room with a beige couch, an end table and lamp, two chairs, and a coffee table with magazines and children's books. I sat on the couch, laid my briefcase across my lap, and waited.

A slender, red-haired woman dressed in a long navy skirt, white blouse, and sage sweater opened the door. She smiled, her blue eyes crinkling with contagious warmth. "Mary Jo?" she asked.

Unexpectedly, I smiled, too. "Hello, Sallie."

She swung her arm toward the inner room. "Please, come in."

Sensing her kindness, I rose and walked into Sallie's office, suddenly struck by the coincidence of carrying a briefcase filled with "baggage."

First, Sallie compiled a genogram, a map of my immediate family members. She concluded and said, "Thank you. This is helpful. Now, how may I help you, Mary Jo?"

I stumbled through my words as I pulled my pages from the briefcase. "It's hard for me to remember all these things, so I've written them down. Can I read this to you?"

"Of course," she replied easily.

I read awkwardly, in a soft monotone, embarrassed and ashamed that I could not simply talk to Sallie like anyone else would. She didn't interrupt me, yet I felt her watch me closely. *What does she see?* I wondered, but I knew: *a pitiful person.* I read faster to finish the narrative, then looked up and said, "That's it."

She nodded her head. "I'm wondering how it felt to read me those pages."

Like a jerk. How would you *feel having to tell this awful stuff? All my life, I've told people what I thought they wanted to hear, but I don't have a clue about what you want me to say.* "Um, I don't know," I finally said, extending my pages to her. "Do you want these?"

She reached out to accept them. "Yes, thank you," she said, and laid them on her desk.

"What do you think about all this?" I asked.

Sallie looked at me kindly for a moment, then said gently, "Mary Jo, I think you are very lonely for yourself."

What on earth does she mean? I wondered, as my cheeks flamed. *I know it's something bad, though. It sounds pathetic.* I was so passive that it didn't occur to me to ask what she meant.

Today I believe that my unbroken monotone told Sallie I wasn't even fully present with her. My utter absence of emotion as I read—no tears of grief, no fist clenched in anger, no smile of happiness—must have revealed how detached I was from my feelings. Could life be any lonelier than being lonely for my self? Not that I know of. I assure my lost young self today that I was not at all pathetic; detachment was merely a coping skill I found to protect me from truths too hard to bear.

Sallie and I concluded the session and scheduled another for the next week. I dropped heavily down each of her stairs, as if I had twenty-pound weights on my feet. When I opened the door into the cold, dark night, I wished I could die because I felt such profound shame. Bad things had happened to me. My core belief that I was bad and stupid led me to believe bad things had happened because I was a bad person. In truth, I felt worse than I had before I'd entered Sallie's office, because now not only did I know what a horrible person I was, she knew, too. I could never have dreamed that Sallie and I had just opened a six-year commitment to do some very hard work together, or that I would one day cut out a gorgeous heart-shaped fabric piece and lovingly stitch it onto my patchwork quilt in her honor.

I hurried to my car to get away. Two miles out of town, I stopped at the mall and walked to the Waldenbooks' Self-Help/Recovery section, in the store's back corner. I hesitantly touched E. Sue Blume's book, *Secret Survivors: Uncovering Incest and its Aftereffects in Women*, slid it from the shelf, and read Gloria Steinem's cover endorsement: "Explores the constellation of symptoms that result from a crime too cruel for mind and memory to face. This book, like the truth it helps uncover, can set millions free." Inside the front cover was an "incest survivor's aftereffects checklist." I quickly scanned the list of thirty-four symptoms; after seeing myself in nearly all of them, I slammed the book shut, shoved it back on the shelf, and strode from the store. As I drove home, I began to gasp for breath. I was having an anxiety attack, something I'd not experienced since Keith's accident, and pulled off the road until I could breathe normally again.

The following week, Sallie and I talked about day-to-day events of my week as I began my long process of learning to trust her. After my appointment, I returned to Waldenbooks and pulled Blume's book from the shelf again. This time my hand was steadier as my mind insisted I must face this, if it was the truth of my life. Standing alone in the aisle, I read each characteristic again, noting the qualifier that *if* I had some of these characteristics, I *may* be an incest survivor. *So I'm probably not*, I thought. Yet, again, I identified with nearly all of the thirty-four characteristics: "Needing to be invisible and perfect"—ouch, I felt like I was pulling a Band-Aid from my arm, tearing away tiny hairs with it. "Splitting, shutting down in crisis, psychic numbing"—another Band-Aid ripped away, more protective hairs gone. "Inability to trust"—a huge ouch! "Boundary issues: control, power, fear of losing control"—my Band-Aids had torn away several layers of skin. "Feeling crazy, different, feeling oneself to be unreal and everyone else to be real"—did Blume know me, for God's sake? "Guilt, shame, feeling worthless, low self-esteem"—my skin felt raw from losing protective layers.

I thought of the false-memory theory and rolled my eyes. *Who would make this sick stuff up? I certainly wouldn't. I want to do other things with my life* . . . I closed the cover, carried the book to the register, and purchased it.

Questions pummeled me as I drove home*: If there was incest, who did it? When did it happen? Where? Why do I feel so dirty? Why do I hate myself?* And mostly: *Why don't I remember?*

In my sanctuary that evening, I carefully detailed my time with Sallie in my journal. I wrote, in part, "When I asked Sallie for my diagnosis, she said dysthymia, a long-term, low-level chronic depression that produces low self-esteem, fatigue, and several other symptoms."

Well, that sounds right, I thought, closing my journal. Then I opened Blume's book and entered the depraved world of incest, a world I would never have chosen to learn about otherwise.

Today I slide *Secret Survivors* from the numerous books I used during my recovery. The pages are yellowed, I notice, as I hold the book as tenderly as I would embrace an old friend. I read the preface and remember how, all those years ago, these highlighted words seemed written just for me: "Countless women do not remember their incest experience. . . . They may be dealing with depression, addictions, anxiety . . . problems with intimacy and sexuality. . . . These survivors need to break through the secret of hidden incest. Only then can they know what those lost years contained and understand the effects of incest."

Lost years? *Where are they?* I'd anguished. *Will I ever know what happened?* I recall a small glimmer of hope that Blume's pages might bring me some answers, some understanding. I keep turning pages, amazed by the extreme number of sentences and paragraphs I marked because they were so meaningful for me. By the end of the book, I'm shocked that only a few of the three hundred pages don't have an exclamation point, a bold star, a dark arrow, or parentheses.

That first night, my tormented self leafed through the first pages until I reached chapter five, titled "Am I Crazy? No, You're Coping"—words that sliced through to the heart of my own aching question. There, I read about women who had no memory of anything, just a terrible feeling. Knowing that others were as mystified as I with this craziness gave me some reassurance and comfort.

These next words resonated so strongly they might have been printed in bold letters: "The first step in recovery for the incest survivor is to acknowledge that the abuse has taken place. Often this acknowledgment occurs before any specifics have actually been remembered. Naturally, this helps the self-doubting survivor to doubt herself even more!"

Several months later, paradoxically, my supervisor asked me to take a weeklong training course to become an agency investigator of allegations of abuse. I also chaired the newly formed Client Abuse Detection and Prevention Committee. No one except me could possibly know just how well-acquainted I was becoming with abuse. As I grew in both my personal and professional abuse education, I could sometimes weave a personal piece of insight into the committee handbook. Other times, the reverse held true.

On March 23, 1992, I completed the investigation of a bus driver accused of inappropriately touching a female client. The investigation was difficult, but careful questioning and examination of numerous facts led to a solid conclusion. I wrote and submitted my report, then left for my evening appointment with Sallie. In the eleven months since our first appointment, our weekly meetings had matured into a relationship of trust that I'd never experienced with anyone else. Sallie was unfailingly respectful of and always fully present with me. She heard all of what I said—bad or good—with kindness and always without judgment.

Another important component of our relationship told me I was working with an excellent therapist. I had read that some therapists told their patients they had been sexually harmed and it turned out some of those patients had not been. I had questioned Sallie a few times about her thoughts of my having been harmed in this way. She looked directly into my eyes and said, "I trust your instincts, Mary Jo."

Sometimes I wished she'd just tell me yes or no, so I could get the process over with and move on with my life. In truth, though, I respected her response, which in time strengthened my trust in myself and gave me courage to push deeper into the unknown. Sallie's wisdom and nurturing further liberated me to grow emotionally, and, at long last, in my sixth decade of life, the dreaded adolescent-report-card comment "emotionally immature" was silently transforming.

I felt agitated and restless as I drove to my appointment. Arriving early, I softly opened Sallie's door, walked to the couch, sat down, quickly got up again, went into the ladies' room, brushed my hair, washed my hands, returned to the waiting room, sat down, picked up a magazine, quickly leafed through it, tossed it down, stood up, and paced. *For heaven's sake, why can't I sit still?* I wondered.

Sallie soon greeted me. I noted her pretty outfit in my journal later: forest-green slacks, a white blouse, a knitted sweater with a green-and-burgundy folklore pattern. I followed her into what I now thought of as my sanctuary away from home and blurted out a jumble of thoughts. I wrote in my journal later, "I wasn't sure whether to talk about events in the present or the past, then said, because so much of the present came from the past, I'd start there. Sallie agreed. Then I went blank and struggled for something, anything, to say."

She's probably rolling her eyes in her mind, I thought, slipping outside myself to see me as she must. I knew my brown eyes were large and serious, that I looked like a woman in mourning with my black slacks, black turtleneck, black dress shoes, and hose. Black was the color of every garment I wore from the skin out. Several months earlier, when I'd needed some new underwear and looked over my choices of bras and panties, I had been drawn to the color black. *Black is sexy, which I certainly haven't felt for quite some time, so why do I want this?* I'd wondered, as I'd looked for my size. Then I'd realized, *Ah—black is the color of grief.* I'd taken my black garments to the cashier, knowing I would purchase all black clothing from then on as a quiet expression of mourning for my lost childhood.

I hadn't prepared for tonight's session, but I'd had some recent troubling flashbacks. I started talking about the one the previous day. I described it in my journal:

> *I wake in terror because someone's hands are all over my body. . . . Don is sound asleep. . . . Shaken, I ask myself who violated me. . . . I want to know. . . . I'm so frustrated I want to scream and punch something so hard I'll be able to smash through the wall that hides me from knowing what happened. Dammit, I'm so sick of all this. Now, right now, I want to know—now! I feel like the undertow is pulling me out into the depths of the ocean, huge waves*

*are crashing over me, pushing and pulling me all over in a
vast helplessness. . . . I will drown. . . . This is so terrifying
I cannot adequately put it into words. . . . It feels like, in
the end, I will die.*

Sudden words spilled from my mouth. "Sallie, I feel close
to something terrifying."

She nodded, repositioning herself in her chair, as if to
prepare.

I said something about my father I couldn't recall later as I
wrote in my journal, then said, "This all started right after Matt
died. *Matt . . .*" I squinted my eyes at Sallie and softly whispered
his name in a question: "Matt?" I repeated it several times, each
in a stronger voice, until finally, in a furious, loud, accusatory
voice, I said, "Matt!" My body was rigid with tension and fury.

A former Long Island girl with lots of seashore time, I'd
experienced the gamut of gentle and powerful waves. I also knew
about tidal waves from my grandmother Davis, who told me about
the eye of the 1938 Great New England Hurricane (aka the Long
Island Express) passing over Long Island, a few miles from her
home on Great South Bay. She and Grandpa watched that tidal
wall gather water and power before it reached its peak, pausing
briefly before it crashed over their house. So did this flashback.

As I tried to let whatever was coming come, a tumultuous
surge of terror filled my body. I pushed my head down, closed
my shaking fists, and shoved them across my clenched mouth,
while also protectively covering my breasts. My stiff upper body
curled into itself as my rigid legs slid under my rocker, and I
pushed myself back, back, away from Sallie, as far away as I
could get. *I have to get away. Get away! Get away!* I was beyond
desperate to do so. My eyes were shut tight, and I screamed
silently over and over, screams that only I could hear in my
head. When I could push away no more because I'd reached
the wall, I kept pushing until my chair moved sideways, tight

against the wall. Then, slowly, my legs lost strength, my silent screams stopped, and my pushing ceased. As I shuddered and sobbed, my head dropped to my knees. My tidal wave had spent itself. I felt battered, broken, and exhausted.

Unknown minutes passed as, deep in shock, I slid into nothingness. In time, I heard Sallie's voice calling, "Mary Jo, come back. You're safe now."

When I could, I lifted my head, opened my eyes, blinked, and stared at her. I thought back to what my words and body had just revealed. Sickening knowledge had just broken into my consciousness with tidal wave force. *My uncle sexually assaulted me?* I could not believe this. Yet I could not disbelieve what my body had just so powerfully asserted.

Sallie was near and silent. I knew she watched carefully to assure I wouldn't hurt myself, and to observe every detail of what was happening. The trust I'd developed for her during the past year had, I'd realize later, allowed me to open the pathway to that day's revelation, to what I believed was my darkest secret, unknown to myself for decades, until now.

"Breathe, Mary Jo," she coached me. I put my hand over my mouth and focused on taking even breaths. After the passing of the flashback, this new information slowly integrated into the now gently lapping, calming waters of my present. I was still, and stared at the floor as I tried to take it all in.

After several seconds, Sallie asked how I was feeling. *How do I feel?* I wondered. Dully, I said I felt numb, paralyzed, shocked, stunned, lifeless. I glanced at my limp hands, one atop the other, palms up, as if in supplication, then looked up at Sallie.

Tears streamed down my cheeks as I whispered, "What's real? Is this real, that my uncle horribly betrayed me? Or is my lifelong belief in him as a kind and caring person real?"

She said gently, "You tell me, Mary Jo. What's real?"

I stared into her somber face, as, in that moment of truth, tears spilled from my eyes, and I eventually whispered, barely audibly, "What just happened here is real. I know from the place deep inside that holds my truth."

She laid her hands tenderly over mine and nodded. "Yes," she said.

I stared away, lost again in fog for several moments, then returned. "Sallie, I've worked with you about so many things, but this—this wipes out everything I've always believed about him being one of the best parts of my childhood."

The door in the waiting room clicked open; her next patient had arrived. I stared at her, still feeling surreal.

"I want you to put this away, like closing a book," she said quietly, forming her hands into an open book, then closing them together with a soft clap, her hands left in a prayerlike pose. "I want you to think about things you like to do, that make you feel happy."

Still dazed by this huge slash through my protective bubble of denial just moments earlier, I could not relate to her suggestion. Instead, I felt as if I were moving between two worlds, which was, of course, exactly what I was doing: shifting between reality and denial, past and present. "I'll try," I told her. "I want to get this work done quickly, but I want to keep my sanity, too."

She smiled, and her eyes sparkled. One day I wanted my eyes to sparkle like Sallie's. "You will. Now, do you need anything before we end today?" she asked.

"I'm thirsty, but I'll get water in the restroom," I said.

"How about a cup of tea?"

I smiled shakily. "Tea would be perfect." Walking unsteadily behind her, I watched Sallie prepare a cup of herbal tea in her lunchroom. "Stay here as long as you want," she said.

"I'll be okay soon," I said, sitting down shakily, hoping that were true, as it usually was with flashbacks. This one, though, had been intense beyond any I'd experienced earlier.

"Can I give you a hug?" she asked, smiling, her blond eyebrows raised.

I always said yes; now I shook my head no. "I need all my energy to hold myself together today, Sallie. Please give me a rain check," I said, surprised I was declining.

"Of course," she replied, and added, "Call me if you need anything." I nodded. She left and I sat alone, sipping my tea, gradually feeling a sense of nurture. About half an hour later, I stood up to test my legs. I still felt shaky and strange, so I walked around the room until my legs felt steadier, then quietly left and drove home uneventfully.

I parked in front of the carriage house at about 7:30 p.m. Don was in the barn; my girls were in the house. Pushing my thin legs up the hill to the side door, I pulled it open. I hugged Polly and Susan tightly, feeling my battered self renew as they smiled and we talked.

Later, after the girls went upstairs, I rushed to my refuge to write my journal note about the day. Although I tried to follow Sallie's instruction to close the book and put this away, I paced back and forth to my computer all evening long, writing down as much of the session as possible, as parts of it returned to me in small fragments. I knew if I didn't write everything I recalled that night, much of it would be lost forever. Even remembering just a few hours later was difficult.

At 10:00 p.m., preparing for bed, I wrote my final entry:

I did put this all away when I left Sallie's. It's still there, but it's away. There's a part of me that feels less angry tonight and somehow cleaner. I haven't forgotten that it happened, and I'm not denying that it did. Something very important happened today.

Now I wonder what on earth lies ahead.

During the early weeks that followed the Matt flashback, new memory slivers surfaced: a small white room where I'd slept, the creepy feeling of someone sliding into my bed, Matt's raspy whisper in my ear—"Shh, don't make any noise"—a hand touching my body, then my genitals. The small blips told a huge story that resonated with chilling truth. Finally, I was connecting with some specifics, a breakthrough that felt affirming, though mixed with unfathomable revulsion and anger.

The night after the Matt memory, Don came to my sanctuary after milking and asked, "How are you tonight?" We hadn't talked much about my breakthrough the evening before. I was too exhausted. But this evening I described the flashback and showed him how my body had responded with that desperate urge to get away. As I did so, my body tensed into another flashback. I curled into a tight ball of fear, my fists pushing against my closed eyes and shuddered, making soft sounds. Don had never seen me have a flashback, and when I dropped my head on his shoulder later, after my body relaxed, he put his arm around me and said, "I'm sorry about this, but it is nice to feel you close to me again."

His words caused me to shudder and bring my hands up to cover my chest. My legs pulled up. In a soft, sad voice I said, "I feel so disgusted whenever I think about being intimate with you. I'm sorry."

"It's okay. I understand this better now," he said. We talked a little more and then, worn out, went to bed. The next morning, we woke early and talked quietly some more. "Jo, I love you; we're in this together. It's going to get better, and I'm with you all the way," he said, and started to move closer to me. I pushed him away. "Listen," he said gently, "this is me. I'm your husband, not your uncle. I love you. I won't hurt you."

He kept affirming these truths in a moment unlike any other we'd experienced. In time, I don't know how long, I became fully present with him and completely relaxed as I felt a powerful surge of love for him I'd rarely experienced. And then it seemed so natural to slide into his arms and tenderly make love, a beautiful surprise for us both—though this exquisite moment was one we would never share again.

Later that morning, I wondered in my journal if I could believe the Matt flashback in the aftermath of such intimacy with my husband. It didn't seem possible to me then that the flashback could be true. Were the strange happenings in my life more related to menopause? I felt schizophrenic again.

That evening, Don and I went out for dinner and I shared that day's battle with wondering again if I was crazy. "You're *not* crazy," my husband said. By the time we returned home, I didn't think so, either. I wrote that I'd made a decision: "I am *not* crazy. I *will* trust what I said to Sallie last Tuesday and I *will* go on from there. For too long I haven't believed in myself. I *believe* in myself. I am strong and brave and . . . very afraid."

The next day, Sunday, I recorded: "I'm shaking as I begin to write. . . . Don has gathered round me with enormous support. I feel stronger today, and his support is why, I know. I'm getting ready to face all my memories."

Although I'd not remembered any abuse by my father, I trusted an innate, strong feeling that—although as yet I could not connect the feeling with a memory—he, too, had violated me.

I hadn't told my childhood family about my first memory yet, unsure whether they'd believe me. As I determined to move ahead and begin talking about my father with Sallie, I called my mother to ask her some questions.

We caught up on recent events, and then she asked how I was doing in therapy. "That's why I'm calling," I said, looking down at the list of questions I'd developed. "Mom, do you remember anything traumatic happening to me in my childhood?"

"Oh, yes," she replied quickly, and described how I'd fallen down Aunt Madeline's basement stairs when I was not quite two. "We took you to a doctor because you couldn't stand up. You were 'out of it.'"

"I remember that," I told her, "though I don't remember the doctor visit. What do you remember about the day you brought Jackie home after her birth?"

"I remember holding Jackie. When you got on the couch with us, you seemed annoyed with her and put your foot on her chest. I told you to be careful, but you kept being rough with her."

"Was my father in the room?"

"Yes, he was sitting in a chair."

"Did he do anything to me?" I asked.

"I don't remember anything," she said.

"I remember that he beat me with his strap because I hurt Jackie."

"It could have happened, and I either forgot or was unaware," she said earnestly.

I was astonished. She was not discounting what I remembered. This was such a breach from our lifelong winner-loser kind of conversation. My mom was supporting and helping me! Feeling heartened and validated, I pushed on. "So, how did he act toward me in general?" I asked, curious to hear her answer.

"He was merciless and demanding," she told me. "He talked down to you all the time, constantly criticized you, and expected you to behave perfectly. He was a morose man and had no sense of humor."

Again, she astonished me with facts that reverberated so deeply in me. I asked my last question: "Were there times when he and I were alone?"

"Probably," she replied. I asked if she ever noticed I was upset when she got home, but she recalled nothing like that. My heart sank. Yet, although we didn't remember all the same things, our memories were in the same ballpark and I found that validating.

I decided to drop the bombshell. "Mom, I've had a memory of Matt molesting me." ("She was pretty boggled by that" was all I wrote later in my journal about her reply.)

"I'm pretty sure my father molested me, too," I said. "I'm going to start digging into that feeling."

"Mary Jo, I never had any inkling, but I wouldn't put it past him," she said. Sexually, he wasn't normal, we concluded after more discussion. Later I journaled, "My mother talked easily and didn't throw up road blocks, as I'd thought she might. She feels comfortable that she did the best she could and seems willing to help me as much as she can. Wow."

In subsequent days, I pondered why this trauma was surfacing at this point in my life. I recalled my anxiety after my father's death, and how Matt's death had brought up similar but more intense feelings. Their deaths, I believed, had triggered the release of memories, for now I was safe, their lives washed away in the sea of time.

Yet there was another important factor, I realized: the farm—its pastoral 170 acres, of which I knew every inch; its century-old weathered buildings; its lovely, aged stone walls; the stream that either trickled or rushed along the front of the house, depending on weather and season; the gently rolling fields and meadows; the rolling hills I loved. There, I had rooted so deeply into the land and the lifestyle that, for the first time in my half-century of life, I possessed a profound sense of home.

I remembered again having played, after Don and I became engaged, John Denver's "Take Me Home, Country Roads" over and over. Not only was the farm home, a miracle in itself, but its embrace had given me a strong refuge as well. I was also more connected to my community than any I had ever lived in until our marriage. I knew unequivocally that there, on that land with my family and those townspeople, was where I wanted to live out my days.

When I went for walks, I saw profound beauty in every direction, in every season. When I climbed to the hilltop across the road, I could look up and down the spectacular valley. One achingly warm and sunny springtime day, I sat on our stone wall and counted the different shades of green I saw on the hillsides, finally stopping at seventeen. I knew where the best wild blackberries were, where mint grew gracefully between rocks by the stream, where the cows hid on the hillside after they calved, where the gopher holes were, and where the most exquisite views languished. I treasured my garden spot, smaller now that I was working off the farm, and my ever-growing raspberry patch.

The solitude and strength of this hilly, rocky land had gifted me with the safest haven possible for this journey into my foggy, troubled past—one as safe as Sallie's space.

I had recently joined a therapy group with women who had done intensive personal work. One of them asked me, "Why go back to the past?" She was new to our group, working on present problems with her spouse, and couldn't understand my need to revisit my childhood. Her brow furrowed as she looked at me over her glasses. "Surely once was enough, wasn't it?"

Good question, I thought, and said, "I have to go back so I can make better sense of my todays." I knew she was unaware of my present nightmare; she didn't have to go back in time if she didn't want to, but I did. After my recent breakthrough, I knew that something deep inside me had silently broken open, like an oil spill beneath the ocean, and would need my time and attention before it all reached the surface.

While I felt much trepidation about what lay ahead, I knew now that I'd opened the door to what Sam Keen called a mythic journey. There was no turning back.

Chapter 25: OCEAN WAVES

Bovina Center, New York, 1992–93

S adly, as I slid in and out of sometimes paralyzing depression at home, Don's and my closeness was short-lived. In part, he wanted me to talk with him about what was happening, to "let him in," as he said. Sometimes I could, while other times I pushed him away.

Anger and frustration floated everywhere in our family life. One day Don exploded because the girls came to the barn late for evening chores. The girls were angry with him because they'd waited at the bus drop-off nearly an hour before he'd picked them up. I was angry because I hadn't been home to help.

Mealtimes, when we shared them, became pick-on-each-other occasions. One evening I detached from talking and listened to the conversation, then wondered why anyone would want to eat at our table. Free-floating anger, as Sallie called it, ruled in our house now, along with ongoing passive-aggressive actions.

Several weeks after the Matt memory, in my sanctuary, I prepared for an appointment with Sallie. Sickening fear told me another memory was close. I'd found a way to break into rising flashbacks by breathing deeply several times, then splitting away from my feelings by dissociation, just as a plumber turns off the water before replacing a commode. Some called this self-hypnosis. I'd close my eyes, put my fingers on my keyboard, and let them start talking to my younger self.

I wrote this note, copied verbatim from my journal: "What are you afraid of?" I typed, letting a free flow of words spill out, without editing or punctuation. When words didn't come, I repeated the last words until new ones arrived. "Tell me its okay you are safe here with me no one can hurt you," I wrote to my isolated child self. She didn't answer; I didn't stop. "Tell me, whats wrong today," I typed several times.

Finally she spoke haltingly:

its dark . . . quiet . . . im in bed . . . Jackies in her bed . . . daddys coming I hear him no no no no no no not him no go away go away I hate you go away I have to hide I have to get away get away get away oh I know ill hide in the closet hurry hurry hurry hes almost here im in the closet now the blankets are all over the floor and im hiding under them oh but im breathing so loud hes going to hear me hear me hear me oh no hold my breath still my heart is pounding so hard hell hear it oh god oh god oh god help me help me please help me I hear the door open oh god hes here help help I hold my breath its so quiet so quiet then he says where the hell is she I can't breathe I shove the blanket over my mouth im so scared whats he doing where is he did he go away I didnt hear the door close.

Then my young self spoke words that sliced through my mind to the core of my psyche, words that, more than fifty years earlier, had sent cataclysmic explosions to my brain that had shattered this moment into oblivion, into the darkest part of my soul, where I would not remember it—until now. The little girl I was whispered her secret: "Jackie is choking oh god noooooooooooo . . ."

Intense rage, which I knew I could not contain, suddenly overpowered my body. I wanted to let out the most primal scream in the history of mankind, but I felt as if my scream would blast the earth into tiny fragments. So I clenched my fists and pummeled a couch pillow, which was as ineffectual as hitting a baseball with a toothpick. I wanted to rip the farmhouse apart with my bare hands and demolish it, yet I knew even that would not diminish my frenzied anger by one iota. How had my body contained all this rage for all these decades? I struggled to breathe slowly, deeply. *God, I have to do what Sallie says: close the book, close the fucking book, until I see her tomorrow.*

I grabbed an open book near me—coincidentally, Ellen Bass's *The Courage to Heal*—and slammed it shut so hard that the reverberations surely trembled through the quiet old house. Acutely aware of how bizarre this moment would appear to any observer, I dissociated and returned to the quiet, calm person I normally was.

The next day, I drove to Sallie's office after work. She smiled, then stopped as she looked into my eyes. I hurried in, gripping the pages I'd written in my sanctuary during and after the previous night's flashback.

"It's a horrific memory," I said. "Jackie and I had a weird closet in our room with three steps up to get in—narrow, no door, about six feet deep; rumpled blankets covered the floor; sometimes I crawled in there to play, tunnel way back; no one knew I was there.

"This is what happened last night," I said, then read my pages to Sallie. I whispered the final words in agony, "Jackie is choking. . . ." I folded up into myself, dropped my pages to the floor, and rocked back and forth, tears leaking onto my cheeks. Minutes later, I raised my head and wailed, "Do you see what happened? I tried to save myself and sacrificed my sister. My *disabled* sister, for God's sake!"

Sallie nodded, her eyes saddened. As always, I felt comfort from her connectedness with me. My urge to scream that loudest scream in mankind's history returned, to scream rage for my father's grisly act that night, to scream pain and guilt for having failed to save my sister, to release the soul-shattering, never-ending scream that had formed within me that night and had been imprisoned in my body for five decades.

"You can scream here," Sallie said gently.

"I can't, Sallie. I'll find a mountaintop somewhere, away from everything, and then I'll scream," I promised, knowing I must get the rage outside myself.

A chilling thought suddenly gripped me. I stared at her. "You know, now I understand how one human being can kill another. If my father was here right now, I would *kill* him," I said, then referenced a meat cleaver and his genitals.

We processed the Closet Memory, and I calmed as our time neared closing. Sallie mentioned she thought I had re-created my childhood closet in my farmhouse sanctuary. Aha! The link between one closet and the other snapped in place. Of course! Just one difference: my sanctuary was safe.

I gave names to the four most devastating memories of my therapy years. Tonight, the Closet Memory joined the Matt Memory.

While driving home that night, I found a secluded dead-end road, parked my car, and screamed into the night until I become so hoarse I was forced to stop. I wasn't finished—I'd scream again and perhaps again, and again, until it all released—but I felt better, for the time being. Voiceless and utterly exhausted, but better. Cleaner.

The next Sunday, I sat in church with Don and our girls. Just before the service, a tall young man whom I'd never seen walked past us. He embraced a sweet little girl, perhaps two years old, wearing a pink dress, lacy pink socks, and Mary Jane shoes. My heart softened at her loving expression when she smiled at her father and touched his hair affectionately. He slid into the pew ahead of us and gently seated her beside him. Tears filled my eyes as I observed their tender love.

Our minister walked to her podium and smiled. "Good morning, everyone."

"Good morning," we replied.

Three pews ahead of us, two-year-old Cassie caught my eye as she stepped into the aisle and walked toward the altar. Her parents had waited many years for their daughter's conception. I watched Cassie turn back to look at them, as if silently asking, *Is this okay for me to do?* Cassie's mom curled her finger and silently beckoned her back. Cassie giggled softly as she hurried back, where they warmly embraced her. These two loving moments between parents and small daughters opened a well of grief so deep, I left the church unobtrusively to sit outside, where my sobs could be private.

I didn't go back to church that day; in fact, I never returned. The grief that drove me from church that day transformed into anger. *Where were You when I was a child, God?* It seemed He was as absent then as I became from church.

As I uncovered my repressed history, the *Boston Globe* steadily broke open the long-term cover-up of pervasive sexual abuse of children in the Catholic Church. In 2016, the motion picture *Spotlight* recounted the story so excellently, it received an Academy Award for Best Picture that year.

On *Saturday Night Live*, Sinead O'Connor sang her song "War," protesting the alleged child abuse by the Church by holding up a picture of Pope John Paul II and calling to her audience, "Fight the real enemy," as she ripped his picture into pieces. This scandal shook me as much as my predatory male relatives had, and begged the question, broadly generalized: If we could not trust family or church leaders, what on earth was left? Not government, I knew. My naiveté shattered, I believed I could trust no one except Sallie and few others.

I slipped further into isolation—not just from church, but I also resigned as town clerk and Planning Board clerk. Essentially, I dropped out of any life beyond my family, my work, and my counseling with Sallie. I lost faith not only in God but also in the world, which I'd grown to perceive as a covertly evil place. I knew there were good people in the world, but I'd learned they could also *seem* to be good when they were not. How could I discern? Whom could I trust? I certainly hadn't done well in the past, so, for the present and future, my solution became to disappear further.

One positive I found in the Catholic Church scandal was that the country's outrage about the church's abuse was as powerful as my own as I uncovered my truth.

I noticed a cycle in my work with Sallie: I would work at easier pieces of healing for several weeks, and doing so would eventually lead to another memory breakthrough. After the Closet Memory, for example, my energy increased; I felt happier, more motivated to be active, and less tarnished by incest. I was realizing how much energy I'd used over the years to repress that part of my past, and now understood why dysthymia, chronic low-grade depression, had tagged along with me most of my life.

I was holding my own in my demanding work environment, yet, by the time I reached home, I had little energy left for my family and none for the farm. Don and I hired no help; our farm was the same family farm it had been five decades earlier, when Don's parents had bought it. Chip had moved away to a new job and was seemingly doing better. Don's father helped Don briefly each morning. The girls fed calves every evening, unless they were away at sports practices or games. Don's family support system lessened so much that *family farm* really became a misnomer. Increasingly more isolated and detached himself, Don began to counsel with our pastor, Karen.

I recall a night when he came in from the barn. I could not miss his troubled aura. He was unshaven, his hair unwashed. He'd also been quieter than usual for the past few days; this night, he stared silently at the table.

I didn't ask what was wrong. I simply blurted out, "Don, let's sell the farm." I would have been stunned, actually, if he'd said yes. He rubbed his graying whiskers and said, "No. Things will get better."

So, two ever-increasingly overwhelmed people, we kept pushing ourselves at a growing cost to our children as we became less emotionally available, more impatient, more weary. Don attended church less, if at all, by then, so our daughters didn't go, either.

"Once your therapy is done, I hope we'll be happy like we used to be," Don said a few times, hopeful for our future. I quietly wondered. Two of the women in my therapy group were working through the end of their marriage. Anne's husband had found a new partner, more like the woman Anne had been before her therapy, and Anne in turn saw that she had grown beyond the level at which the marriage had comfortably functioned.

Don and I had been on fairly equal footing emotionally when we fell in love, yet my slow purge of buried trauma had freed me to grow, while Don was still Don. Although he was going to counseling, which offered the hope that we might each grow, would that happen? Could my journey cost us our marriage? That was the last thing I wanted.

One, then two years passed. I forced myself to rise each morning, the girls and I prepared for school and work, I dropped them downtown at the bus stop, drove over the mountains to work, returned home or attended therapy twice a week, prepared dinner and spent time with my family, cleaned up, retreated to my sanctuary to journal. At night, desperately weary, I fell into bed, where I often woke from flashbacks or frightening dreams.

One recurring dream, in particular, I recall to this day in vivid detail. In the dream, I was a small child living in Hitler's Germany, alone in the night, outdoors on back streets. In terror, I hid behind lampposts; when I was sure no one was near, I'd scurry to the next post, and the next. I didn't know where this lamppost-to-lamppost journey was taking me, as I always hid in the shadows to avoid the Gestapo, but I knew life was utterly terrifying and joyless. When I recorded this dream in my journal the first time, my tears fell on the page. I easily understood the symbols and grieved for that little girl so alone in the dark.

I began aching to work part-time, to be home more with Polly, now fifteen, and Susan, thirteen, worried because I knew they needed more attention. In late 1992, I saw a potential solution: our two vehicles—Don's truck and my car—would soon be paid for, out of my paycheck. One night, sitting with tea at the kitchen table with Don, I said, "I'm thinking about talking with my employer about working half-time."

He stared at me. "Jo, we can't survive without your income."

"I'm exhausted. I cannot go on like I have in the past few years," I said shortly. Didn't he care about me? I pulled out the budget I'd been working and showed him the figures that made my half-salary possible once the car and truck payments were completed.

He was taken aback. "Well, that might work," he said.

"That's what I think. Tomorrow I'm going to talk with Barb about reducing my hours," I said. He nodded, though his expression remained doubtful.

For the past decade, I'd been the on-site director of a satellite program for disabled and mentally ill adults, earning a good salary for a Delaware County woman, a fact that our farm's lack of prosperity masked. When I broached half-time employment with my supervisor, she listened closely, then said, "You know I need a full-time person in this program." I nodded.

"Would you be interested in a half-time social worker position in the Walton program?"

"I would love that," I replied without hesitation, pleased about returning to my long-ago work in Cooperstown. This would also mean not traveling the terrifying two major mountains each way.

We fleshed out the details, and I started my new position. Despite the fact that I was home and could meet the girls on the afternoon bus, and that we could do more together, the pleasure soon diminished as both Don and I continued our downward slide. Therapy was getting harder to struggle through, and for Don, the endless farm challenges were always at the forefront of his thoughts.

Sometimes I shared with Don what I was uncovering, yet other times, after a difficult session with Sallie, which I then recorded in my journal, I felt too exhausted to go through it yet one more time with Don. Sometimes I pushed him away and asked him to leave me alone. The intimate parts of our life were now practically nonexistent.

"Don't shut me out, Jo," he told me, and I heard warning in his tone, yet also believed I was doing the best I could. When he embraced me in the night, I, shattered by the ongoing betrayals I uncovered, could not bear to let him close. I knew it was unfair and was hyperaware of his sadness about the cost he—and our whole family—was bearing for my childhood traumas, but it was a heartbreaking truth.

Sometimes—irrationally, I knew—I even wondered if I could trust Don, as I wrestled with a new question: Do all men betray? My father did. My uncle did. My first husband molested my sister. My husband might betray, too, although I had *no* reason whatsoever to feel this way. No, I was being crazy. Or was I?

Aside from insights I was gaining in therapy, I found others in unexpected places. When I read Elizabeth George's first novel, *A Great Deliverance*, my growing radar told me in the novel's early pages that there was incest in that family, long before the reveal. Each red flag chilled me: the father who married a six-teen-year-old girl, who took complete control of caring for his daughters, Gillian and Roberta, eight years later. The mother left soon after Roberta's birth, leaving him alone to raise the girls, whom he homeschooled, enforced rigid religious practices upon, and kept isolated on the farm.

I met myself in the teenage character Gillian, who was portrayed to the inspector in hugely varying ways, depending on the townsperson describing her: "She was wild, ungoverned. She was an angel, sunshine. She was a cat in heat. She was the loveliest creature I've ever seen. It was as if there were no real

Gillian at all, but only a kaleidoscope that, juggled before view-
ing, appeared different to each person who gazed into it."

When the father's horrific incest was revealed in the final
chapters, the inspector asked the psychiatrist how Gillian had
survived.

"It appears to have been . . . dissociation, a way of subdivid-
ing the self so that she could pretend to have or be those things
which she couldn't really have or be." He explained that when
a person dissociated as Gillian had, "she couldn't feel anything
her father did to her because she was not a real person." The
inspector noted that every villager described her as a different
person and the psychiatrist confirmed that as the exact behavior.

Thus, Gillian felt familiar to me as she adapted to become
whatever each person in her life needed or wanted her to be. I
examined a long thread back through my life: whether a parent,
relative, teacher, classmate, friend, librarian, school advisor,
employer, or whoever, I always figured out who that person
needed me to be and became her.

In rereading George's novel more than twenty years later,
I found what could be a partial clue about the why of my father's
and other abusers' behavior: Gillian's father pushed his wife
out of his bed after both daughters were born because he was
"threatened by women, I should guess, the feminine represen-
tation of the entire adult world that he feared," the psychiatrist
theorized to the inspector. In my situation, I can envision this
reasoning as believable, knowing my father's, uncle's, and
grandfather's attitude. I don't feel it's complete, because they
all had relationships with adult women, as well as children, but
I sense it may be a compass needle.

Chip had gotten a job on a nearby farm. One day I invited him
out for lunch and talked frankly about my early lack of good

parenting skills, my—until now—having raised my children predominantly as I had been raised, and my recently learned-about dissociative behavior. Chip said, "Mom, I know you did the best you could," and I easily saw he meant this from the bottom of his heart. While his words soothed my sorrowful soul and eased my guilt temporarily, they couldn't remove the profound grief of the two-edged sword I bore: that while I *had* done the best I could, I had wounded my own children.

The painful knowledge didn't stop there. Many years later, another powerful question rose for me: What harm and trauma happened to the adults in my childhood family to cause their aberrant behavior? The fact is, I have learned, that children often absorb the trauma their parents have experienced. How many generations had this been going on in my family?

I asked my mother about her childhood a few times. She recounted the adoring relationship my grandfather's mother had had with her, after mothering four sons. Mom also felt that her own mother and father were a bit distant but otherwise good parents.

Unfortunately, by the time I could have begun working on that question with my father's family, there was no one left who could have known. I wished that Aunt Madeline, sister to my father's father, had been alive when I'd developed the courage to have those difficult conversations. Aunt Madeline might have helped me uncover that history if she had experienced or observed it in her childhood family. Or she might have been a victim herself.

My daughter Susan was a year old when Aunt Madeline departed this world, more than ninety years old. To you, dear reader, and always with my life writing groups, I emphasize being vigilant in gathering your family's stories. When those relatives leave, they take their stories with them. Forever.

I'd begun to think about *my* dreams. While I'd supported Don's goals and wishes, I had never thought about what mine might be. How could I weigh in now, after half a century of life, to find the woman beneath my exterior identities of mother to three living and two deceased children, farm wife, employee, daughter, sister, cousin, neighbor, and more? I returned to Sam Keen's questions and pondered: *What do I have to offer the world? What are my gifts? What do I really want to do? What is important to me? Then, once I know these answers, how can I earn my living?*

I had no idea.

I began a voracious self-help reading program. My earliest reading focused on being the child of an alcoholic, long before the Matt Memory confirmed the sexual abuse I suspected. Janet Woititz's *Adult Children of Alcoholics*, Wayne Kritsberg's *The Adult Children of Alcoholics Syndrome*, and Judith Seixas and Geraldine Youcha's *Children of Alcoholism: A Survivor's Manual* each gave me so much valuable information about the syndrome, validation that I was not crazy, and the knowledge that there was a healing path through it all—in another word, hope. Another phase I focused on was relationship healing. Janet Woititz's *Struggle for Intimacy* and Emily Marlin's *Relationships in Recovery: Healing Strategies for Couples and Family* were my favorites. They gave me a step-by-step overview of and methods for traversing the difficult road to healing my and Don's relationship.

Peter A. Levine's ground-breaking book on his then quarter-century of work with PTSD, *Waking the Tiger: Healing Trauma*, was published in 1997, several years after my early flashbacks. I discovered it shortly thereafter and ever since held his book as the most meaningful of all that I read. A favorite passage that reassured me over and over during the years was, "If you are experiencing strange symptoms that no one seems to be able to explain, they could be arising from a traumatic reaction to a past event that you may not even remember. You are not alone. You are not crazy. There is a rational explanation for what is happening to you. You have not been irreversibly damaged, and it is possible to diminish or even eliminate your symptoms. In trauma we know that the mind becomes profoundly altered. For example, a person involved in an auto wreck is protected initially from emotional reaction and even from a clear memory or sense that it really happened. These remarkable mechanisms ([i.e.], dissociation and denial) allow us to navigate through those critical periods, hopefully waiting for a safe time and place for these altered states to 'wear off.'" In time these words taught me to fully trust my body.

And during times of feeling overwhelmed, these wise words re-grounded me to my healing goals many times: "While trauma can be hell on earth, trauma resolved is a gift of the gods—a heroic journey that belongs to each of us."

I treasured Alice Miller's research and writings about the causes and effects of childhood trauma: *The Truth Will Set You Free: Overcoming Emotional Blindness and Finding Your True Adult Self*; *The Drama of the Gifted Child*; *Banished Knowledge*; *Breaking Down the Wall of Silence*; *Thou Shalt Not Be Aware*; and *For Your Own Good*. When I knew for certain I'd been sexually assaulted, after E. Sue Blume's book, I purchased Beverly Engel's *The Right to Innocence: Healing the Trauma of Childhood Sexual Abuse*, a seven-step self-help program. Later, I read Janet Woititz again, this time her *Healing Your Sexual Self*—a little book for survivors and their loved ones—packed with helpful information about resulting behavior, dysfunctional family systems, perpetrators, enablers, ways to cope, the impact of abuse, how to work with the powerful emotional stages, post-traumatic stress disorder, and much more. Wendy Maltz's *The Sexual Healing Journey* is also a well-worn book on my shelf. In *Reach for the Rainbow: Advanced Healing for Survivors of Sexual Abuse*, by Lynne Finney, herself a survivor and therapist, I bookmarked the section she devoted to my traumatizing fear that someone would find out I had been sexually abused, a terror and shame I lived with for decades, until I finally decided I would write my full story, with the hope it would find others who have had or know someone who has had a similar experience.

I decided to start out by nurturing myself at least as well as I'd tried to nurture everyone else in my life, a step Marlin wrote about eloquently in discussing what she called the Pioneer Stage. Initially, that felt incredibly selfish, yet I was learning that until I cared well for myself, I could not care well for others. *So how do I find my self?* I wondered. *Perhaps by listening to my heart pleadings?* Marlin encouraged me to start having some fun, begin to respect myself after years of self-denial, and seek some change, and she provided concrete ways to do that. I needed her suggestions, for I had no idea how to care for myself and hadn't known I should even be doing that.

By midsummer 1993, Marlin had nudged me to listen to myself better. I again yearned for solitude, time away from family, friends, and work, for two weeks—to me an unthinkable concept. I talked with my family, and, while they were uneasy, Don and the children once again agreed. I scheduled two weeks of vacation and accepted my friend Deni's offer to stay at her Goodyear Lake camp when she and her family drove home to Virginia after Labor Day. She and Tom asked that, at the end of my stay, Don and I winterize and close up the camp. We had a deal.

I pinched myself as I prepared for the precious time I felt so starved for. On September 11, 1992, I packed my Chevy station wagon with basic groceries and drove forty miles to the camp. Simplicity was my primary goal, along with freedom to follow my heart's desires: reading, sitting by the water, outlining a young adult novel I wanted to write, and enjoying the exceptional experience unlike any I'd ever had.

I wrote my first journal note four days later: "On Saturday (the day I arrived) and Sunday I did anything I wanted, primarily read. Then yesterday morning I got up (when I woke up, no alarm clock!) and prepared to work on my book. I worked nearly all day on the outline and then filled in ideas. I'm pleased with my progress. This morning I did some more work—it's beginning to come alive, and I'm excited."

Later that day, I noted, "After outlining chapter 1, I knew I needed to put the writing away and prepare for my session with Sallie. Fear arrived. I decided to talk on paper to my fear: "Tell me what you are afraid of today. Go ahead and feel your fear. . . . It's okay, you are safe here at the camp. . . ."

As I self-hypnotized and let the words flow onto the paper, my fear and stress increased, my handwriting grew larger, until, at the height of the memory unfolding through my pencil onto paper, my normally small letters were an inch high, four to five words on a line. I wrote disjointedly about my father, often in deep conflict with that inner voice who knew truths that I didn't want to face right then. But that little girl inside was ready and kept pushing. Finally, I yelled, "No," threw the pencil down, and slammed my journal shut. I began walking in circles around the fireplace room, scuffing one foot after the other, the way I did at home sometimes when I felt very, very old. Then I wrote, "I feel in shock. I'm going outside, away from this dark place in my notebook."

Walking beneath the late-afternoon sun, breathing deeply to center myself, I thought, *I'll just close the book and go through this flashback with Sallie.* The memory surfaced easily the following day with her, exceptionally filled with terror and rage, loathing and disgust, as I remembered my father forcing me to hold his erect penis, then my gagging a few minutes later.

I stared limply at Sallie afterward, again encapsulated in that deep shock I'd had following the Matt Memory. That day I named the Claw Memory, returned to my solitude at the camp, and wrote I felt "shocky and sick to my stomach." On subsequent days I noted that I had felt "dizzy, light-headed, and somewhat nauseous ever since my September 17 appointment."

At home a few weeks later, I'd note that the memory "must relate to the night I read the *Newsweek* article, the night my hand formed into a claw."

After the Claw Memory resurfaced, unknown triggers caused my hand to frequently become a claw in the weeks ahead. Sallie administered a newly developed, nonverbal treatment technique, eye movement desensitizing and reprocessing (EMDR), which would, after three or four sessions, blessedly end my body's claw response. EMDR proved to be a highly effective treatment for post-traumatic stress disorder, a second diagnosis I was given at the onset of my flashbacks.

I was determined not to let this horrific memory steal what I'd sought in coming to the camp. I used the remainder of my days preparing good food, walking, writing, resting, enjoying the lake from shore, and treasuring each day of sunshine warming my body.

All too soon, on my last day I noted, "I'm letting go, with regret, for this solitude has meant so much to me. It has been time to be free, to be close to the water, to live simply but well, to take excellent care of myself, but, most of all, time to feel and to be."

Don and the girls arrived, and we winterized the camp in half an hour. We walked down the long steps to the lake and enjoyed a little time together by the water, and then it was time to go. I left with a renewed commitment to my husband and children in my heart, as well as to that little girl within.

About halfway home, I said something to Don—I didn't record what—and he didn't answer. I waited and mentioned something else a little while later, and when he remained silent a second time, I knew he was annoyed about something, though I had no idea what and knew he wouldn't tell me. I decided I wouldn't plead repeatedly with him to tell me what I'd done to offend him until we started fighting, as I usually did. I simply became quiet and let it go.

Chapter 26: STORM AT SEA

Bovina Center, New York, 1993–94

I drove to Sallie's one afternoon without an appointment, accompanied by my now-familiar sidekicks, acute fear and agitation. I knew a memory was building to tidal wave proportions. "Do you have any time for me today? I'm on the cusp of another memory and am close to crazy with anxiety. Mary Jo," I wrote on the small note I taped to her door. Returning later, I found her reply: she had a 2:00 p.m. cancellation.

During the next hour, a ghastly memory of my grandfather—Dad and Matt's father—emerged. Despite all the years that have passed, as I write my previous sentence, my hand rises to cover my mouth. Always my first instinct is to keep the secret, too terrible to tell. I force my hand back to the keyboard.

My grandfather took me for a ride when we visited him and Aunt Mary in the Bronx, probably at Thanksgiving. Snow was on the ground. I was about seven, wearing a dress and coat and high white socks with my patent leather Mary Jane shoes. Powerful body memories emerged as I described to Sallie clear fragments of him hitting and yelling at me because I cried and struggled to get away as he painfully molested me.

Stunned and sickened as I was by a third family abuser, I was not completely shocked that he had done that. While I had always liked my mother's father, I'd never liked the short, round, hard-eyed man who was my father's father, and that day I suddenly understood why. When I drove home after my appointment, my thoughts were so deep into a new, horrific question that I slid off the road near the top of Meredith Mountain. The ditch propelled me back onto the road and into a ninety-degree spin and, miraculously, back into my lane. Instantly, I was wrenched back to the present, trembling from the near-disaster, as well as from my new question: Did my mother marry into a family of pedophiles? But I slammed that book of thought shut and focused on getting home safely.

Shortly after my birthday in 1993, the pain, the unresolved problems, and anger simmering beneath the surface of our family's life for far too long was about to explode like the recent car bomb in the World Trade Center's underground parking garage, which shook that institution with the force of an earthquake.

Father's Day 1993 dawned on a warm, quiet morning. Don and I rose early. He dressed, thumped down the stairs, clicked open the door to the basement, *thunked* the door closed behind him, and walked to the barn. I descended quietly to the peaceful kitchen, smiling as I prepared a fragrant cup of Red

Rose tea. I planned to create a special meal to honor Don and his father and began by stirring yeast into a little warm water for my onion bread.

Polly and Susan soon trotted downstairs, dressed in barn clothes, and headed out to feed calves. "Tell Daddy Happy Father's Day," I reminded them.

"We will," they replied.

By 1:00 p.m., the kitchen was filled with a fragrant mixture of onion bread, hearty pot roast and gravy, orange sauce for the carrots, and blackberry pie. Don and his dad sat at the big oval table, talking about a sick cow, as I prepared to mash the potatoes. Then Don said to Sue something that caused her to get angry with him. Though I didn't record in my journal what it was, I know their anger erupted like an unexpected thunderbolt.

"Hey." I moved between them and said quietly, "Can we talk this over later, so we can enjoy a nice meal together now?"

They ignored me and kept arguing . . . and then Don hit Sue. I was momentarily stunned, for he had rarely hit the children in all our years together. Time paused, life stopped, and then Sue stomped up to her room, crying and furious. I followed her to be sure she wasn't physically hurt. "I'm not hurt," she told me. "I just want to be alone." I returned downstairs, wondering if there was any way to salvage our day, but, of course, it was ruined for everyone.

Wordlessly, I put food on the table. A heavy cloud of unease hung over us as we ate in silence. The food was tasteless to me. The conversation did not go beyond "please pass the gravy." The little food I ate landed like lead in my belly. Don's father drove home right after he finished eating. Polly helped me clear the table. I loaded the dishwasher. Don went into the living room to read the paper, silent and uncommunicative. This would, I realized with devastation, never be talked about.

I climbed to Susan's room every few hours. She lay on her belly, facing the wall, and when I spoke, my fourteen-year-old told me, in a pained, muffled voice, "I don't want to talk, Mom. Please leave me alone."

I put my hand on her shoulder and said, "Okay, just know I'm here, Sue."

Although I'd sometimes spanked my boys—as a young mother repeating how I had been disciplined in my youth—I now hated hitting and believed it taught that violence was a solution to anger. What happened earlier, I knew, was a detonation of the growing anger and frustration that had become a full-time resident in our home. We couldn't go on this way. I knew about the cycle of violence and that unless something changed, this would happen again. And again.

Suddenly, rage about the childhood baggage I had unknowingly brought with me into the home I'd created with my husband and children shot through my veins with a *whoosh*. My past had stolen, and continued to steal, so much from my family every day of our lives. *What more*, I wondered, *can I do to erase it? I just want it gone.*

My hopes for my adult life had been simple and uncomplicated: to nurture my children into happy, educated, contributing adults; to be a good partner in a healthy marriage; to have an interesting and contributing career; to be an active part of the little community that I loved.

But I didn't have time to sit and ponder any further that night. The next day was Polly's sixteenth birthday, and I was having a party for her and several friends. I strode out to the kitchen to make her cake.

Later, after Polly and Don went upstairs and as the day closed, I went one last time to Sue's room. "I want to say good night, Sue," I said.

She replied sadly, "Good night, Mom."

"I love you." I kissed the back of her head, rubbed her back, and left her room. She was silent.

The next morning, I woke Polly with a hug and sang "Happy Birthday" to her. She grinned and said gleefully, "Thanks, Mom."

When I went to Sue's room, I gave her a back hug and said, "Time to get up, Sue. You okay this morning?" She nodded, and I trotted downstairs to prepare breakfast. Polly soon came down, and when Susan didn't, I returned to her room. She lay on her back beneath the pink, blue, lavender, and white patchwork quilt she and I had created together a year earlier. "Sue, aren't you coming down for breakfast?" I said, sitting down on her bed.

She turned her head toward me and mumbled, "Mom, I've done something really bad."

Fear flooded my body. I whispered, "What have you done, Sue?"

"Before I went to sleep last night, I swallowed a whole bottle of Tylenols."

My world spun uncontrollably as I tried to process her words. Then my emotions shut down and in slow motion I thought, *Oh God, what do I do?*

"How many tablets were in the bottle?" I asked, praying it had been nearly empty.

"I don't know," she replied in a dull voice. "A lot, I think."

"How do you feel right now?"

"I'm sleepy," she said, "and my stomach hurts."

I kicked into action. "Okay, Sue, we've got to get to the ER right away. Can you get some clothes on?"

She inhaled deeply. "I think so."

"Good. I'm going to tell your dad and Polly what's happening." I started to leave, and when I reached the door, Sue said softly, "I'm sorry, Mom. Now I wish I hadn't done it."

Me too, I anguished. My brain raced: we had a thirty-minute drive to the Walton hospital. We would drive because that would be quicker than the volunteer ambulance crew could get to us and then to the ER. I alerted the hospital that we were coming. When we arrived, two nurses were standing outside the ER entrance with a gurney. I was so terrified Sue would die, I dissociated. If I'd been in a courtroom at that moment, a reporter would have said, "The defendant showed no emotion."

The nurses slid Sue on the gurney, wheeled her inside to a curtained cubicle, and took her vitals. She was conscious. *Thank God—that has to be good, right?* Someone came in with a page of questions for Don and me. I answered everything with meticulous honesty, inwardly dying from shame and the belief that I was an utter failure as a parent.

A blur of events unfolded around us. Tylenol, we were told, could cause severe liver damage. They were assessing that now. The doctor was mandated to contact Social Services whenever a child attempted suicide. *Yes, of course. Sue must be protected from her bad parents.* I remembered working for Social Services in child welfare and investigating abuse allegations, never dreaming I would one day be a person investigated. A caseworker arrived and talked with us a long time. A nurse came in to ask a question. The doctor returned.

What will happen to us now? I despaired. Our troubled family's problems had ruptured beyond our walls. Other people were making decisions about our lives now, outside our control. That was beyond terrifying, yet, ironically, very soon tiny, growing waves of relief would replace my terror as helping hands reached out to our family in many healing ways.

Polly had stayed home, and we had talked through the morning. She still wanted to have her birthday party that afternoon. Don said he'd stay with Sue. I didn't check with Sue to be sure she was okay with that plan; I simply believed it would be. I hugged her and drove home to greet our guests for Polly's sweet-sixteen party, subdued but praying these lovely girls wouldn't notice. *Oh, Polly, I'm so sorry this all broke wide open on your special day.*

The following day we learned, with tremendous relief, that Sue would recover physically. She had also been referred to the Benjamin Rush Center in Syracuse, a private facility known as the finest in our area, and which took our health insurance.

During the strained days that followed Polly's birthday, I experienced new, bizarre symptoms at home: I was highly agitated and unable to be still. If I sat down, I rose quickly and paced. *Do I need to be in perpetual motion in order to feel some control over my life?* I wondered. I called Sallie and whispered that another of my children had almost died, describing Sue's attempted suicide.

"Sallie, I'm coming unglued." I described my inability to be still or to sleep. "I can't believe I'm saying this, but I keep thinking I need to admit myself to the psych unit at Bassett Hospital. What do you think?"

Following a lengthy conversation, Sallie agreed to start my admission process. Much later, I realized I was no longer functioning as I had just a few days before: it didn't occur to me, for example, to wonder if Sue was uncomfortable with being alone with Don at the hospital without me, nor did I consider the need to make arrangements for someone to be with Polly, who looked shell-shocked whenever I saw her. She would be alone with Don while Sue and I were hospitalized. Don had retreated even deeper within himself, yet I trusted he would not hurt her. Nor could he give her the emotional support she needed, I knew, but, fortunately, my mother and sister Bonnie came to stay with Polly, opening a new chapter in their long-distance relationship, which strengthened in a way that endures to the present.

When Sue was discharged from Walton Hospital two days

later, Don drove her to the Benjamin Rush Center. As they traveled to Syracuse, I drove myself to Cooperstown to self-admit at Bassett Hospital. I was soon checked in and taken upstairs, chilled to hear the lock click behind me after I stepped into the ward, knowing I had no key. I shivered and wondered what waited here for me—for us all.

A nurse handed me over to another nurse at the station, who welcomed me and said, "Let me show you to your room. It's a double, but the other bed is empty right now."

"That's nice," I said, glad to be alone. We walked down two doors from the station and into a pale green, medium-size room with two freshly sheeted beds. I chose the one by the window, where, after I unpacked and put my clothes into small drawers, I sat and stared out until my dinner tray arrived. I picked at my food. After I took my tray to the cart in the hallway, I walked to the social room, where several men and women watched television, played solitaire or other games, read, or sat, doing nothing. I felt as numb and shocky as I had after the Matt Memory, and as out of place as if I had entered a third-world country where I didn't know the culture or the language. A few people acknowledged me by looking or smiling at me; I smiled wanly or said hello to those who looked at me, then returned to my room. In a while, I decided to write my first journal note:

I am in the psych unit at Bassett Hospital. Susan overdosed on Sunday. I feel dead and want to sit here and stare out the window forever.

I called Sallie yesterday morning because something was so wrong: I couldn't be still; I had to keep moving; I couldn't feel. I wanted to run away again, go away alone and it suddenly seemed that a hospital was the right thing to ask for. I was crying like a child when I asked her if that was the right thing. And here I am. Now I'm officially mentally ill. Not crazy, but not in good shape, either.

Later, a nurse brought my evening medications. I tipped the thimble-size paper cup holding three small pills into my mouth, then drank the lukewarm water she handed me. "I couldn't wait for the little white Ativan to swim into my blood-stream and achieve its mission: oblivion," I wrote.

The next morning, I awoke disoriented, until I remembered the previous day's drive. A bevy of thoughts swirled in my mind. Never had I envisioned myself in a psych ward at age fifty-one, lying on a narrow white bed, unable to gather an ounce of energy simply to sit up. I reflected: I was a program director for a local nonprofit organization, I'd earlier been a church elder, a church-school teacher, a playschool mother, the elected town clerk for several years, and clerk for our Planning Board. When my children were small, I operated a quality day care program in my home. *How did all that hard work and commitment bring me here?* I shook my head, disbelieving.

Then the food cart's slow, low rumble approached. Breakfast. The short, stocky aide brought my tray, her cheery "Hi, how are we doing this morning?" causing me to smile vaguely at her as I forced myself to sit up. I dimly wondered why no tempting coffee aroma arrived with her, then looked at my tray and realized each plate and beverage container was tightly sealed. Like I was shut away from the rest of the world now, like that tablespoon of Smucker's strawberry jam entombed in the tiny plastic container on my breakfast tray. And that was exactly where I wanted to be.

I ate little and soon slid into a fog, recalling a recent dream I'd had just before coming to the hospital:

I was alone in my farmhouse kitchen, washing dishes at the sink, head down. Suddenly, a spark of bright light caught my eye and I saw a fire blazing around the edges of the chimney damper. I grabbed an empty milk bottle, filled it quickly with water, and ran to the old woodstove. When I pulled open the damper and dumped the water in, the fire quickly died.

I returned to the sink, exhaling a huge sigh of relief. That was a close call.

I scrubbed some pots, until another flash captured my glance. Another fire! Terror clutched my belly as I repeated my previous actions and again put out the fire. But within minutes there was another fire, then another, and another. They were endless, until I woke up, trembling.

I'd always feared a fire in the old farmhouse, knowing it would burn to the ground in mere minutes. But I also knew from a place within, where my deepest truths resided, that the fires in my dream were merely symbols of other fires I'd been putting out for years.

My days fell into a routine of regular meals, group therapy, craft activities, meeting with my psychiatrist, free time for socialization or isolation, and talking daily with my primary psych nurse. His name was Bill, a medium-height, slender, soft-spoken man whom I liked, which was good because men were not my favorite people then.

I journaled daily about my conversations with my team, my feelings, and my insights. The gray Formica counter in my hospital room held my neatly closed black binder with my pencil precisely parallel to it.

Do I really belong here? I asked Bill. Gently, he said yes. My supervisor from work called, misses me, do I have a sense of time when I'll be back, I don't know, now I feel pressure, stress, and guilt. . . . The minister told me that despite what has happened, I have worked very hard to raise Susan as well as I'm able. I need to keep that focus! Bonnie, Mom, and Don visit. Bonnie tells me my house is filled with angry people . . . it's everybody's fault and

nobody's fault . . . Susan doesn't want to come home . . .
Polly is angry but doesn't want to talk about her feelings
. . . Bonnie wants to take the girls home but also feels we
must work things out as a family. I used to take care of
everything. Now I've stopped and it's all fallen apart. My
nurse Stephanie tells me things can get real rocky before
they get better. I have an anxiety attack. Sallie calls. Tell
Bill. I do some anger work with him. He says I have huge
anger; it can take years to get rid of that anger, he says,
adding that as long as I'm angry with my parents and
can't forgive them, then I can't forgive myself. . . . I hold
a pillow as if it's a baby. Is this Jocelyn? Or Keith? It's not
Susan because she wants to die, too. I'm afraid to love her
anymore. My psychiatrist tells me I'm not taking actions
to show Susan I love her. What is that block? If the staff
can't see my emotions, how can Susan? I put a big arrow
by her next words: Not showing emotion will lead to dis-
tance, then more and more separation.

I wrote: "Dear Susan, I have loved you so much. I'm
trying to understand why I'm not reaching out to you. If
you had died in a car accident, I'd be devastated. But to
attempt suicide was to throw back at me all I've tried to
give you over the years. That act shattered my heart—the
ultimate refusal, the ultimate rejection. Giving you your
life was a profound gift I was thrilled to give. The love I
gave you was not perfect, I know, but you know I loved
you. Yet how can I love you when I cannot love myself?"

I do not mail the letter I wrote to Susan, but now
I can see the problem more clearly and what I need to do.
I talk with Bill about it. We plan for me to call Sue. She
agrees. We talk about where she is, what she's doing, is she
okay, essentially a good conversation, nothing deep. It's
time to say goodbye. I want to say I love you but find my
throat closing over the words. I'm terrified to say I love

you but force myself to. I'll call back in a few days, I tell
her. Okay, she says. I think she means it.

My journal steadily fills with a kaleidoscope of thoughts
and feelings and flashbacks that show me the inner workings of
my confused mind. I am falling apart, just like my family.

Next to my black notebook lay a small, carefully folded
patchwork tablecloth. During evenings at the farm, I'd begun
piecing brown calico and muslin scraps into a wild goose chase
pattern, aka flying geese. I'd thought I would quilt it at the hospital, but the fabric remained untouched on the counter, where,
instead, I felt as if I were on a wild goose chase as I wrote page
after page about my hospital days in my notebook. I had other
notebooks, too, in particular a mauve one concealed at the farm
where no one could find it. I had kept these secrets for years,
which was probably one reason I was in this hospital. But here
kind nurses were with me during flashbacks in the night and
reassured me that I was safe, that I had to deal with terrifying
events when I was small, but no more.

During the six weeks I lived on the ward, the circle of people
who expressed kindness and support for me, both in and outside
the hospital, helped me slowly, like a turtle, gain a little more
understanding, a little more strength, a little more about how to
cope, and a little more hope and trust that things would work out.

A few days before I was discharged, as I wrote some pages
after dinner, a sudden thought jolted me: *I need to write a book*
about all this.

When I graduated from college, I wanted to write a book one
day. I thought it would be a mystery, a genre I'd always loved.
But there, on the psych ward, I began to write an outline of
what took me to the hospital and it quickly became crystal clear

that my hospitalization and all that led to it was the story I needed—indeed, had—to write. In many ways, it *was* a mystery—my story—for, during recent years, I had solved puzzles that had curiously shrouded my life for decades.

Recently the Unabomber had set off a bomb at nearby Yale University, profoundly injuring a science professor, and I wondered if the victim would heal from his awful wounds. Similarly, the recent explosion within our family caused me to wonder if we could heal. I believed I could never reenter the painful world on the other side of my window.

Yet, in fact, I would leave that hospital in six weeks and return to my family—with encouragement from my psychiatrist, the hospital staff, and other patients whose journeys had intersected with mine. They said I was "strong" and would "make it out there," hopeful words that I prayed were true.

Sue and I were hospitalized for about the same amount of time. Once the difficult first phone call was behind us, she and I talked a few times each week, conversations that were light and newsy. She'd formed a new friendship with a girl who lived north of us in Watertown; they hoped they could visit when they both returned home. I said we'd try. Her best friend, Lisa, had called her. She was glad to hear from her and her parents. I was pleased; they were good friends to Sue. Yet an invisible wall prevented me from asking the questions that were so important but that I couldn't allow into my mind yet: Why did you try to take your life, Sue? Will you ever do that again? Can we work out a system for you to let me know if you ever feel so desperate again? My terror about her near-death overtook all my other emotions for her and left me paralyzed to talk about it.

I returned home shortly before her discharge; then Don and I went to the Benjamin Rush Center for family meetings with her doctor. These were positive; there, I found the courage to tell her doctor my borderline-phobic fear about Sue's return home. Would she try to take her life if she got upset again? If she did, would she succeed this time? Her doctor reassured us Sue had well learned some very good coping skills, and his words bolstered me.

We entered family therapy with Sallie when Sue came home, and began to work on the unspoken anger that had so long permeated our home. Taking baby steps, I set healthier boundaries with the girls. One night, for example, they returned from the barn fighting. I don't remember which girl grabbed the other, but I hollered, "No hitting!" The aggressor dropped her hand and looked angrily at me, causing me to remember words my mother had said to me when I was my daughters' ages, furious and looking at my mother similarly: "If looks could kill me, I'd be dead."

"Sorry," I said to my daughters, "it's a new rule." I found they accepted my new boundaries in time because I was also becoming more consistent. A few weeks later, Polly and Sue returned from the barn, again angry about something. "Remember, no hitting!" one yelled at the other. I couldn't help it. I burst out laughing. When they heard me and stared at me, the argument ended. But they were expressing their anger, and that was positive.

I learned how terrified of anger I was—a fear I'd acquired in childhood. I saw my role in our anger problems more clearly and struggled to let people express anger within boundaries and to share my own in more respectful ways. After several sessions, the girls wanted to discontinue therapy and we all agreed to put it on hold for a while. And so, as our lives continued on in some new ways—such as healthier expressions of anger, and many old ways, such as my exhaustion and unavailability for Polly and Sue at the end of the day—I could not shake a gnawing feeling that we were simply in a holding pattern, that the metaphorical next fire in the chimney would return, that it would be bigger and more powerful, and that this time I wouldn't be able to put it out.

On our twentieth anniversary, June 29, 1993, Don and I went out for dinner, a rare event. We engaged in small talk as we ate our well-prepared food at the Hobart Inn in the next town down the mountain. As we finished our chocolate cream pie, I gazed at Don, noting his attention was elsewhere and wondered what he was thinking. As I looked at him, an unacknowledged truth burst into my mind: *I don't even know this man anymore. He's become a complete stranger.*

"We" didn't exist any longer, I realized, and gazed away sorrowfully. *What happened to us? Where did those two happy young people go?* I'd known our recent years might take a heavy toll on us and that my therapeutic work, depression, and PTSD might harm us. Yet I was not prepared for the moment of truth that arrived that night. These recent years *had* driven the final, fatal wedge between us. I could no longer hide behind my illusion that if I just worked a little harder, things would get better. Sadly, I tucked that knowledge away for a little while longer.

Months later, several inches of snow blanketed the ground when my phone rang at work. "Mrs. Doig, this is Shelley, a nurse at the Delhi emergency room."

Terror clamped my heart. "Oh, God, is something wrong with Sue?"

"No, we have your husband here." He'd been thrown by a horse his cousin boarded at our farm. "Can you please come?"

Diagnosed with a punctured lung and bruised ribs, Don was transferred to Bassett Hospital in Cooperstown. I followed the ambulance for the fifty-mile trip. When the hospital staff completed their exams and assessments, then admitted Don, I drove home, arriving about 2:00 a.m. It was already the next day and I needed to go to work, but there was no one to care for our dairy. I called Chip, living in nearby Delhi; miraculously, he could come and help me.

After four hours of sleep, I rose to a frigid house. When I pushed up the thermostat, it didn't click on. I hurried to the basement. The oil tank was empty. Okay, I'd start the wood furnace but found no wood indoors or outdoors. I called the oil company and asked for a delivery. They would come if I'd give them a check for the past-due balance and the present delivery. I agreed, discomfited because this was a bill Don paid.

The following day when I came home from work, I found a disconnection notice from the electric company and an overdue notice for my auto insurance in the mailbox. I was so stunned by the breadth of Don's problems with his share of our bills that something inside me snapped. *No! This is not the way I want to live. This is not who I am. I will not exist on the edge anymore.* My moment of astonishing clarity had arrived in the mailbox.

Months later, Don told me that when I visited him that evening at the hospital, he saw in my eyes that things were over between us, though he didn't yet know why. He was right. I had decided to say nothing until he was home and healed again. So much for trying to delay truth.

One morning as I prepared for work, Polly asked, "Can Sue and I eat the leftover cheesecake for breakfast?" I hesitated, then, to their delight, agreed. Later, driving to work, I was intrigued by the idea of creating a nutritionally sound breakfast food resembling cheesecake. I'd also been wanting to create some new, happy memories in a family quite short of them recently. Polly,

Sue, and I made several variations over the next several days, until we agreed on one.

Not long afterward, our area *Daily Star* newspaper's annual cooking contest sought entries. I decided to enter the breakfast cheesecake recipe. Happily, it qualified for the cook-off. The girls and I drove to Oneonta together, bringing with us four chilled earthenware bowls of cheesecake for the judges to sample, since it tasted best when chilled. As they lifted the bowls from the car, three fell to the ground and shattered. Tears filled their eyes as I reached into the car, where the fourth bowl had remained intact. "Don't worry, my daughters. One bowl will be enough—and besides, you are more precious than any bowl of breakfast cheesecake." They wiped their tears away.

At the end of the day, back home, I was called by a contest judge, who told me the recipe had placed third. Our prize was a lovely Noritake china service for eight, yet, best of all, the event transformed into a wonderful memory.

Chapter 27: BUTTERFLY

Delhi, New York, 1994–95

As Sallie and I continued to work together, she suggested Don and I see another therapist to work on improving our relationship. He agreed easily. Toward the end of our first session with Justine, she gave Don an assignment: to initiate a date with me before our time next week. *Wow*, I thought, a *date*. Rarely did we go anywhere, and never did we call it a date. I smiled as he drove us home, feeling good about the idea and wondering what we might do.

Since Justine had given the asking assignment to Don, I said no more. One day, then another, then a third and a fourth, and then the entire week passed. As we drove to Justine's for the next appointment, we barely talked. When we seated ourselves in Justine's office, she smiled at us and said, "How did your week go?"

Don was silent, so I said quiescently, "We didn't have a date." I felt my cheeks start to burn, ashamed that we'd failed her first assignment.

Justine looked from one to the other of us with knitted brows. "Why not?"

Don didn't hesitate. "I was so mad at her, I didn't want to ask her for a date."

Justine asked, "What were you angry about, Don?"

"I heard Jo and Polly talking about the Bobbitt family. I'm sick of the women in my house being so negative about men," he said. (The John and Lorena Bobbitt story had made worldwide headlines that week, in late 1993: John came home one evening, and Lorena claimed he raped her. After he fell asleep, his wife got up and went to the kitchen for a knife, then reentered their bedroom. As John slept, she cut off his penis at its base, took it with her when she left the house for a drive, and flung it out the car window into a field. It was subsequently reattached successfully.)

I couldn't believe what I'd just heard Don say. *What is he talking about? I always know when he's angry with me, don't I? I've had no sense of his being angry.*

I can only hypothesize about what Polly and I had said about the Bobbitts, because, instead of noting that conversation, I wrote in my journal that Don had sat with Polly and me that night and that we'd talked about an hour and I thought it was a really positive time.

Whatever the reason, Don decided not to do the assignment.

"I understand that you're tired of my all-too-often-negative attitude about men," I told him in our counseling session, "but what is so creepy is that you got angry and I didn't even know it because you didn't tell me."

"Why didn't you tell Mary Jo how you felt?" Justine asked.

"It wouldn't have changed her mind," he said.

In my journal that evening, I wrote, "Yes, I understand now why it happened. Don feels powerless to change things.

He's given up. And I'm so overwhelmed. I see black undercurrents that run beneath our relationship that can sabotage us at any moment. It feels so crazy-creepy-crawly to me because they are as covert as what happened in my childhood home."

Justine gave us another assignment for the following week: for Don to initiate a conversation about one responsibility we could share, then listen to my thoughts, and then for us to let her know what we'd decided to do. The following week, as we left for our next appointment, Don asked, "Do you remember what our assignment was?"

Instant fury gripped me. "You just don't care, do you? You wait until the last minute, and then you forget, for God's sake! This is why I feel like I'm at the bottom of your priorities." This was another failure—an F for therapy homework!

At Justine's, I said I didn't think I could live this way much longer. We couldn't put together a simple date the previous week, and this week was even worse. Don remained quiet for the rest of the session and the ride home.

I made an appointment with Sallie for just myself the following week. By late summer, I knew I couldn't continue in our marriage. I believed the kindest way to open this conversation with Don was to propose a trial separation in Sallie's presence, to help make the discussion as positive as it could be. Sallie pushed me to closely examine this idea. Was it really the right solution? I heard her well, yet, in the end, I listened to my heart.

A week later, Don and I returned for another session together with Sallie. "Don, I want to propose we try a six-month trial separation," I said gently. "It would give us time and space to figure out if we can stay together."

He replied, without hesitation or surprise, "I think that's a good idea."

Again, although I appreciated his agreement, I was stunned. "I feel like you've thought about this yourself," I said, my head tilted.

"I have, but I would never have been the one to say it."

I wanted to roll my eyes.

We planned a family appointment the following week with Sallie and Justine to share our decision with our daughters. When I gently told Polly and Sue about the trial separation, they were speechless—until their anger spilled out. They refused to live with me; they both would stay on the farm with Don.

I moved to a small two-bedroom apartment in the next town. Mom and Bonnie kept in close touch with the girls. Within a month, they all agreed the arrangement for the girls and Don was not sustainable. Bonnie arranged private boarding placements for each girl, Polly with one of her teachers and Sue with an aide at her school. Our family was now in fragments.

I trudged from the old farmhouse down the long slope to the stone wall steps, my arms embracing the final cardboard box. Light drizzle misted my bifocals, causing me to gaze at a blurred world. I placed each foot carefully so I would not slip on the wet brown leaves beneath my worn sneakers.

During that final trip down the hill, I reflected that when Don and I had said our vows more than two decades earlier, we hadn't known that *until death do us part* might also include the death of the relationship. When I reached the stone wall, I stepped down three broad stones placed more than a century ago by Scots settlers and thumped my heavy box onto the wall. I walked to the dusty station wagon parked at the faded red carriage house that housed now-rusty milk cans and other memorabilia from another farm era. As I grasped the handle that opened the car's storage area, a loud, imploring *meow* startled me. Staring up at me was Harriet, a barn cat.

I felt sudden compassion for the large, long-haired Maine coon cat, who had arrived in our barn a few years before and had never left. Her bushy tail had become a briar patch, and her dark-furred body was a tangle of burrs and knots. I wiped moisture from my glasses with a tissue as I realized this cat looked like I felt.

The question spilled from my mouth before it formed in my mind: "Do you want to come with me, Harriet?" I reached down to scratch her head, but she backed away from my hand. When I walked to the rear of the car and shoved the box into the last open space, Harriet—who had never in her life been in a car, to the best of my knowledge—jumped in, meowing loudly. She hopped over into the backseat and began pacing back and forth, as I had done in my kitchen before my hospital admission.

"Okay, little girl," I said, sliding into the driver's seat and looking at her, "we'll take this trip together." She stared into my eyes. I slammed the door shut and turned the ignition key. As I drove down the country road, away from my life of twenty-plus years, I talked softly to her, aware that my car was filling with a pungent stench that blended fine inside the sagging barn behind us but would be offensive in the small apartment ten miles ahead. My landlord had made no mention of pet rules. I decided not to inquire.

I thought of the thick carpeting in the apartment. "Harriet, the first thing I have to do is give you a bath when we get to our new home." I glanced over at her wide, lime-green eyes, knowing how much she'd hate it. Perhaps it was best that she didn't know what lay ahead. The farm had been her only home for so long.

We arrived, and I carried her inside, directly to the large kitchen sink. The prospect of bathing her and brushing the thick knots from her long fur was daunting, yet it had to be done. In two inches of tepid water, she struggled through that bath with me, detesting every second. When I applied shampoo, she squirmed desperately to escape. My hold was firm, my words soft and reassuring. After a thorough rinse, I attempted to brush her hopelessly tangled fur and knew right away that scissors were the only solution. Before she reached the end of her endurance, I'd cut away a dozen matted, walnut-size clumps. Then I enveloped her in a clean brown towel and held her close, inhaling her fragrant scent, and murmured, "Okay, little girl. It's over."

I felt her desperation to be free, so I placed the toweled bundle onto the floor and loosened my hold. She leaped from the towel, fur clumped wildly by dampness, and disappeared into an unknown hiding place in the apartment. I didn't see her again for three days.

Our first trip to the vet revealed that she was pregnant. "Just one kitten," the vet told me, adding, "That's very unusual." I smiled and noted that the bald places in Harriet's fur were beginning to fill in with new growth. A healthy sheen was starting to show on her coat. I looked at her and thought, *Harriet, the courage you gathered to leave behind everything familiar and journey to an unknown place is beginning to show good results.* I wondered what she would say to me about it all if, for just a few moments, she and I could talk.

Our days slipped by, until the middle of the night before one of the most difficult Mother's Days of my life. Something woke me, and, passing slowly through fuzzy layers of confusion, I realized Harriet was curled in the circle of my extended arm. *That's odd*, I mused hazily. *She's never slept this close to my head. She's always near my waist or my feet.*

Then I realized that something was different. She was restless, and her breathing sounded unusual. *Wait a minute*, I thought, *I never hear the sound of her breathing.* And in another moment, I was filled with awe as I became aware of sounds and movement that told me she was about to give birth.

My first impulse was to jump up and move her out of my bed and onto a clean blanket somewhere else. After all, this would probably be messy. Yet I couldn't bear to interrupt or distract her from the important work she was doing, so I lay still in the silent darkness, listening and thinking, fully drawn into the moment. Then a powerful intensity enveloped Harriet and me as I realized that, by choosing to give birth so close to me, she was obviously inviting me to share her miracle. Profoundly moved as time stood still on this dark night, I listened to the sounds and felt the movements within the circle of my arm. When I heard a tiny whimper, I smiled. The new kitten had arrived.

I listened to lapping sounds. Then, ever so slowly, I moved my index finger in one direction and then another, drawing a mental picture with what I touched in the blackness. There was Harriet, her head moving rhythmically as she gently bathed her newborn. Tracing a path forward from her head, I lightly touched the damp, cigar-shaped body that lay between Harriet's front paws. With the lightest touch, I stroked the kitten's tiny forehead, desiring to communicate a wondrous, warm welcome to the world.

A small, squeaky sound emanated from the kitten, and intense joy surged from my bursting heart to my vocal chords. Tears slid down onto my pillow as I whispered, "All is well, Harriet."

I missed not living with my daughters and hoped they would work through their negative feelings in the near future and stay over occasionally. I purchased a sturdy oak bunk bed for the second bedroom, but it remained unused. I went to their athletic games, despite their distancing from me, because I wanted them to know I loved them unconditionally.

At work, I applied for a promotion: director of the residential program. When I'd resumed full-time status the year before, I'd become house manager for a large residence of high-functioning disabled adults. The new position would mean I'd provide leadership for all six agency homes in various parts of our county. I was aware when I applied that part of what I could give my residents was the nurturing that my children could not presently accept.

In one of my four interviews, a program director asked me to describe myself in one word. "Would you accept three words?" I asked.

She smiled. "Sure. Go ahead."

I'd thought about this question—one of many the agency used to tease out qualities a résumé couldn't reveal—as I'd prepared for my interview. I'd pondered about which word would now capture my essence; many came to mind, yet each fell short, until I decided a three-word phrase was exactly right.

I knew none of my interviewers could possibly understand the intense work that allowed me to say that day, "Good self-esteem."

It may have seemed an unusual answer to them, but for me—possessed all my life with a dreadful self-image and absence of self-worth—the words celebrated taking that journey back in time, facing truths I still worked on, learning to respect and honor myself, and shedding the constricting snakeskin of my perception that I was a bad person pretending to be a good one.

I got my promotion and dove enthusiastically into the huge job. Meanwhile, passing weeks brought glimmers of reconnection with my daughters: Polly called me a few times on the phone; Susan came over to say, "Hi, Mom," for the first time after a basketball game. I felt cautiously joyous. Polly would soon graduate from high school and leave for Mexico for a year as a Rotary Exchange student. She had bought a car and occasionally drove to my apartment to visit; sometimes Sue came with

her. We shared alternating times of good visits with a few difficult ones, such as the time I met the girls by chance in a Delhi
store and I said something that made Sue angry; she yelled at
me and ran back to the car. Yet, overall, we were slowly healing
our fragile connection.

Following six months of separation, I called Don one evening.
"Do you want to meet somewhere and talk? It's been six months."

He agreed. I arrived early at McDonald's, and, as I waited
and watched people come and go, former friends, a Bovina
couple, walked in.

The husband smiled and said, "Hi, Mary Jo," while his
wife pointedly ignored me. I'd heard from the Bovina grapevine
that she believed I was a terrible mother who'd deserted her
children. I wondered if anyone knew the truth: that Don and I
had agreed to a six-month separation and that the children had
chosen to stay with him. But I was learning I no longer had to
please everyone and let the snub, which would have been hurtful
months earlier, pass by.

Then I saw Don pull into the parking lot, step out of his
Ford pickup, and amble to the entrance door. He walked uneasily, out of rhythm, which told me he was uncomfortable, as he
approached the bench where I waited.

We said hi and got cups of tea, then slid into a booth opposite each other. It was late, about 9:30 p.m., and we'd not talked
in several months. Our attempts at small talk were awkward, so,
deciding to get to the point, I said softly, "Well, we both know
why we're here. . . ."

He nodded slowly, his hazel eyes large and serious, and
looked away from me.

Pausing briefly to form the words, I gently said something
like, "Don, I've thought a lot about us these past six months,

and . . . I know of no way to rebuild our relationship. We've tried therapy. . . . The therapist supported our plan to separate. I never wanted this to happen to us, but it has. . . . We don't even know each other anymore."

He sipped his tea silently.

"What about you? Do you feel the same? Or differently?" I asked, now wondering if I'd made a mistake by sharing my feelings first.

"It doesn't matter, does it?" he replied quietly.

"Of course it matters," I said. "I'd like to know your feelings."

He tipped his cup, finished the last of his tea, and stared at the container. "Why would they matter?" he said, crumbling his cup. "If you don't want to get back together, it's not going to happen."

I had no answer. Pale and somber, he slid from his seat, said a hasty goodbye, dumped the cup in the trash, and strode quickly through the door.

I glanced around. My former friends watched Don leave. *Can they sense the gist of our conversation?* I wondered. I stared through the window at Don, sitting tall and alone in the cab with his hands on the steering wheel, then watched the truck lights come on, back up, and move forward, small red rectangles that disappeared quickly in the darkness.

I sat there a long time, wondering what Don's feelings were about us. His words echoed in my mind: *If you don't want to get back together, it's not going to happen.* He was right in one sense, I believed, yet feelings always mattered. I rubbed my forehead and eyes with my hand, then rose, tossed my tea container in the trash, and walked through the shadows to my car. I never did learn what Don's feelings were about us, but if I had to guess, based on his words, body language, and actions, I'd say he might have wanted to try again. He may still have felt that marriage vows were forever. Or that I'd get better in therapy and he'd wait until I returned to being the woman he'd fallen in love with all those years ago. He'd be right that I was better, but I was no longer the person he'd fallen in love with. I was someone who now knew brutal betrayal by men who had been my would-be nurturers, and I still had to figure out if I could ever again join with a man in a close relationship.

My years in Bovina totaled twenty-three before life tugged me elsewhere. Those sweet Bovina beginnings—of quilting bees, of rich attachment to my community, of women gathering, working, sharing stories, and nurturing together—all slipped away when I moved from Bovina. Yet, along with the appliquéd square I created for the Bovina quilt, much of my heart and spirit remain there to this day, stitched for eternity into the fabric of that community—where I'd planned to live out my days—and all that we exchanged with each other.

While I traveled new roads on my patchwork journey, those beginnings resurfaced in a different way, through my writing, which I did not recognize at first. Nevertheless, I rekindled them and they in turn gave me two sacred gifts: they played a significant role in my healing and became an unexpected passion.

Chapter 28: CONNECTING DOTS

Delhi, New York, 1996–98

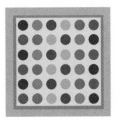

Don and I each retained an attorney and tackled dividing our assets while turning the farm over to Don—a two-year process.

After graduation, Polly left for Celaya, Mexico, through our local Rotary Exchange program. We wrote to each other regularly. Her early letters reflected joy with her distance from the Catskill Mountains, a deep relief to be away from family turmoil and have her own positive experience. Rotary required that family not visit until several months after she left. Ten months later, during the two weeks I was there, we shared wonderful sightseeing trips, visits with her three sets of host families, positive and healing conversations, and delightful shopping, most memorably in San Miguel de Allende. A few old conflicts surfaced, yet were rare.

When she returned home, Polly lived with me and enrolled in our community college in order to reground herself on American soil and figure out her major and where she might transfer the following year. Sue, distanced from me during Polly's year in Mexico, occasionally visited again.

Sue had moved from her first boarding home to another, with a former schoolmate of Don's, who didn't hide her opinion that I was a terrible parent. Sue was forced to choose between us, and I believed I had lost my youngest daughter forever. When Polly arrived home again, though, her presence offset some of the negatives Sue heard in her boarding home. I was cautiously, quietly joyful to find Sue's and my relationship slowly healing with time and care.

Work challenged me, requiring long hours and deep dedication. One morning at home, I wrapped myself in my Irish cable-knit afghan and wrote in my journal, "My marriage has ended, and now I'm questioning my career. I used to feel I'd stay with this agency until I retire, but lately I don't think so. Some days I don't want to go to work. Why not?"

I stared at the paper, and my eyes grew wide at the next words that flowed: "Why not? I'm tired of this work. The work hasn't changed nor have the people. It's me—I've changed."

I was startled. What would I do if I didn't work with the disabled? How would I use the skills I'd mastered? As I stared at my red carpeting, the Closet Memory returned. After all these years, I heard Jackie choke again and became as paralyzed as I was that night in the closet. I'd thought the screams about that memory were all outside me. They weren't. Having no neighbors who could hear me, I screamed until I was hoarse. The flashback passed; then I slept.

When I woke later, I wrote more. "It's a fact that I direct a residential program for disabled adults. I'm responsible for their safety and well-being. I am passionate about this responsibility."

I wrote faster. I underlined *passionate*. Twice. Suddenly, the Closet Memory exploded into my thoughts. I froze for several minutes. When I could write again, my words were "I couldn't protect my disabled sister from my father." A sudden question erupted: "Is that why I chose this career? So I could do, as an adult, what I couldn't do as a child? Am I every day trying, by caring so conscientiously for my residents, to make up to my sister for the fact that, by saving myself from him, I sacrificed her?"

I stared at my words and drew in a breath so deep it sounded like a sob. Then I sat still and stared dead ahead.

Yes.

It made absolute sense.

Time stood still as this profound realization seeped through my body like pure, cleansing water. My career and the Closet Memory were inextricably linked. As I assimilated this connection, relief at finding my truth quieted my body.

I stared out the window to the snowy meadow, think-ing how grateful I was for my greatest healing tool: writing. How could I have worked through the tremendous fear and anxiety I experienced during a flashback without writing about it? Without ultimately understanding its roots, as I just had in uncovering the link between my work and the Closet Memory? When these recollections returned later, I grew to understand I was safe, in my own home or my therapist's office, and that gave me courage to travel through the flash-back, powerfully defusing those overwhelming emotions, instead of running. They had never fully left, but they rarely interfered in my life anymore.

I returned to the couch with a cup of tea. A recent work memory returned. One of my residents alleged a counselor had held his bedroom door shut one morning, preventing the resident from leaving his room, a restraint not allowed in our program. The resident screamed to get out, but the counselor held the door tightly closed. An investigation proved the allegation true. I was furious and also hyperaware that my rage was far out of proportion with the event. I didn't know why then, but this day at home, I understood: someone for whom I was responsible had been abused and I hadn't prevented it. *Just like Jackie.*

Even as a skilled program director, I could not protect all my residents at all times. Tears streamed down my cheeks as I wrote my next thoughts: "I am so exhausted, and today's realizations are just one reason. I'm exhausted, yes: from carrying secrets for decades; from trying to please supervisors who recently observed I wasn't doing enough at my job; from working fifty to sixty hours each week; from the never-ending responsibility of my program. Mostly, though, I'm exhausted from having cared so inadequately for myself."

When I reread the words, I accepted the truths that, until that day, I'd either not taken the time or not had the courage to face—or both.

Now I had reached the heart of the matter, the eye of the hurricane:

I was abused as a child. But did I have to continue to abuse or neglect myself as an adult? No. I couldn't protect my little sister when she and I were small, but did I need to spend the rest of my professional career making up for it? No!

During the next few days, I dug further into my shifting feelings about my work and discovered more insight when I read *The Addictive Organization: Why We Overwork, Cover Up, Pick Up the Pieces, Please the Boss, and Perpetuate Sick Organizations,* by Anne Wilson Schaef and Diane Fassel. Our organization was highly committed to excellence, one reason I was so drawn to being part of it. This day, I saw the equation easily: Excellent agency + I work there = I am an excellent employee.

My reading showed me another perspective that clearly described me. In the chapter "Four Major Forms of Addiction," there I was: a workaholic who was compulsive, perfectionistic, and controlling. Also a depressive who harbored feelings of guilt and inadequacy. The next section spoke further to me:

> *Thomas Peters and Robert Waterman noted in their book,* In Search of Excellence: Lessons from America's Best Run Companies, *that being part of an excellent company can be exhausting because "dedication to the quest for excellence" is tiring. Many "passionate activists" give up family time, entertainment, and most other pastimes; marriages could fall apart if a spouse is so devoted to a cause or job that all else is shoved aside. "Excellence is a high-cost item."*

Yes, my job had been high-cost for me. I didn't perceive this as a negative label of our organization, but I clearly saw my own unhealthy behavior in those pages. As I rose through the ranks to program director, I had proven to myself that I was good enough—I could do it. Yet I had used time that my family needed, and I had neglected myself.

Now I no longer needed a job, an organization, a portfolio, a Mercedes, or a mansion to define me as excellent or anything else. Ironically, somewhere in the past, my commitment to excellence and personal growth had transformed into a solid value within me and was now part of my soul and DNA.

Before I returned to work, I wrote my resignation, giving generous notice to find and train my replacement. When I took my decision to my supervisor, I left our conversation with one certain feeling: I had reclaimed another part of my life.

This event brought another stunning realization: suddenly, I felt free to move anywhere in the country or the world. Like the traveler in Robert Frost's poem "The Road Not Taken," the road I'd traveled in recent years had brought me to a fork that graced me with a choice: continue my present path or gather my fragile courage and bear off onto a new, grassy trail.

Knots of apprehension twisted my stomach as the metaphorical road relentlessly beckoned my soul. After weeks of introspection and research, I decided to move to central Virginia's stunning Blue Ridge Mountains, five hundred miles away.

A few weeks later, I recorded this dream:

I was alone in my car, driving on a quiet road with lush green grass on each side, parallel to a superhighway. Vehicles hurtled by steadily. At one point I turned left to enter the highway, but the road didn't connect. I continued on and, a little later, turned left again. Again, the seeming on-ramp did not connect to the superhighway.

I decided to park, got out of my car, and began to walk along the blacktop pavement, enjoying the warmth and green growth on both sides of the road. My hand embraced a small, smooth gray stone that I'd had for ages. It was incredibly important to me, and I always kept it with me. Suddenly, a uniformed policeman, medium build, about five foot ten, walked up briskly behind me. I should feel afraid, I thought, as he caught up with me, but he strode right past, seeming not to notice me. I felt no apprehension or fear, just peace and confidence.

Then I dropped my stone. Immediately I bent down and rubbed my fingers through the grass. I knew precisely where my stone had landed, but it had disappeared. My distress increased as I searched more, until suddenly my eyes widened. A thick, solid new plant shoot was emerging from the exact spot where my stone had fallen. The shoot was strong, with a rich, deep green bud that grew as I watched. A lovely burgundy color banded the outer edges of the still-curled petals. As I stared, I knew from that place within that recognizes my truth that what I had let go of—my stone—had transformed into beautiful, healthy new growth.

I woke smiling, feeling peaceful and deliciously right with the world.

Chapter 29: BRICK WALLS

Center Moriches, New York, 1999

Daffodils bravely pushed their sunny heads through lingering patches of snow four months later, after I'd spent my fifty-seventh winter preparing for my move to Virginia's Blue Ridge Mountains. I'd done a lot of reading, writing, and reflection about where I would start my new life and career.

I'd chosen the Blue Ridge, similar in ways to the Catskills but with more warmth and less winter. I'd fallen in love with the Shenandoah Valley during the years I visited my daughter Polly as she attended Washington & Lee University in lovely, historical Lexington. I had no job waiting but knew I would work that out when I got there.

As I sorted clothing one afternoon, placing items in either the small "keep" pile or the larger "give away" pile, the phone rang.

"Hi, Sister." Bonnie's voice, always upbeat, quivered.

"What's wrong, Bon?"

"Mom fell this morning and broke her back."

"Oh no," I cried.

"Thank God we got that medic-alert necklace last month. The emergency crew got there in ten minutes."

We talked somberly. Mom was comfortable in the hospital, with a long medical journey ahead. We considered her possibilities, wondering if she could ever again live independently in the cute bungalow her grandfather had built decades earlier on the Great South Bay inlet. By the end of our conversation, I decided to pause my Virginia move and return to Long Island to help Mom get back on her eighty-two-year-old feet, if that was possible. Bonnie and I believed that because Mom so loved her life on Adelaide Park, she would be highly motivated to return.

Within the week, I hugged my son Chip goodbye in his small home on a farm where he worked with the owner, his friend Rob. Chip was also building an electrical business of his own. Then I bade farewell to Susan, who was working on a nearby dairy farm as a milkmaid while she decided her next steps in life. Polly, in Virginia, was supportive of my plan and, as with Chip and Susan, planned to visit me at Mom's. I was feeling content with where each of my three children presently were in their unfolding lives. Lastly, I said a quiet farewell to Keith at the Bovina cemetery, telling him of my move as I pictured him with other sweet little angels. "Peace, my small son," I whispered, as I turned to leave. Walking to my car, I remembered Jocelyn's grave was in Center Moriches. I'd get to visit her soon.

The next morning, as I prepared my cat, Hilary, for the trip, I said one more silent farewell: to her mother, Harriet, now buried in Delhi.

I packed my car with necessary, meaningful possessions: a small box of dishes, glassware, and silverware; bedding; my computer. Stacked in another box were carefully chosen books: Kenneth Ruge's *Where Do I Go from Here?*, Susan Wittig Albert's *Work of Her Own*, and Richard Bolles's *What Color Is Your Parachute?* Thick towels safely embraced graduation portraits of my three children. In the remaining trunk space, I tucked four window boxes to plant flowers for my mother's carport. We were ready.

Hilary stared from her carrier as I backed out of my drive-way. Once under way on our 250-mile journey, I suddenly wondered if I'd lost my senses by moving back in with a parent with whom I still had issues. I always forgot about them when we were separated. *Stop it! This is for Mom*, I chided myself, *to help her become independent again.* Yet the closer I got to Center Moriches, the less I felt like the competent adult I'd worked so hard to become and more like the insecure, anxious-to-please, dread-filled child I used to be. *Will things be different this time?* I wondered. I hoped Mom and I would share pleasant, memo-rable days. I wanted this to be good for her. Yet I flashed back to moments when her impatient, degrading words had left me feeling shamed and worthless. I'd done much personal work to grow; would I react in an adult way now?

Then I remembered that Mom had insisted I go to college and how hugely that had influenced my life. Yes, it had taken me a decade to complete, but I had earned that degree. Without it, given the direction my life had taken, I imagined myself going through life leaning on others, probably unhealthy men, to care for me, rather than care for myself. I was forever grateful to her.

Doubt crept back in, though. Would the old winner-loser pattern still be the solution for problems that came up? Would this, would that, would the other thing happen? What had I gotten myself into?

I guessed I'd soon find out.

I stared at the highway as my car, but not my heart, sped for-ward. Too late now to turn back, I was—for the first time in my adult life, to my complete discomfort—homeless. I'd vacated the ranch house I'd leased and stored my belongings and now had no other place to go except to the tiny house my grandfather had sold to my mother for $1 after she'd divorced my father three decades earlier.

Her short, sandy driveway hushed my arrival as I pulled into the carport. The house was silent and dark as the overhead sky. I was glad to have a few days to settle in before she came home.

As I unlocked the aluminum storm door and pushed open the inside heavy wooden door, I wondered, as I had dozens of times, why my mother locked the flimsy storm door—so easy to break open—and not the sturdy wood door. It was a niggling reminder that she and I had, through the years, found little common ground upon which we agreed.

I carried Hilary inside and turned her loose; she immediately hid, likely overpowered by the scents of Mom's two cats. Weary, I brought in the few things I'd need that night, then locked the car, screen door, and inside door.

I slept fitfully but woke the next morning with a keen wish to walk to the water. I tugged yesterday's clothes back on, fed the cats in three different rooms behind closed doors, and stepped out the door into the warm Long Island morning. A slight breeze blew off the water. I closed my eyes, lifted my face to the sun, and inhaled the salty air, feeling close to heaven. It had been so long since I'd been here.

I walked to the bulkhead, enthralled to hear small waves gently lap against the buttress. Out on the pier, I sat on a low piling to savor the deep pleasures I so loved: the fresh, salty air filling my nostrils, the bright sun warming my body. Then a seagull screamed from atop a tall piling, drawing my eyes instantly upward to watch as he lifted off and powerfully flew away. I realized he'd just emulated my actions yesterday, lifting up and away—the gull from his comfortable perch and I from my home, from Chip, Keith, and Susan, from my work, from my whole familiar Catskill world.

I wondered again what lay ahead as I rose and moseyed back to the little house on Adelaide Park. There, I unloaded the remaining boxes from my car and stacked them in the tiny guest bedroom that was now my temporary space in my mother's home. Sitting on the twin bed, looking around at the comfortable room now cluttered with boxes of my stuff, I realized that I'd unwittingly taken an important step in my inner journey.

I'd come home.

That afternoon, I visited Mom at the skilled nursing facility in Riverhead and was delighted to see her.

"Hi, Mary Jo!" she said with a beatific smile, her eyes dancing. "I'm so glad you're here and that I'm coming home tomorrow." Mom was encased like a mummy in an armpit-to-thigh white body cast that fit over her clothing, which caused her to move carefully yet clumsily and grumble about the device she would wear for two more months.

As I hugged her, an aide walked in and said, "Hi, Mrs. B.—it's time for your physical therapy."

Mom rose from her chair. She and I followed the aide to the PT room, where I stood and watched closely as she walked, really quite well, with her cane. After the half-hour session, she was noticeably tired when we returned to her room. Once she settled onto her bed, we removed her brace and chatted a bit; then I said, "Mom, I'm going to leave now, okay? I have things to do at home to get ready for tomorrow."

She smiled wanly. "I'm so tired."

I hugged her, feeling much compassion for her and the huge challenge looming ahead. I squeezed her hand and said, "I'll be back in the morning for your discharge meeting."

She nodded and closed her eyes. I left for home, where I baked some corn muffins, changed Mom's room around to accommodate her present needs better, and eagle-eyed the entire house for anything that might cause her to trip or fall. I found no hazards.

The next morning at ten o'clock, Mom's SNF team, along with Bonnie and me, gathered around the conference table. I quickly saw how much the staff loved her. *Everybody Mom meets loves her*, I thought. *Why am I so cautious?* I dropped the question, though, and listened. The physical therapist reported, "Overall, Mrs. B. has progressed well with her walking while she's been with us, and my prognosis is cautiously optimistic." I looked at my sister, and we smiled at each other. Soon the review was completed and follow-up appointments given. All team members said warm and caring goodbyes to my mother, as she beamed, her eyes watered, and she thanked each person warmly.

"I'll drive my car to the front entrance," I told the nurse who wheeled Mom to the front door. Then we tackled the complex task of helping Mom into the passenger seat. When she was settled, the nurse placed her portable oxygen tank on the floor and I clicked the seat belt around her body cast. We thanked the nurse, and I started the engine.

"Well, here we go, Mom," I said cheerfully, glancing over.

Her short gray hair wisped upward from her ears. "I hate this damn cast," she said.

"I'd hate it, too," I agreed. "Thankfully, you can take it off during the day."

She nodded, rolled her eyes, and sat wretchedly for the half-hour ride home, where a technician waited to deliver a full-size oxygen tank and a commode.

Our first few days were busy and exhausting as we worked out new patterns for her multitude of daily needs: meals, medications, inhalers, bathroom assistance, and more. On day two, a home health aide, an RN, and a physical therapist visited, introduced themselves, described their respective roles, and set up their visitation schedules.

Hilary generally hid under my bed, petrified of my mother's twenty-pound *Lion King*–lookalike cat, Buster. If Hilary bravely ventured out when Buster was in another room, Zipporah, my mother's creamy, chocolate-tipped cat, hissed, spat, and snarled as she chased Hilary back under the bed.

I stood in the hallway, watching, and thought, *Okay, here we go!* And rolled my own eyes as I smiled.

I'd worked hard to lessen my potent lifelong need to be in control. Now I lived with my mother, who, while she always had and still needed to be in full control, found herself dependent on others for all aspects of her care. It was frustrating for her. *Well, this will be fun*, I mused, as the first few days passed and I managed to keep compliant and pleasant, with my mouth shut.

In a short time, though, we developed good routines that worked well. One afternoon, after I'd mowed the lawn, culled the raspberry and blackberry bushes, then gone for a long bike ride by the water while my bread rose and a chicken roasted, I was feeling great and my mother was having a rather good day herself. As I stood at the kitchen stove and turned on the gas beneath a pan to make gravy, it made an initial loud, rapid clicking sound as the pilot flame caught, then kept clicking.

From her bedroom, my mother screamed frantically, as if a murderer held a knife at her throat, "Turn the gas down," just as I was doing exactly that. I bit my lips, trying to puzzle why I felt so instantly furious. My answer? Just as when I was a child, her screaming caused me to feel humiliated and utterly incompetent.

Later, as we ate together, I explained how I felt when she screamed at me. Tears brimmed my eyes as I realized how much I had needed to be talked to with kindness as a child, but I didn't say that.

She listened, then said what she'd always said: "You shouldn't feel that way. You're too sensitive."

I said something new. "But I *do* feel that way, Mom. Our relationship is important to me, and these feelings are a real barrier. If I don't share them with you now, when can I?"

She berated herself. "I don't know why I yell like that, Mary Jo."

I wish that she—or I—had smiled just a tiny bit as she said her next words: "Why don't you just turn on the stove the right way—my way?"

I would have burst out laughing, as I do at this moment while I write. We could both have had a great laugh. But she was serious: her way was the right way, the only way. And I was serious, too; I needed to feel respected and competent.

"Because I'm different than you," I said quietly, wanting to smile and cry at the same time.

Something squeezed inside me as she apologized. "I will never do that again," she said.

"Thank you. Please don't beat on yourself, Mom. I just want you to understand how I feel when I'm screamed at." She nodded and became silent.

Some bricks tumbled down from our wall.

The next morning, Mom pointed out her bedroom window at her treasured half-acre of woods. They were dense with low growth, and that year an aggressive, kudzu-like vine had crept over the wooded floor and into the trees.

"If you want to clean out some of that mess, it would be nice," she said. I knew she didn't want me to work too hard and get overtired from my busy days, yet I knew how she'd labored at keeping her woods clear and now could not.

That afternoon, relaxing as warm sunshine seeped through

my shirt and onto my bare arms, I clipped and ripped away vines. It was going to be a huge job, I saw, yet I was well satisfied with the improvements just my first few hours of work had wrought. I also saw the silent, metaphorical layer beneath my physical work: the symbolic clearing-out of years of undergrowth from Mom's and my relationship.

The following day, the nurse called to reschedule her visit for another day. Mom didn't like her routine changed and said, "Do you think Ellen is disorganized?"

"More than that, Mom, I think she's very busy," I replied.

Mom looked away, signaling that she thought, because I hadn't agreed with her, that I was being critical of her.

I returned to the woods and tore some vines from a tree. In my woodsy solitude, I realized that I was guilt-ridden because I wasn't feeling the way my mother wanted me to feel. This, I saw, had been a lifelong dance between us. I ripped off more vines and dug out pesky undergrowth near another tree. I finished up a few hours later, went in and showered, then wrote about my new insights. After writing, I thought I heard a couple more bricks tumble from our wall. I could cope, I saw, when I understood the deeper level of what was going on between us.

As our days and weeks passed, we encountered nearly all of our past negative patterns in our varied interactions. After each time, I revisited the woods and pulled out kudzu while trying to figure if I could bring the current conflict to a healthier place. Sometimes I talked with Mom; sometimes I figured it out on paper. Meanwhile, the outdoor work benefited me physically as well as mentally, as I gleaned new understandings beneath the sunshine. The woods were becoming noticeably clearer, too.

On the sunny morning of July 17, I headed outdoors to scrub down the yellow aluminum siding on Mom's house. As I worked, I heard a small plane droning overhead, a common sound on a Long Island summer day. When the sound returned again, and then a third time, I felt sudden apprehension. I went into the house, where Mom sadly informed me that John F. Kennedy Jr.'s small plane was missing, with him, his wife, Carolyn Bessette, and her sister, Lauren, onboard. The aircraft returned several times that day and the next; each time I heard its drone, I prayed that they would be found, alive and safe.

Four days later, the fuselage was found. The following day, their bodies were recovered. To this day, the sound of a droning plane never fails to take me back to that July day at Mom's house, when our former president's son, wife, and sister-in-law left us.

The house siding was sparkling clean; the window boxes were brimming with Mom's favorite blue petunias, red geraniums, and red and white impatiens; and I'd cleaned the carport.

"Would you like to eat lunch out in the carport?" I asked one warm but not humid morning. Mom had difficulty breathing in high humidity.

She beamed. "That would be wonderful."

I made sandwiches and iced tea and set them on a folding table. I put two lawn chairs on each side of the table and helped her outside. Mom sat down and caught her breath. She hadn't been outdoors since the previous fall, and now she looked around at the woods, the house, and the carport.

"Wow, this place is beginning to look like someone actually lives here," my mother said happily. Her words gave me insight into how deep her frustration had been about not being able to do those tasks.

"I've been thinking about bringing Jackie home for a weekend," I said. "Are you up for it?" My sister's dual diagnosis (intellectual disability and mental illness—schizophrenia) caused her to be either very sweet or very miserable, a true Jekyll-and-Hyde personality, and she usually showed both sides of that coin when she visited.

Mom looked at me. I knew Jackie came home one weekend each month before Mom's fall. Her visits could be challenging, though, particularly when Jackie was out of sorts.

"Are you up to it?" she asked. I knew that Jackie would be both relieved and reassured to see how well Mom was doing, and that Mom would be glad to see her, too.

"I can manage, Mom," I said, then smiled and raised my eyebrows. "Remember all those years of working with my residents and their behaviors?"

I knew this was a vague unknown to my mother, yet in my field I had been considered highly skilled in behavior management techniques. I enjoyed working with my positive principles to increase positive conduct. We arranged a visit.

I drove to Hampton Bays and brought Jackie home on a Friday night. She and Mom were delighted to see each other.

"So, anybody hungry?" I asked.

"Yes!" Jackie said.

I walked out to the kitchen, then called out, "Jackie, want to come chop some onions for the meat loaf?"

"No, I don't want to," she said. Mom was silent. My screw-up, I realized, had been framing that as a question, rather than a statement. I was too used to my program's expectation that residents be compliant and actively involved in household activities if they had those abilities. Jackie's IQ was borderline, about seventy-six, and she was a high-functioning woman, despite her disabilities. She had great fine motor skills and did precision chopping of vegetables, meticulous embroidery, handwriting, and so much more. She was also highly skilled at avoiding anything she perceived as work. I'd long grieved that in her residential program she and the other residents were waited on, instead of being encouraged to join in. It was easier and quicker for the staff. If Jackie was pushed to participate in household responsibilities, she flew into an abusive rage, which resulted in everyone's caving in to keep peace, then feeling relieved when she went to her room.

I was chopping onions when Jackie called out, "Yuck, Buster just barfed under the table." She and Mom were sitting right there as I grabbed a paper towel. "Here, Jackie. Please wipe it up while I chop? Mom can't bend over."

She looked at the towel, then away, and said softly, "No, I don't want to." Mom was silent. She understood my approach and my deep belief that we all, disabled or not, build self-esteem from accomplishing things we are capable of.

I ignored Jackie's comment, wiped the floor, washed my hands, and resumed dinner preparation. I was quiet, but I was getting annoyed with her and started tossing around mental ideas about how to balance things without upsetting my mother, who hated confrontation. I asked nothing more of Jackie the rest of the evening.

The next morning, emerging from a good night's sleep, I woke to hear Mom say, "When Mary Jo gets up, she'll make you some eggs."

"Oh, good," Jackie said.

Eyes closed, I started to fume, then figured out how I was going to handle the two helpless women who waited for me to take care of them. One, I knew, needed me to do that; the other was being manipulative, and Mom was enabling it.

I got up, dressed, and walked out to the kitchen, where someone had made tea for them both. "Good morning," I said, and smiled at them.

"Ma said you'd make me two eggs for breakfast," Jackie said. Mom was quiet; she knew how I would feel.

"Jackie, you know how to make wonderful scrambled eggs. You've done it so many times. Remember?" I talked through the process with her.

She scrunched her nose and slowly shook her head. Mom remained silent.

"Well, let me know when you're ready to start the eggs, and I'll give you a hand," I said. Jackie stared out the window. I was encouraged because she often got angry and started yelling at that point. I would be kind and respectful, but I wasn't backing down—the lines were drawn, and the ball was in Jackie's court. I well-remembered my childhood years, how we were all so manipulated with anger, both in general and by Jackie's anger in particular. I could never live that way again.

I puttered around, unloaded the dishwasher, cleaned the counters and sink. I made a cup of tea for myself and sat at the table to talk with Mom and Jackie.

Several minutes later, Jackie said softly, "I guess I'm ready."

"Great. Let's do it," I said, as we both rose from the table.

As I stood nearby, complimenting her on each step, she got two eggs from the refrigerator, broke them perfectly into a bowl, and beat them with a fork.

"You know how to use the gas stove?" I asked.

"Yeah," she said happily, fully engaged in her task. I watched her turn on the burner, oil the cast-iron frying pan, then scramble the eggs in the pan.

I got her a plate, she scraped the eggs onto it, and I put it on the table.

"Want juice?" I asked.

"Yeah," she replied, smiling.

I poured orange juice and put the glass on the table as she put her first forkful of eggs in her mouth.

I smiled at her. "So, how do your eggs taste?"

"Good," she said, giggling.

After breakfast and cleanup, I darted out to the woods. As I tugged away more kudzu, I pondered. Mom always found it easier to do things for Jackie, and I understood better now, given all Mom had dealt with, why that happened. I'd learned how to manage behavior effectively to obtain the best from capable disabled people, but Mom hadn't had that opportunity. So what did that mean? Well, I decided, we were different in our approaches and each of us was doing the best we knew how.

I wished with all my heart that my sister had been well challenged to use the fine skills she possessed, but that had never happened and would not now happen. I had to accept that, along with the fact that Mom wasn't going to change, either. As I yanked out a particularly stubborn vine, another fact clicked into place: I needed to do better at respecting what my mother *had* accomplished with my sister. In 1945, when Jackie was born, Mom was encouraged to institutionalize Jackie because, in theory, her life expectancy was short. (As I write today, Jackie has just celebrated her seventy-third healthy birthday.) My mother would not hear of institutionalization, and I knew how her choice had created a long, difficult, and lonely road for her, with few supports to help her meet Jackie's complex needs.

After a few hours in the woods, I decided to talk with Mom about how much she had accomplished with Jackie, how different our approaches were, and my hope we could simply respect those differences. Later, over a cup of tea together, she listened to me and agreed we were very different. I sensed she accepted this, though she said no more.

By the end of the weekend, several situations between my mother and sister had stirred up all kinds of old stuff for me. Each time, I quietly returned to the woods, where, in my seemingly unending kudzu battle, I cried or raged or grieved about the past, which had been so damn hard. But by weekend's end, as I drove Jackie back home, I reflected on the infinite wisdom of the Serenity Prayer: "God grant me the serenity to accept the things I cannot change, courage to change the things I can, and wisdom to know the difference."

The following day, in the woods, I thought back to the weekend as I sat on the soft ground. I picked up a nearby fallen oak leaf and traced its edges with my finger. *I choose you to represent Mom and Jackie's relationship and their relationship with me.*

Then I stood up, climbed a tree, and sat in its first forked limbs, which were as high as I dared climb. I held the leaf out, slowly released it, and watched it flutter to the ground. I wrote later in my journal, "I am letting go of my attempts to change what cannot be changed." I silently blessed the falling leaf, my mother and sister's relationship, and my relationship with them both.

My heart softened.

I stayed with Mom for her nine months of healing, and during that time we worked out several old conflicts, both mine and hers. For instance, there was the day she kept saying, "I can't do this; I can't do that."

"Mom, let's take the word *can't* out of your vocabulary," I said.

She snapped, "Okay, I *can* walk to town, then."

"No," I said, "I mean that words like *I can't* keep you feeling helpless and weak, when you can do so many things. Let's focus on what you *can* do; each day you do a little more, like taking your six a.m. meds independently this morning. That's a big deal."

Silence.

I went outside to work in the woods and think. When I returned, I said, "You know, I need to clarify. I'm not implying you can do things you're not able to do; I'm just talking about how language can either weaken or strengthen us."

"I've thought more about what you said, and I understand what you mean," she said, nodding. We went on to talk about other solutions to situations that made her feel helpless.

"Your mind is so good; you're not losing cognitive skills, and you're so fortunate," I told her. We decided we could do better. I noted in my journal, "Today I'm feeling good about being here, that I can be helpful in positive ways and that I also can grow. I can help Mom focus on being more positive, and I believe I can learn from her also."

Then there was the day Sue called to say she was coming

to visit. I was delighted, as was Mom, who said, "I've always resented that you lived so far away with my grandchildren."

"What?" I said. "I've always been under the impression that you resented them when you came to visit me, because I needed to spend time with them also."

She looked away, then said, "Yes, I wanted you to myself... but I guess the reason the kids turned out so well is because you spent lots of time with them."

My eyes widened. "*Wow!* Thanks, Mom!"

On another particularly challenging day, she argued with everything I said. Following one of my responses, she told me, "You're so heavy, Mary Jo." She was not talking about my weight.

"I'm sorry," I said, "but this is the person I am right now."

"I try to be light," she replied, "but you're always so weighty."

An old, familiar pain flowed through my body. "Excuse me for a while," I said. I left the table to ask myself what that pain was as I started cleaning the cat box. In time I reached a core understanding: *I have never felt accepted by my mother (or father, for that matter) as the person I am. I must come to terms with that. I must accept that I am not the person she wanted, that she has not been able to love and accept me unconditionally. What can I do? I can't change her, but I can value and honor myself. I can claim my life from today on, the right to be who I am; it all starts with me.*

My journal spilled over with our multiple moments of old conflict, many of which she and I talked through, or, if not that, from which I gained the understanding I needed to accept what was, and to let it go.

When she became able to care for herself again, in January 2000, I resumed my plan to move to the Blue Ridge Mountains.

Mom's and my separation was emotional, our relationship was healthier and more harmonious, and we had even developed the ability to laugh at ourselves. One afternoon shortly before my move, I carefully made tiny, love-filled stitches around the large heart flower for Mom on my quilt.

On January 2, 2000, I packed my car. An important question still nagged at me, though: *Why* didn't Mom know about the abuse? Yet, given her medical frailty and my gratitude for her belief and acceptance of my memories, I decided not to ask. Instead, I later researched the phenomenon of why a woman could be unaware of incest happening in her home, and found denial to be a primary reason.

Roland C. Summit, assistant professor of psychiatry at Harbor-UCLA Medical Center, who defined child sexual abuse accommodation syndrome, said, "As someone substantially dependent on . . . the father, the mother in the incestuous triangle is confronted with a mind-splitting dilemma. . . . Either the child . . . or the father is . . . lying and unworthy of trust. . . . The mother's whole security and life adjustment and much of her sense of adult self-worth demand a trust in . . . her partner. To accept the alternative means annihilation of the family and a large piece of her own identity."

I accepted this as the probable explanation for my emotionally inundated mom, whose primary goal in life had been to be a wife and mother. The prospect of everything falling apart without my father's basic support, shaky as it sometimes was, would have terrified her. Right or wrong, this insight put my question to rest.

I knew when I backed out of her driveway, leaving on my five-hundred-mile trip to Virginia, that I would never regret my nine-month detour. Mom lived out her remaining six years in her beloved little home, as my amazing sister Bonnie and brother-in-law, Bill, provided all the support she needed. Tenderly, I fastened their heart flowers near Mom's and Jackie's on my patchwork quilt.

Whenever I think back to that summer and fall of 1999, I smile with deep gratitude. Clearing my mother's woods was one of the best things I could have done for our relationship. They looked remarkably good, too.

Chapter 30:

CABIN IN THE BLUE RIDGE

MOUNTAINS

Lexington, VA, 2000

I lived briefly with my daughter Polly and her roommate, Eszter, and worked as a temp at the Health Department while seeking a rental home and permanent employment.

A local newspaper listing—"small 1 BR cabin in secluded setting, close to Lexington"—reached into my heart and led me to Osprey Lane, halfway up a mountain in a wooded setting surrounding a simple cabin in a small clearing. I signed the lease for my 589 square feet of living space, the size of a one-car garage, on February 5, my fifty-eighth birthday, and celebrated that I was no longer homeless.

The following day, I carried boxes through my back door into the off-white kitchen and living room area. Behind doors and in drawers, I stashed silverware, earthenware dishes, two pots, a pan, a cast-iron frying pan, dish towels, and potholders. In the cabinet above the stove, I stowed glasses, mugs, and a few other necessities. On the faux-oak countertop, I placed a radio that I would rarely use, deferring instead to the sounds of nature.

Beyond the door to the bath and bedroom were my mattress, on a box spring, and a lamp on a small plant stand. As I made up my bed, I recalled the lovely carved antique oak high-frame bed I'd left at the farm, covered with my handmade quilt, a fence-rail pattern in shades of apricot, green, and muslin, and matching quilted drapes. They were elegant compared with this simplicity, but that was then and now was different.

One day my son would bring me the bed frame, my overstuffed couch, my oak coffee table and end tables, and some other basic furniture. For now, I didn't miss them. Material possessions meant little; fewer possessions gave me greater freedom to pursue my simple yet challenging goal—find my new career, my day job, as I birthed what I now believed was my life's true work: writing, which I was anxious to begin.

The living room's picture window framed a scene of trees stretching bare branches high into the sky, silently inviting me to center my computer/dining table before it. I covered the thick pine board supported by concrete blocks with a sky-blue tablecloth and slid Grandpa Davis's maple desk chair in front of it.

I gazed wistfully at the melting snow outside my cabin, recalling my long-ago cabin dream when my sons were small, after I'd earned my degree and achieved financial stability again. I'd planned to build a cabin among trees overlooking peaceful Arnold Lake near Cooperstown, New York. My throat ached as I remembered the tragedy that shattered that dream. *Strange,* I reflected, *how life fulfills a dream so differently than the way one imagines.* All these years later, here was this country-blue, white-trimmed cabin on a Blue Ridge mountainside.

Reluctantly, I carried in my final possessions: two three-inch-thick binders, one black, which I started when I was hospitalized, and one mauve, in which I'd written prolifically each day as our earlier family life crashed down around us. These journals contained detailed entries of the past decade of my life that I'd kept locked in my car since I'd moved.

I hoped they would not contaminate the sweet, clean air in my cabin with the terrible secrets that I felt others needed to be shielded from. I shoved the binders beneath the table and shrouded them behind the tablecloth. Then I reminded myself that my journals contained the truths of my life, that my truths showed me I was not the odious person I'd always believed. I *was* a good person.

Lately I'd felt my stories trying to ooze through the pores of my skin. Now, the final part of my healing had arrived: to get my story outside me once and for all; to face, embrace, and integrate that long-dissociated part of myself. Carrying the notebooks indoors was a simple but profound first step on the next part of my journey.

Late on moving-in day, I sat before the picture window at my computer desk. Feeling apprehensive, yet tenderly surrounded by silent trees and solitude, I wrote my first words.

I needed to be employed as I lived on the mountain. Subsisting on my modest savings, I gave myself the gift to explore several kinds of work outside my recent career path. This frequent change of jobs may have wrecked my formerly pristine résumé, but that did not concern me. I was searching, and I'd know my work when I found it.

I worked first with women and children through the Health Department, and next in a college library, where I learned that, while libraries had always been my favorite places, I preferred reading books to checking them out to others. When the local free clinic hired me part-time, I liked the work immediately. Life had, it seemed, come full circle. I was helping others move ahead on their difficult journeys, as some kind people had helped me when I was a young, impoverished, and discouraged mother.

The health department rehired me part-time to teach adolescents ways to make healthy life choices. I liked that work also, hoping I could influence others to make better life decisions than I had. Fairly soon, though, my two half-time jobs grew to about thirty hours a week, more time than I wanted to work, becoming thieves of my writing time and solitude. I talked with both supervisors, explaining that I needed one full-time, benefited position. While the grant-funded Health Department position could not provide full-time hours or benefits, the free clinic and I worked out a satisfactory arrangement. This was the outcome my heart truly desired. I was delighted and grateful that, after a year without health insurance, I was fully covered again.

Eight months after moving to Virginia, I was well settled in my new career and routines at home, especially a regular writing schedule. As I moved through my first Virginia seasons, my awareness of the natural world that surrounded me broadened and deepened. I'd moved into my cabin when light snow covered the ground, crunching as I walked from my car to the cabin. Sometimes the icy air hurt my nostrils when I inhaled, yet soon winter transformed into a glorious springtime, revealing an abundance of new, sensuous gifts of nature that I'd never previously connected with, although surely they'd always been there. Gentle breezes lifted my hair so tenderly that they felt like a sweet caress, as spring transformed into summer. Through the sparkling picture window in my bedroom, I discovered abundant redbud trees when their heart-shaped leaves unfurled. The third picture window, by the back entrance to the cabin, framed numerous loblolly pines, some diminished from lack of nurture by sunshine, others full and vibrant.

Never an enthusiastic early riser, I got up with the sun, pulled on sweats, and greeted the day by stretching on my deck. I listened to birds who welcomed me by freely giving every gorgeous note of their melodies. Behind the cabin, pathways circled the wooded area and led, mazelike, in several directions, including toward the top of the mountain. It was a natural aerobic spa right in my own backyard, a lovely outdoor space to nurture me. I fast-walked up and around my mountain for half an hour, learning all the little ridges, inclines, and places where rocks had broken through the ground like molars on a toddler's gums. I looked for unexpected surprises as the dawn drew me in. One day it was a tiny new lavender ground flower that opened up and whose name I didn't know, but that didn't matter. She gave me her beauty in full, and I gave her my unabashed awe for her brave appearance. Sometimes I sighted a doe raising her white tail when she heard me, followed abruptly by the sound of crackling brush as she ran deeper in the woods. Other times, a groundhog waddled quickly back into his hole or a sweet bunny scurried silently away. By then I was fully part of the new day, my spirit open and vibrant, my lungs drawing fragrant, clean air into my body. I returned to the side deck, stretched again, then showered quickly—a necessity with a five-gallon water heater!—and prepared for work.

During the summer, I lived more on the L-shaped deck that started at the back door and wrapped around the front of the cabin than in the house, where I hung out with Mother Nature, read books, or wrote stories. I planted red and white impatiens around two small boulders near the cabin and delighted in the contrast of the bright colors against the pale gray stones and green lawn. The sweet aroma of wild honeysuckle in my small clearing transported me back to my childhood, to the bush that grew in our side yard in Mastic and whose scent I treasured.

I recalled that the first bottle of perfume I ever bought was honeysuckle. When I mowed the small lawn, the grassy scent reminded me of newly cut hay on the farm, always one of my favorite summer scents.

One summer afternoon, a whirring hummingbird hovered close to my front deck and sent me out to buy a feeder. Soon four hummingbirds visited daily, two with brilliant, fluorescent-green bodies. Summer also brought dense humidity, during which bugs buzzed endlessly, some with a never-ending cadence, others stopping and starting. When I listened carefully to their summer songs, I could discern at least three different sounds that lasted until long after darkness.

Later in the summer, I found clusters of tiny butterflies hovering on the ground, their inner wings colored like apricot jam, their outer wings etched in patterns the shade of milk chocolate. I stepped carefully around them, wondering if their morning gathering was a butterfly staff meeting during which they decided where their fluttering flight would take them that day. Or did they simply go where the wind sent them?

In fall, the breezes intensified, the pine branches creaked, and my redbuds shed their drying leaves and rustled to the ground. The heightened breezes blew my hair across my face, and when I pushed it back into place, the wind asserted that it, not I, was in control.

And so, as the seasons cycled around again, each picture window generously bestowed kaleidoscopes of sky, clouds, sun, storms, moon, and galaxies of stars for the next few years. Through each, I experienced my world to be as still and charming as a Currier and Ives painting.

During my second spring at the cabin, I saw more significant changes in myself. I treasured the springtime fingers of sunshine dropping through the pines, placing dappled designs on the soft-needled floor. When I touched a daisy petal or a fragile wild rose petal, I marveled at the sight, feel, and texture of each unique bloom. Years before, on the farm, when I was so busy working hard to suppress what I didn't want to know, I was not mindful of the lush natural gifts that surrounded me there. Now they nurtured me intensely. I was slowing down; the race was over. I didn't have to please anyone, just myself—and I was so easily pleased by the finite beauty of a single wildflower. Inside my cabin, this slow, steady healing gave me ever-increasing energy to make good progress in writing my stories.

One cloudy afternoon during that second spring, I was hiking near the top of the mountain when a storm arrived unexpectedly and emptied buckets of rain on me. Instead of frantically running for shelter, as I had done my entire life, I stood stock-still in the wide-open grassy field, honoring the new response my heart pleaded for: *I want to experience what it's like to be fully present in a rainstorm. Kids always look like they have such fun in the rain; let's see what's here. . . .*

With my writing, I'd been working on developing sensory descriptions, so I focused on my senses in those moments. I looked upward to see what falling rain looked like from the ground, rather than falling outside a window. I saw just a nano-second flash before I immediately and involuntarily clamped my eyelids shut when giant drops hit like little water bombs, but I'd seen the amazing sight briefly, and now it was mine. Eyes tightly closed, I listened to the sound of the rain and realized falling rain sounds very different when you're standing beneath it than when you're hearing it hit a roof.

Dripping wet then, yet smiling like a child who didn't know she should run for cover, I opened my mouth to taste the cool outpouring, letting the water nurture me just as it nurtured the ground. For the first time in my life, I opened myself to feel the rain hit my skin, soaking through my clothes, molding my T-shirt and jeans to my body. And then I amazed myself with an involuntary action: I raised my arms as high as I could reach—I, who had always kept my arms close to my body in probable covert protection to keep myself safe—and strained to touch the dark sky above me, as if that were even possible, and then the heavens beyond, and, once again in my life, I felt something break free within. I stood dripping in that place a long time, not wanting to let go of the moment, which I could not yet process but knew was deeply significant. When the rain subsided several minutes later, then stopped, I slowly sloshed home, my socks soaked, my sneakers filled with water, as wet as if I'd just been baptized in a lake.

As I traversed down the slippery mountainside, a memory returned. Not many years before we separated, Don asked me, "Do you remember the first time I kissed you, when I put my arms around you, that your arms stayed down at your sides?"

I didn't remember but was horrified by what that passive response revealed about me to him then and exposed to me now. I saw a clear snippet of how I'd been molded into absolute passivity by those who'd misused their power when I was small.

Later that evening, I wrote about the storm in my journal and explored the deeper meaning of my afternoon in the rain.

I have been running away from storms, and not just thunderstorms, for far too long. Today I stopped. I learned today that I can face anything—losing two children and nearly a third, abandonment, poverty, divorce, the terrible betrayal of a mentally ill father and his family—and face each challenge as I encounter it. I have nothing more to fear. I have fully bonded with my Creator, who is everywhere I look now: in my natural surroundings, in my work, in my life.

I remembered when I was on the cusp of returning to the Catholic Church and then the sickening sex abuse scandals broke open. I was filled with revulsion; I could not go back then, not now, probably not ever.

Alice Walker once said in a conversation with Clarissa Pinkola Estés and Jean Shinoda Bolen, "Mother Nature is my goddess, and the Earth is my sanctuary." Her words resonate deeply with me; I believe that my church community is composed of every single living being whom I encounter each day, whether at work, in a store, or passing by anonymously in a motor vehicle.

I never found in any church what I was discovering, little by little, on my mountain. My soul was unreservedly content and fully connected with my Creator. In those seemingly ordinary woods, with their serene and silent gifts, I was crafting a richly colored quilt that embraced me with profound peace.

When you reach the heart of life, you see beauty in all things.
—*Kahlil Gibran*

Epilogue: TWINKLING STAR

Lexington, VA, Nine Years Later

I am one of twelve just-selected jurors seated in wooden chairs before a judge in our Rockbridge County courtroom. Lean, with sparse gray hair, the judge looks at us over narrow glasses low on his nose and begins to speak. "This trial is about rape. The accuser has charged the defendant, Sam Jones, of raping her on or about March 17, 2009."

Rape? My muscles instantly clench and want to curl into a fetal pose. I freeze so they can't, because I have to appear normal here. *My God, how can I do this?*

Now, wait, my adult self interrupts. *This trial is not about your history.*

I force myself to breathe deeply. *Inhale, exhale, inhale, exhale.*

Sam Jones sits by his attorney, and I compel myself to look at Jones's back. He's brown-haired, medium height, broad, stocky, dressed in jeans and a T-shirt. *He could easily overpower someone,* I think. He turns his head, and I see his blunt features, his blemished skin, his expressionless blue eyes.

Don't you dare judge him yet, my grown-up voice warns.

I don't care what you say. I don't like his looks. He's cold, big, and beefy and looks like a bully. I'll bet he raped her!

My grown-up self shoots back, *You know you want to be a responsible juror. Don't let this old crap get in the way. This is about today.*

Tears want to gather behind my eyes, but I control them. I take more breaths. *I can do this. I am stronger than my past.*

The judge interrupts my inner battle, saying he will ask us several questions. "I'll ask if you know the defendant or the accuser, if you know any case facts, if anything in your background might prevent you from making an unbiased decision. . . ."

That last statement hits my gut like a bowling ball scoring a strike. *Breathe*, I remind myself. *You want to serve.* I've always been honored when summoned to jury duty. But the turmoil that roils in my body now, the nausea, the closeness to flashbacks . . . And suddenly the very atmosphere in the courtroom begins to change for me as I slide back in time. I feel terror rise like fog around me. The judge's voice fades as I hear a girl softly cry out, "No!" I feel rage and helplessness, then hear a man's low, cold words: "Stay still!" I listen to the stifled wrestling sounds of forced sex and see the girl go numb with powerlessness.

I struggle fiercely also to hear the progression of the case before me. The judge is asking easy questions, which we twelve answer in unison: yes, yes, and yes. Then he asks, "Is there any reason that might impair your ability to judge this defendant fairly?"

Say yes! my younger self shouts.

Now, wait—maybe you can do this, my grown, healed self replies. *You know how hard you've worked to overcome your past.*

My eleven peers reply in unison, "No." No one notices my silence, and the judge goes on, asking more easy questions. Yes, yes. Then he says, "Have any of you had an experience in the past that could cause you to be biased? If so, I won't ask for details but will accept your answer at face value."

My moment of truth is here. *What will I say?* I ask myself, not even knowing which word, *yes* or *no*, will come from my mouth.

"No," my peers say in unison. I hesitate a second, before I say quietly, "Yes."

The judge looks closely at me and says, "You are Mary Jo Doig?"

I nod, my throat closing, my tears starting.

"Ms. Doig, you are excused."

I nod my head in acceptance, rise shakily, and leave the courtroom, hazily aware that another person is already being sworn in.

Outside, dazed, I sit on the court steps for several minutes, trying to process what just happened. It all feels unreal. In time I rise and walk numbly to my car. When I start the engine and pull out onto the highway, it strikes me: I am driving home with an old, forgotten friend—dissociation. In late morning, I enter the sanctuary of my home and drop onto the soft couch, utterly depleted. I sleep for hours.

Later, I rock gently in my front porch swing, staring at the beautiful Blue Ridge Mountains across the road, absorbing the day's remaining warmth. I reflect that, despite the passage of decades since their deaths and my intense years of personal work, my father and his family have stolen yet another day from my life. My lips press into a hard circle, and my eyes narrow as I watch the sun disappear behind the mountains. I now understand that those three men—who are stitched into my quilt near the stem bottom, their heart-shaped leaves browned and unopened—lacked enough sunshine and rain and sweet breezes to nurture their leaves open so they could thrive, so they could know the richness of healthy love.

I watch my beloved mountains darken as twilight arrives in full. Mere moments later, a twinkling star tugs my eyes skyward. As I stare at the cosmic gift, I feel my mouth soften and my eyes moisten. Then a corner of my mouth moves upward as I smile, remembering that those days are ever so rare.

Acknowledgments

To those who have helped and supported me as I moved through my life and through many revisions of my story, please know you are each lovingly stitched among the abundant heart-shaped leaves on my office quilt.

To Susan Wittig Albert, for her decades of unending dedication to women with stories to tell; and for birthing the Story Circle Network where I found courage to tell my story.

To my Work in Progress writing sisters and to all the women I've worked with throughout the years of my SCN journey.

To Pattie C. S. Burke, in loving memory, who first told me this story must be shared.

To Linda Hasselstrom, talented author, fellow country woman, and early editor, whose treasured encouragement kept me committed and, when I had to walk away from the story, returning again and again.

To Annie Tucker, an extraordinary editor who brought me to the finish line with a delightful sense of humor, grace, and wisdom.

To Brooke Warner, for her remarkable vision and deep commitment to publishing independent women authors, and the team of wonderful women at She Writes Press.

To my writing circle members (Ellen, CeeCee, Mona, Diane, Jo Ann, and Mariclaire), who show me every other Friday the profound gifts of sharing our stories.

To Stephanie Barko, a smart and kind publicist who led me through the miasma of marketing with patience and grace.

And especially to you, dear readers, with the hope that, if parts of your story should thread with mine, or if mine is stitched to portions of yours, that we can talk at www.maryjodoig.com.

About the Author

photo © Polly Davis Doig

Mary Jo Doig has been editing life writing and facilitating women's writing circles for twenty years. Her stories have been published in *Inside and Out: Women's Truths, Women's Stories* and *Kitchen Table Stories*. She writes in solitude near Charlottesville, VA in her home by a huge window that looks out at the gorgeous Blue Ridge Mountains, where she also enjoys quilting, gardening, hiking, and time with her family, friends, and rescue pets.

Patchwork is her first book. Visit Mary Jo at

www.maryjodoig.com

Selected Titles From She Writes Press

She Writes Press is an independent publishing company founded to serve women writers everywhere. Visit us at www.shewritespress.com.

Say It Out Loud: Revealing and Healing the Scars of Sexual Abuse by Roberta Dolan. $16.95, 978-1-938314-99-5. An in-depth guide to healing the wounds caused by sexual abuse, written by a survivor who's lived the process firsthand.

Fourteen: A Daughter's Memoir of Adventure, Sailing, and Survival by Leslie Johansen Nack. $16.95, 978-1-63152-941-2. A coming-of-age adventure story about a young girl who comes into her own power, fights back against abuse, becomes an accomplished sailor, and falls in love with the ocean and the natural world.

Secrets in Big Sky Country: A Memoir by Mandy Smith. $16.95, 978-1-63152-814-9. A bold and unvarnished memoir about the shattering consequences of familial sexual abuse—and the strength it takes to overcome them.

Raising Myself: A Memoir of Neglect, Shame, and Growing Up Too Soon by Beverly Engel. $16.95, 978-1-63152-367-0. A powerfully inspiring and unflinchingly honest story of how best-selling author and abuse recovery expert Beverly Engel made her way in the world—in spite of her mother's neglect and constant criticism, undergoing sexual abuse at nine, and being raped at twelve.

Don't Call Me Mother: A Daughter's Journey from Abandonment to Forgiveness by Linda Joy Myers. $16.95, 978-1-938314-02 -5. Linda Joy Myers's story of how she transcended the prisons of her childhood by seeking—and offering—forgiveness for her family's sins.

Baffled by Love: Stories of the Lasting Impact of Childhood Trauma Inflicted by Loved Ones by Laurie Kahn. $16.95, 978-1631522260. For three decades, Laurie Kahn has treated clients who were abused as children—people who were injured by someone who professed to love them. Here, she shares stories from her own rocky childhood along with those of her clients, weaving a textured tale of the all-too-human search for the "good kind of love."